THE COMPLETE
REMOTE PILOT

Bob Gardner and David Ison

AVIATION SUPPLIES & ACADEMICS, INC.
NEWCASTLE, WASHINGTON

The Complete Remote Pilot
by Bob Gardner and David Ison

Aviation Supplies & Academics, Inc.
7005 132nd Place SE
Newcastle, Washington 98059-3153
asa@asa2fly.com | **www.asa2fly.com**

Visit the ASA website often, as any updates due to FAA regulatory and procedural changes will be posted there: www.asa2fly.com/textbookupdates
See the "Reader Resources" page at **www.asa2fly.com/reader/rpt** for additional information and updates relating to this book.

Cover photo: iStock.com/golubovy

ASA-RPT
ISBN 978-1-61954-562-5

Printed in the United States of America.
2022   2021   2020   2019   2018   9 8 7 6 5 4 3 2 1

Library of Congress Cataloging-in-Publication Data:
Names: Gardner, Bob, 1928- author. | Ison, David C., author.
Title: The complete remote pilot / Bob Gardner and David Ison.
Description: Newcastle, Washington : Aviation Supplies & Academics, Inc., [2018] | Includes index.
Identifiers: LCCN 2017052466| ISBN 9781619545625 (trade pbk. : alk. paper) | ISBN 1619545624
     (trade pbk. : alk. paper)
Subjects: LCSH: Drone aircraft. | Drone aircraft—Government policy—United States. | Drone aircraft—Study
     and teaching—United States. | Air traffic rules—United States.
Classification: LCC TL685.35 .G37 2017 | DDC 629.132/52—dc23
LC record available at https://lccn.loc.gov/2017052466

Contents

Foreword

I have always loved stuff that is up in the air. When I was a child, my father was also a big fan, so we went to air shows, flew model airplanes, and would pull over and stop alongside the road in our rural area to watch big Stearmans spraying the farm ground. My fascination with model airplanes never left, and many years later I find myself making a living out of my hobby. If you're considering the same, this publication is for you.

You can fly sUAS (small unmanned aircraft systems) platforms professionally, but there are required steps you must take and information you have to know. In fact, you have to become an aviator. The lines between a UAV (unmanned air vehicle) flight and a piloted aircraft are really becoming blurred. To fly an sUAS, you will need to understand weather, the National Airspace System, airport operations, and other items previously held for manned aircraft. One of the largest tasks ahead will be learning a new language. Aviation has its own terminology, and to make it even more challenging, so much of it is referred to with acronyms. Authors Bob Gardner and David Ison have laid all of this out for you, organized it well for future reference, and included great graphics.

I remember watching an entire battalion surrender to a drone on the nightly news in late 1990 and thinking that all of those bad guys threw their hands up to a model airplane. Well, sort of…. The connection is real, and it's been very gratifying to see so many drone pilots for the military come out of the model airplane ranks. Today, the technology of multi-rotors and their built-in stabilization allow flying by many more operators with fewer "stick and rudder" skills. This knowledge, however, is still a major part of being an aviator. David Ison and Bob Gardner have written a great flight plan to obtain all of the aviation knowledge required for becoming "The Complete Remote Pilot."

Enjoy your flight!

Bill Pritchett
Director of Education
Academy of Model Aeronautics

Getting Started

INTRODUCTION

by David Ison and Bob Gardner

It is hard not to want to explore the possibilities of becoming a drone pilot. Drones, officially referred to as unmanned aircraft systems (UAS), provide tremendous opportunities for commercial and personal use. They provide a unique view of our world, are relatively simple to use, and have become increasingly affordable. While UAS have often been viewed as toys, they have become very sophisticated vehicles capable of performing a range of tasks. This increase in capabilities and utilities has resulted in more common use of UAS, with them oftentimes sharing airspace with manned aircraft. Thus it is necessary for UAS operators, or remote pilots, to be aware of the various requirements, regulations, and operational principles associated with manned aircraft so as to safely and responsibly operate in the airspace above the United States (referred to as the National Airspace System or NAS).

For many of you, this may be the first time you have been exposed to the sometimes confusing and complex nature of aviation and piloting knowledge. Even if you are a manned aircraft pilot, you may be unfamiliar with the intricacies associated with UAS operations and how they fit in with manned aircraft. Reading this book is your first step in the path to become a competent, knowledgeable, responsible, and safe remote pilot as well as prepare for the Federal Aviation Administration (FAA) written knowledge test.

The first step is to collect some information that is readily available from the FAA. Since UAS operations are covered by FAA regulations, it is a good idea to get your hands on a copy of these important documents. Since these rules have been fairly dynamic, I would suggest you visit the Electronic Code of Federal Regulations website (eCFR) at www.ecfr.gov and peruse Title 14, which covers everything aviation-related. In particular, you will want to read through 14 CFR Parts 91 and 107. Part 91 covers general operations requirements for aircraft and pilots, while Part 107 is specific to UAS. It is also recommended that you read FAA Advisory Circular (AC) 107-2, *Small Unmanned Aircraft Systems (sUAS)*, which expands upon the various requirements for sUAS operations in the United States.

For those of you who are seeking to fly only recreationally, you technically do not need a Remote Pilot certificate, but it is wise to familiarize yourself with the aforementioned information. Additionally, you will want to get a copy of FAA Advisory Circular 91-57, *Model Aircraft Operating Standards*. You may also want to join the Academy of Model Aeronautics (AMA), which provides tremendous resources for hobbyist pilots.

While the FAA provides some free online training and documents for aspiring remote pilots (including those who already hold a manned pilot certificate), a more comprehensive reference is necessary to gain a full understanding of UAS and how to safely use them in U.S. airspace. Thus, this book was written to help guide you through the process to become an educated, responsible, and safe remote pilot.

REMOTE PILOT CERTIFICATE

There are two primary pathways to becoming a certificated Remote Pilot. First, if you are not a current manned aircraft pilot (e.g., Private Pilot, Commercial Pilot, or ATP with a current flight review), you will need to successfully pass the FAA Remote Pilot knowledge exam. (Note that a Student Pilot certificate does not suffice.) This exam covers a range of topics, many of which are likely to be unfamiliar to both manned and unmanned pilots. Therefore, you will need to do some studying before attempting the exam. Studying is critical to success. At a cost of more than $100 for each attempt, you do not want to have to take the exam more than once; moreover, the FAA requires you to wait 14 days to retest if you fail. In order to take the Remote Pilot exam, you must be at least 16 years of age, and you must receive a score of at least 70 percent to pass. Prior to taking the exam, you should create an Integrated Airman Certification and Rating Application (IACRA) account by visiting iacra.faa.gov. After passing the exam, you will complete your IACRA application for the Remote Pilot certificate with an sUAS rating. A temporary certificate, good for 120 days, will be issued. Once your application has been officially processed, you will receive a permanent certificate in the mail.

The second pathway applies to certificated manned aircraft pilots (excluding Student Pilots) who are current per 14 CFR §61.56. Additionally, you will need to complete the FAA's online Part 107 training course which, upon completion, will provide you with a certificate as evidence of the achievement. You will then need to apply via a Flight Standards District Office (FSDO), designated pilot examiner, airman certification representative, certificated flight instructor, or other person authorized by the FAA administrator. You will be issued a temporary certificate that is valid for 120 days, after which you will receive a permanent certificate in the mail.

WHAT WILL THIS BOOK DO FOR YOU?

A quick search of the Internet and popular online retailers will display almost endless numbers of resources to study for the Remote Pilot exam and to prepare for flying UAS recreationally or for business. Unfortunately, most miss many of the nuances associated with aeronautical knowledge and often simply regurgitate, in overly terse text or outline form, what the FAA has released. These resources don't provide the most efficacious or efficient way to become a competent remote pilot. This text is designed to not only prepare you for the exam, but also to help you learn how UAS fly, how to intelligently talk about them and their components, and to be well-versed in the aeronautical knowledge required to fly these systems in the same airspace as large commercial jets.

Our goal is to provide important details in down-to-earth language. Whether or not you already know a thing or two about flying, this book will bring things into perspective specifically for the remote pilot. Aviation has its own language, much of which remote pilots need to know to understand the intricacies associated with flying. Sometimes the terms, maps, and reports available to the manned aircraft world are somewhat complex and confusing. That's what this book is for—to guide you through this unfamiliar territory (or refresh your memory about it) so you never have to feel lost.

Here are some examples of things you need to know, but may not yet be prepared to perform:

- Did you know that you should not typically fly UAS within 5 nautical miles of an airport with a control tower?
- How do you know you're within 5 nautical miles?
- What is a nautical mile?
- How do you know if an airport has a control tower?

These are just a few examples of questions you will be able to answer with the help of this book. And this is just one tiny bit of aviation knowledge from the plethora of information with which you must be familiar. Fear not, however, because we'll guide you through it all. Best of all, each lesson has review questions to ensure you understand the material, as well as to help prepare you for your written exam. You may also want to purchase ASA's *Remote Pilot Test Prep* book to focus in on the exam itself, and refer to the reader resource page for that book: **www.asa2fly.com/reader/tpuas**.

Well, let's get started!

Unmanned Aircraft Systems: Learning the Language of Drones

A VERY BRIEF HISTORY OF UNMANNED AIRCRAFT SYSTEMS (UAS)

Here is a question to get us started: when was the first drone (which we will refer to as UAS) flown? What's your guess? Would you believe that it was in August of 1849? While the Austrians were laying siege to the city of Venice, Italy, they concocted a plan to send balloons with attached explosives to bombard the city. While one could argue that these were not UAS as we imagine them, they were one of the first uses of an aerial system to complete a mission of sorts. Similar tactics were employed during the U.S. Civil War but were not entirely effective. In 1896, Samuel Langley launched an unmanned aircraft, the Aerodrome, off of a catapult housed on his floating barge. It wasn't until World War I that a guided, pilotless winged aircraft was flown. Between 1916 and 1917, the first of these types of aircraft were flown—some to serve as targets and others to deliver bombs, the latter which were referred to as aerial torpedoes, guided by rudimentary autopilots.

World War II brought forth a slew of UAS from both Axis and Allied forces. Germany's V-1 "buzz bomb" had a simplistic guidance system that would cut the engine when assumed to be in the target area. The United States also experimented with remote control technologies to convert existing manned aircraft into UAS. One example was Project Aphrodite, in which B-17 bombers were made into flying bombs. Pilots were on board to take off and to arm the warhead. After remote control was engaged, the pilots would

parachute out. Probably the most prolific use of UAS during this period was as targets, with more than 12,000 target drones used to assist aerial gunners and pilots practice their shooting skills.

Most of the UAS activity from World War II to Vietnam continued to be in the form of target flights or flying bombs. Eventually, the latter evolved into the modern-day cruise missile. UAS were later used for reconnaissance, typically launched from an airborne platform such as a Lockheed C-130 Hercules. Following the Vietnam War, the United States dramatically slowed its drone research and production, but other countries, notably Israel, made leaps and bounds, paving the way for the UAS age as we know it.

Around 1990, the United States became increasingly interested in using UAS to perform missions that would typically be too boring or dangerous for manned pilots. Thanks to the Global Positioning System (GPS) and advances in sensors, computational power, and other components, UAS could be accurately guided to precise target locations and perform a range of missions from reconnaissance to attack. By 1994, companies were producing unmanned war machines. UAS such as the now-familiar Predator and Global Hawk came to fruition. Since 2000, the U.S. military has rapidly increased its use of UAS to perform tactical missions across the globe. Today, headlines frequently highlight the U.S. military's use of UAS. However, these types of UAS are not commonly seen in the United States (although they do fly here—for training, special missions, and border protection purposes), and they do not resemble the types of systems most remote pilots will operate.

While militaries were figuring out how to utilize UAS for war, radio-controlled aircraft as we know them today were concurrently being developed. In fact, the technologies went hand in hand. The ability to control an object via radio came about in 1898, thanks to Nikola Tesla. A more sophisticated control system was tested in 1903, using radio waves to execute specific commands on a robot. By 1917, such technologies were being used in UAS. Throughout the period of the World Wars, remote control aircraft became more sophisticated and popular. In the 1950s, gas- and battery-powered, remote control aircraft truly sparked the hobby flying market. By 1968, there were even remote-controlled helicopters. As batteries have improved, computers and other components have shrunk, and as prices of these items have become more reasonable, the world of remote control flying has become more accessible to a wider audience. While much of the remote control flying done before the early 2000s was for recreation or as a hobby, it quickly became apparent that UAS has much more capability and potential. Fast-forward to today, and UAS are technologically advanced tools that can be used to perform a very wide range of functions, from simple photography to assisting farmers through the use of precision agricultural sensors. There is no limit to what modern UAS can do. The only limit is your imagination. Of course, a UAS is only as good as its pilot, so let's start digging into the details on how to become one.

TERMS AND ABBREVIATIONS

Both the manned and unmanned aircraft worlds have their own set of terms and abbreviations. Wouldn't you be a little nervous if you asked a doctor, "Hey doc, what are the results of my thoracic CT scan?" and he looked at you puzzled, responding "A what kind of scan? What is a CT?" Similarly, you want to be able to use and understand the UAS/aviation talk. This is essential to being a knowledgeable remote pilot, but it can also be a critical part of communication with other UAS operators and personnel as well as conversations you may need to have with pilots and air traffic controllers.

Below are some of the most common UAS and aviation-related terms and abbreviations that will be important for you to know.

AC   Advisory Circular—an advisory document released by the FAA to provide additional guidance on important subjects that goes beyond the explanations in the regulations and other documents.

AGL   Above ground level—the height, in feet, of an object (e.g., tower or UAS) above the underlying local area terrain.

AIM   *Aeronautical Information Manual*—An FAA publication applicable to all types of aviation/aerospace operations. Provides detailed information on topics such as air traffic control, weather, airports, and other subjects critical to remote pilots.

AIRMET   Airman's Meteorological Information—a current and forecast weather warning covering a specific area that is applicable to small aircraft and UAS (e.g., for windy conditions, turbulence, low visibilities).

AOA   Angle of attack—the angle between the middle of an airfoil (i.e., wing or rotor blade), referred to as the chord line, and the relative wind. Relative wind is opposite to the direction the aircraft/wing/rotor is moving.

ATC   Air traffic control—a service provided by ground-based personnel in charge of separating aircraft in controlled airspace. Remote pilots may have to contact ATC in specific situations.

ATCT   Air traffic control tower—a facility responsible for handling departures, arrivals, and ground operations at an airport (or airports).

ATIS   Automatic Terminal Information Service—a continuous broadcast of non-control aeronautical information. Provides weather information for the transmitting airport.

CFI   Certificated Flight Instructor—an individual who is licensed to provide flight and ground instruction.

CFR   Code of Federal Regulations—the codification of the general and permanent rules and regulations published in the *Federal Register*. Title 14 of the CFR applies to areas of operation and certification of UAS and other aviation/aerospace vehicles.

COA   Certificate of Waiver or Authorization—a special waiver or authorization by the FAA to allow operations beyond those defined by Part 107. Operators with COAs are allowed to continue to operate under them until they expire.

CT   Control tower—*see* ATCT.

DPE   Designated Pilot Examiner—a person designated by the FAA to represent the administration in the issuance of pilot certificates and to conduct practical exams.

FAA   Federal Aviation Administration—government entity charged with regulation, enforcement, and promotion of the aviation/aerospace industry in the United States. Also charged with ensuring safe operations in the NAS.

FPV   First-person view—the ability of a remote pilot to utilize a camera onboard a UAS to see from the perspective of the UAS in flight. The view is displayed on a screen that is part of the controller, on a tablet/smartphone, and/or in FPV goggles worn by the remote pilot.

FSDO   Flight Standards District Office—a local field office serving as a representative of the FAA, providing services and handling compliance relating to aviation/aerospace for a specific geographic area.

FSS   Flight Service Station—the provider of flight and weather services to pilots. FSS can be accessed via the Internet or phone.

GCS   Ground control station—the ground-based means of controlling a UAS. Also known as the controller.

GPS   Global Positioning System—a U.S.-based network of satellites that provides very accurate position information to aircraft and some UAS. GPS is one of several Global Navigation Satellite Systems (GNSS). For example, Russia has its own system called GLONASS.

IFR   Instrument flight rules—the set of FAA rules that applies to aircraft flying on IFR flight plans and that allows aircraft to fly in poor weather (less than 3 SM visibility and cloud heights below 1,000 AGL; referred to as instrument meteorological conditions, or IMC). IFR aircraft primarily navigate with sophisticated instruments and navigation systems, such as GPS.

KTS   Knots—nautical miles per hour.

METAR   Aviation Routine Weather Report—a weather report, usually distributed each hour, from airports with weather observation capabilities.

MOA   Military Operations Area— a type of special use airspace, designed to separate military aircraft training and activities occurring in the designated area from non-military air traffic. sUAS typically should avoid operating in MOAs.

NAS   National Airspace System—the various types of airspace as well as the airports, ATC facilities, technology, and related rules and regulations that exist in the United States.

NM   Nautical mile—a distance of 6,076 feet or approximately 1.15 statute miles. NMs are used for most aviation navigation distance measurements.

NOTAM   Notice to Airmen—a notification of a change to expected or documented procedures or operations. Examples may include if a control tower frequency has changed or airspace is restricted due to the President being in the area. Be sure to check for NOTAMs before each flight to avoid unwanted attention from the FAA or law enforcement.

NTSB   National Transportation Safety Board—the government agency in charge of investigating transportation accidents in the United States.

PIC   Pilot-in-command—the person in charge of the operation of an aircraft. In the case of UAS, they are referred to as the remote PIC. Note that the remote PIC does not necessarily have to be at the controls of the UAS.

RPAS   Remotely piloted aircraft system—the term used by many countries outside the United States to describe UA or UAS. RPAS is generally synonymous with UAS.

RPIC   Remote pilot-in-command—the person in charge of the operation of a UAS. Note that the remote PIC does not necessarily have to be at the controls of the UAS.

RWY   Runway—pavement used by manned aircraft for takeoff and landing.

sUAS   Small unmanned aircraft system—a UAS that weighs less than 55 pounds (25 kg).

SIGMET   Significant Meteorological Information—a weather warning covering a specific area and that is applicable to all types of aircraft and UAS (e.g., for extreme and dangerous conditions).

SM   Statute mile—a distance of 5,280 feet. Commonly referred to as miles in non-aviation contexts. SM are sometimes used for distances in aviation, such as in aviation weather reports (METARs and TAFs).

TAF   Terminal Area Forecast—an aviation weather forecast for a specific airport.

TFR   Temporary Flight Restriction—a restriction to flight operations issued via NOTAM. Flight into a TFR can have dramatic consequences usually involving law enforcement or government agencies. Be careful to avoid these.

TSA   Transportation Security Administration—the government entity charged with the safety of transportation in the United States. The TSA will vet potential remote pilots prior to the FAA issuing permanent certificates.

TWY   Taxiway—pavement used by manned aircraft to taxi to and from runways.

UA   Unmanned aircraft—term used to describe the actual aircraft that is part of a UAS (i.e., excludes the ground station/controller).

UAS   Unmanned aircraft system—the total system associated with an unmanned aircraft, including the ground station/controller, sensors, processors, and other components. UAS is also used generically to refer to a drone or remote-controlled aircraft. Previously referred to as unmanned aerial vehicles (UAV).

UTC   Universal Time Coordinated—a standard time used in aviation operations based upon the time in Greenwich, United Kingdom, uncorrected for daylight saving time. Given in 24-hour (military) format. Also referred to as Zulu time. UTC is used in communications, NOTAMs, and weather forecasts.

VFR   Visual flight rules—the set of FAA regulations that dictate operations by aircraft not flying under IFR. VFR flight requires good weather conditions (i.e., more than 3 SM visibility and cloud ceiling heights above 1,000 feet). VFR aircraft navigate with the assistance of visual cues.

VLOS   Visual line-of-sight—the ability of the remote pilot to see the UAS without any aids to vision (such as using FPV or binoculars).

VOR   Very High Frequency Omnidirectional Range—a navigational aid used by aircraft, often to define aircraft routes or position.

WX   Weather—a common abbreviation used when referring to aviation weather conditions.

TYPES OF UAS

Just as there is a cornucopia of manned aircraft, UAS come in various sizes, shapes, and configurations. With few exceptions, at least in the near-term, most civilian UAS remote pilots will be operating small UAS (sUAS), which are defined as those weighing less than 55 pounds. This text will focus on sUAS operations, though most of the details outlined are also applicable to larger UAS.

UAS are divided into two primary categories: fixed-wing and rotor-wing. Fixed-wing UAS generate the lift necessary to fly from a wing, just like a conventional aircraft. Rotor-wing UAS generate the lift needed to go aloft through rotors (essentially propellers oriented horizontally to provide lift vertically), just like a helicopter. Rotor-wing UAS are classified by the number(s) of rotors that they utilize for flight; for example, a UAS with a single rotor is considered a helicopter, while one with several rotors is referred to as a multicopter. A common configuration of four vertical propellers/rotors is referred to as a quadcopter. Figure 1-1 shows typical UAS configurations.

UAS use one of two types of engines to produce power to fly—internal combustion or electric. Internal combustion engines are typically used in larger UAS as well as in hobby/model aircraft, while electric seems to be the power source of choice for sUAS, particularly for multicopters. Obviously, internal combustion engines require some kind of fuel, a means to store it, and a way to induce combustion. Electric engines require a fuel of sorts, as well, in the form of batteries (or even solar panels). Because most of the various components needed for sophisticated sUAS use electricity, and conserving size as well as weight is important, batteries are the ideal choice for powering sUAS.

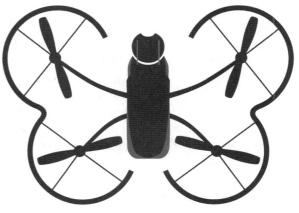

QUADCOPTER

UAS COMPONENTS

Just like manned aircraft, UAS are comprised of numerous subsystems that allow for controlled flight as well as more utilitarian functions such as providing navigation and position information, speed and altitude measurements, and the ability to take pictures and videos. Figure 1-2 shows the "guts" of a typical quadcopter. While internal components of sUAS vary in regards to size and capability, in general the innards of UAS are very similar. For example, all UAS have flight controllers, systems to manipulate the engine(s), a power source (battery or fuel), and a means to communicate with the ground station/controller, which is used by the remote pilot to fly the UAS.

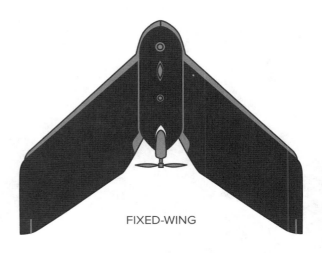

FIXED-WING

/ Flight Controller

The brain of the UAS is the flight controller. This device interprets the inputs from sensors and the remote pilot's controller commands. Onboard sensors often include GPS, an inertial measurement unit (IMU), an altimeter, and a magnetometer (i.e., a fancy compass). Additionally, some UAS have autopilots to allow for autonomous navigation, which can be programmed to fly pre-planned routes, circle objects, or follow the remote pilot. The flight controller manipulates the speed of the motor(s) to execute the commands of the remote pilot or autopilot. It also is used to manipulate other sensors, such as the onboard camera.

If installed, a GPS module can provide extremely accurate position information that can be used to superimpose the UAS position on a map (such as on a controller display or in FPV). GPS is available just about anywhere on Earth as long as the UAS has a clear "view" of the sky, thanks to the constellation of satellites that constantly transmit the data needed for

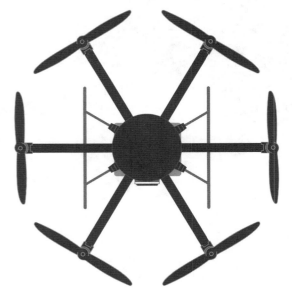

HEXACOPTER

Figure 1-1. Typical UAS configurations.

the GPS module to determine its location. Obviously, GPS will not work indoors, so remote pilots should familiarize themselves with any limitations to UAS use when GPS is not available. Many UAS use GPS to stabilize their positions, making it very simple to fly and essentially allowing for "hands off" loitering. Some UAS can become less stable when GPS is unavailable. Another useful feature of GPS is that it allows a UAS to note the position where it launched and automatically return to this "home" location if commanded to do so or in abnormal situations (such as controller signal loss or getting too far from the controller transmitter). One caveat is that the Return to Home function of most UAS is not aware of trees or buildings that may exist between the UAS's current position and the remote pilot. You do not need much imagination to understand how that could ruin your day. When beyond visual line-of-sight (BVLOS) operations are

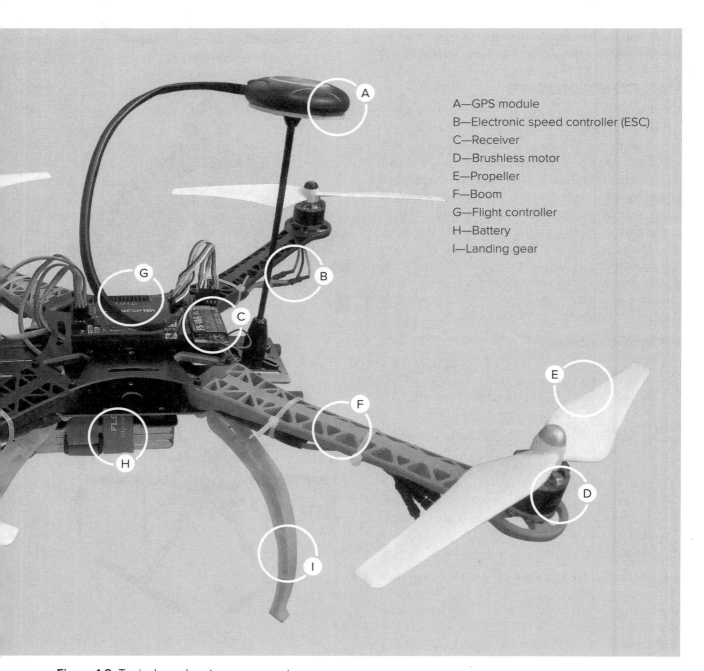

A—GPS module
B—Electronic speed controller (ESC)
C—Receiver
D—Brushless motor
E—Propeller
F—Boom
G—Flight controller
H—Battery
I—Landing gear

Figure 1-2. Typical quadcopter components.
(Halftermeyer; https://commons.wikimedia.org/wiki/File:Parrot_fleet_of_Drones.jpg; CC BY-SA 4.0)

permitted, GPS can assist the remote pilot in flying the UAS long distances from the launch point and in tracking specific routes. For example, a UAS operation could include the UAS launching from a safe vantage point, flying over a dangerous chemical leak, loitering, taking pictures or video, maybe even using infrared or other sophisticated sensors, and flying home—all with little or no input from the remote pilot.

/ Communications Components

For the UAS to communicate with the ground station/controller, it must have an antenna and a receiver. The antenna may be obvious, appearing like a little pencil or whip extending from the top (or other part) of the UAS, or it can be integrated into the structure of the UAS. The receivers on most UAS are the types used on remote control (RC) aircraft, with different numbers of channels based upon needs. (Channels are necessary to send different messages to components, such as motors and cameras.)

/ Batteries

Both electric and internal combustion UAS utilize batteries. For UAS with electric engines, the battery is the primary source of power for the engine(s), flight controller, servos (if applicable; these move flight controls or other parts), autopilot, and sensors. Some UAS have a stand-alone camera with its own battery while on others, the camera is powered by the primary onboard power source. On simple, internal-combustion UAS, fuel is used to power the engine, but batteries are still used to power servos and other onboard components. Sophisticated, combustion-engine UAS may employ onboard electric power generation through a generator or alternator. UAS batteries must be lightweight and able to deliver enough power to operate the vehicle for a reasonable period of time; thus, they are generally high-capacity nickel-cadmium (NiCad) or lithium polymer (LiPo) types. LiPo batteries have gained popularity with sUAS because they are lighter, have larger capacities, and can deliver higher discharge rates. Unfortunately, LiPo batteries must be used with caution because if damaged or mishandled, they can explode or catch fire (see Chapter 10 for more details).

Batteries are marked with various numbers that provide details about their capabilities. A LiPo battery cell has a nominal voltage of 3.7 volts (V). To increase capacity, multiple cells are combined inside a battery, and this will be indicated on its cover. For example, a 2S battery indicates that two cells are installed in series

(S) giving a total voltage of 7.4 V (3.7 V x 2). Electric motors are rated by kilovolts (kV), which translates to rotations per minute (RPM) per volt. More volts equals higher motor speeds. Battery capacity is measured in milliampere-hours (mAh), which can be thought of as the size of the "fuel tank." Capacities vary depending on the manufacturer and UAS platform type. If a battery is marked with 5,000 mAh, this means that the battery can provide one amp (A) for an hour for every 1,000 mAh (after all, a milliamp is 1/1000 of an amp). Thus a 5,000 mAh battery can supply 1 A for five hours, 2 A for two and half hours (5,000 mAh ÷ 2 A = 2.5 hours; remember, 2 A = 2,000 mAh), 5 A for one hour, and so forth.

Another number you will see on batteries is the discharge capacity, denoted by the letter "C." For example, 50C means that the discharge capability of the battery is 50 times the capacity in amps. If we have a 5,000 mAh (i.e., 5 A) battery with a 50C discharge rating, it can sustain a maximum continuous output of 250 A (50 x 5 A = 250 A). Battery charge rate, also noted on the battery, is rated in terms of "C." Utilizing the same aforementioned formula, if a 5,000 mAh battery has a 5C charge rating, it can safely be charged at 25 A (5 x 5 A capacity = 25 A).

A battery monitor is often installed on a UAS to track the status of the battery, providing feedback to the remote pilot. The current battery capability is typically displayed somewhere on the controller and/or causes the UAS to perform certain commands (e.g., return home) when the battery is low. As is evident from these descriptions, batteries are complicated components of UAS, and further discussion is beyond the scope of this book. It is wise for remote pilots to become familiar with the various attributes and capabilities of the batteries onboard their specific UAS.

/ Electronic Speed Controllers

Electronic speed controllers (ESCs) for each electric motor are connected to the flight controller. ESCs convert onboard direct current (DC) power to the alternating current (AC) used by UAS motors. They also control the motor speed and direction. Each ESC is connected to the motor it controls. Motors attach to the frame (fuselage) of the UAS via motor mounts. The latest technology uses brushless motors, which are quieter and more reliable than older motors that employed brushes.

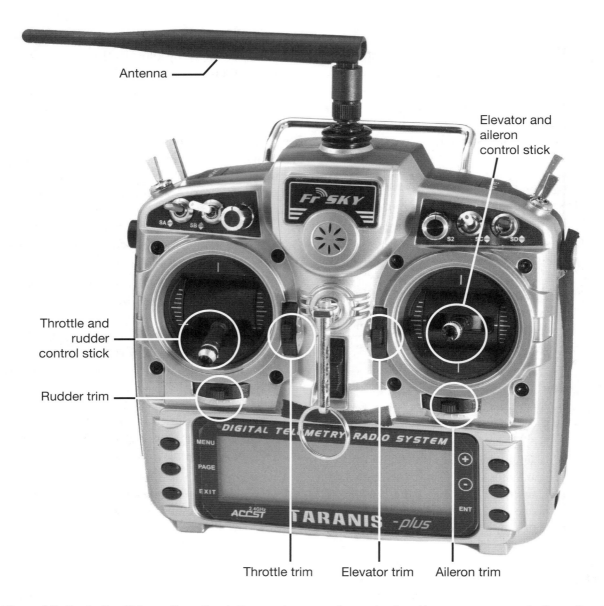

Antenna

Elevator and aileron control stick

Throttle and rudder control stick

Rudder trim

Throttle trim

Elevator trim

Aileron trim

Figure 1-3. Controller. This configuration is the most commonly used setup. However, some controllers allow for customization of switches and stick functions.

(Lucasbosch; https://commons.wikimedia.org/wiki/File:FrSky_X9D_Taranis_plus_2.4_GHz_handheld_RC_transmitter.jpg; CC BY-SA 3.0)

Fixed-wing UAS have very simple motor arrangements, rotating propellers to either push air (when the propellers are mounted on the back of the UAS) or pull air (when mounted on the front). Multicopters have more complex setups with multiple motors spinning propellers in different directions to counteract torque. Considering Newton's third law—for every action, there is an equal and opposite reaction—if all propellers rotated in the same direction, it would be problematic to control the UAS. Also, the propeller rotation is arranged so that some propellers push and others pull. In a quadcopter, the propellers in the "front" of the UAS pull (also referred to as tractor propellers) and the ones at the rear push. Multicopters with more motors become more intricate. Of course, a propeller that rotates in a clockwise direction cannot be the same as one that rotates counterclockwise. Essentially, the propeller blade angles are reversed so that thrust (lifting power) is appropriately generated. UAS manufacturers mark the propellers and motors to ensure they are properly matched. For fixed-wing UAS, control comes from the movement of flight controls similar to manned aircraft. These are electrically actuated by servos linked to the flight controller/receiver.

/ Additional Component Options

UAS usually have some type of landing gear, which can be as simple as a skid or a pole, or more complex involving wheels or the ability to retract (or both). Additional features may include a camera or other sensors. Simple UAS have cameras fixed to the body of the aircraft, giving them minimal utility since the remote pilot must aim the aircraft appropriately to get the desired picture or video. Advanced UAS employ cameras that can be controlled by the operator via a gimbal motor and control unit, providing the ability to tilt the camera left and right, and perhaps up and down. The ideal installation includes a gimbal, which is a stabilization feature that helps dampen vibration effects and potentially keep the camera image level as the UAS maneuvers. Some cameras are integral parts of the UAS (i.e., provided by the manufacturer), while other UAS allow for the attachment of a user-provided camera or other sensor.

/ Controller

The controller serves as the interface between the remote pilot and the UAS. Figure 1-3 shows an example controller. While controller features vary, they commonly all have two primary control "sticks." These sticks control the motor(s) and movement of the UAS. In the "standard" configuration (Mode 2), the left stick controls the motor (thrust) and the yaw (nose left/right) of the aircraft while the right stick controls the pitch (nose up/down) and bank/roll (wing and side angles left/right) of the aircraft (Figure 1-4).

With the left stick, pushing it forward (up) increases motor speed, and pulling it back decreases motor speed; pushing the stick to the left yaws the aircraft left, and pushing it right yaws the UAS to the right.

When manipulating the right stick, pushing forward will cause the UAS to move forward (multicopter) or nose down (fixed-wing), and the opposite occurs when the stick is pushed backward. Pushing the right stick left or right will cause the aircraft to move or bank in the same direction as the stick is pushed.

Individual controllers may include various other extra buttons and controls. On some models, there is a switch to change between control modes, which typically include a more stable mode or modes for beginners and a less stable mode or modes for those with more operating experience. A common feature is a "headless" mode, which allows the user to control the aircraft without having to consider which way it is "facing" (i.e., the joystick on the controller will direct the UAS to the right, left, forward, or backward from the user's perspective, regardless of the UAS's orientation). This may be helpful because without headless mode, when the aircraft is flying towards the remote pilot, the left/right control inputs need to be reversed, because a stick input for a right bank/movement will cause the aircraft to move towards the remote pilot's left (since the aircraft's right is to the user's left).

Additional control features may allow for flying with or without GPS inputs (if installed), although flying with GPS inputs typically provides much more stability and the capability to fly "hands off" the controls. Additional switches or controls may be available to control the gimbal/camera, if installed. Some controllers have status screens or even first-person view displays. It is also typical to have control "trim," which allows for fine adjustments to the yaw and turning controls in case the aircraft drifts when the remote pilot releases the controls.

COMMON USES OF SUAS

Flying sUAS can certainly be a fun hobby. The advent of first-person view (FPV) technology allows the user to be fully immersed in the aircraft. Also, sUAS provide a means to take photographs and videos from perspectives not previously possible without spending lots of money or becoming a manned aircraft pilot. Even "drone" racing has caught on to the point that it is receiving sponsors and television coverage. In addition to the many fun things you can do with sUAS, these devices have many practical applications, as well:

- Real estate agents are using sUAS to survey and photograph the properties they are selling.
- Farmers are using these systems for precision agriculture, allowing them to see which crops need more water or fertilizer and even which crops are being weakened by pests.
- Search and rescue personnel use sUAS to find lost hikers and missing animals.
- Game wardens employ sUAS to protect endangered species and track down poachers across the globe.
- Scientists use these systems to monitor the environment, study animal life, and collect other types of data.
- Companies deploy sUAS to inspect and monitor their assets such as powerlines, plants, and transmission towers.

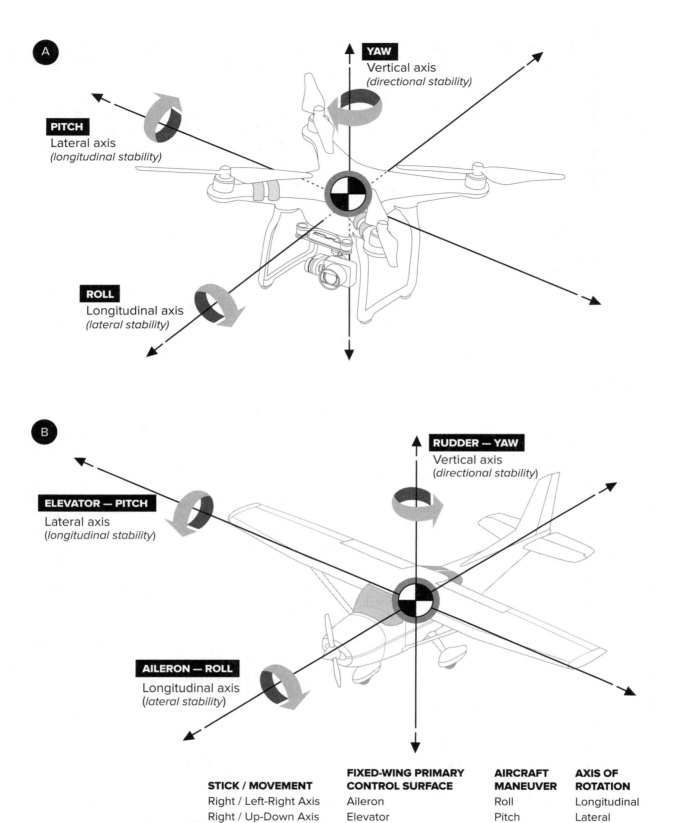

STICK / MOVEMENT	FIXED-WING PRIMARY CONTROL SURFACE	AIRCRAFT MANEUVER	AXIS OF ROTATION
Right / Left-Right Axis	Aileron	Roll	Longitudinal
Right / Up-Down Axis	Elevator	Pitch	Lateral
Left / Up-Down Axis	Throttle	Thrust	—
Left / Left-Right Axis	Rudder	Yaw	Vertical

Figure 1-4. Control inputs and axes for (A) multicopter and (B) fixed-wing UAS.

- Security and law enforcement personnel utilize both fixed-wing and multicopter sUAS to provide surveillance and monitoring to protect the public or specific assets.
- News crews are adopting sUAS to assist in aerial coverage and to provide unique aerial perspectives.
- Film makers also utilize sUAS for aerial views, providing amazing footage that otherwise would have been impossible or would have required elaborate equipment or manned aircraft.

This is by no means an exhaustive list; many other potential uses exist. Essentially, if you can imagine it, you can probably do it with an sUAS. The only real limitations are those imposed by aircraft performance as well as federal, state, and local regulations.

SUMMARY

Now that you have been introduced to the basic sUAS terms, components, and uses, the next step is to explore the specifics of aeronautical knowledge with which remote pilots should be familiar. It would certainly be much more fun to simply go fly our systems whenever and wherever we wanted, but this would not be a responsible way to operate. Just as we would not hop in a car without learning the rules of the road, signage, and basic safety practices, we cannot launch into the same airspace occupied by airliners full of people without learning the various particulars and peculiarities of the environment.

REVIEW QUESTIONS

Lesson 1 — Unmanned Aircraft Systems: Learning the Language of Drones

1. The _____ is responsible for the operation and safety of an sUAS.

   A — owner

   B — operator

   C — remote pilot-in-command

2. The concept of keeping an sUAS within visual sight of the remote pilot-in-command is referred to as

   A — VLOS

   B — VSPIC

   C — UASVS

3. An sUAS has a maximum weight of _____.

   A — 55 kg

   B — 55 lbs

   C — 55 oz

4. What is the nominal total voltage of a 3S LiPo battery?

   A — 3.7V

   B — 3V

   C — 11.1V

5. If your sUAS battery is rated at 7,500 mAh and consumes an average of 30 A per hour, how long will the battery last?

   A — 120 minutes

   B — 30 minutes

   C — 15 minutes

Regulations: Remote Pilot Certificate sUAS Rating Privileges, Limitations, and Flight Operations

GOVERNMENT REGULATIONS AND OTHER PROCEDURES PUBLICATIONS

As you progress with your pilot training, you will come across what will seem to be a never-ending series of instructions, procedures, methods, restrictions and advisories, and you will wonder how you will be able to remember it all. You don't have to. The Government Printing Office (GPO) distributes hundreds of publications on aviation subjects and you should become familiar with what is available. All government publications are available from the Government Printing Office in Washington, D.C., and GPO bookstores in major cities, but you will find that your local pilot supply store carries many of them. Private publishers offer reprints that are more convenient to use and considerably less expensive than the government publications (but no less official). The ASA editions of the Federal Aviation Regulations and *Aeronautical Information Manual* are excellent examples. The FAA publications are also available in electronic form, which has the additional benefit of the search function (so you can search any single or multiple documents for a specific word or topic). Many of these publications are available online. The web addresses in this book are only suggestions—there are many sources. You can find almost any FAA publication by going to www.faa.gov and typing the name of the desired publication into the search window. *Warning:* Do not rely on the accuracy of FAA documentation provided by third parties for use on electronic devices. Those sources are frequently found to be incomplete. Always refer to the FAA website for the latest information.

/ Aeronautical Information Manual: Basic Flight Information and ATC Procedures (AIM)

The *Aeronautical Information Manual* (AIM) contains information on a host of aviation subjects and is an essential reference for both manned and unmanned flyers. This list of chapter headings will give you some idea of the extent of coverage. (For each, I've indicated in parentheses if it has low, medium, or high relevance to sUAS; note that *no* section is irrelevant).

1. Navigation Aids (*low*)
2. Aeronautical Lighting and Other Airport Visual Aids (*medium*)
3. Airspace (*high*)
4. Air Traffic Control (*high*)
5. Air Traffic Procedures (*high*)
6. Emergency Procedures (*high*)
7. Safety of Flight (*high*)
8. Medical Facts for Pilots (*medium*)
9. Aeronautical Charts and Related Publications (*high*)
10. Helicopter Operations (*low*)

Figure 2-1 is an example of the type of detailed information on procedures available in the *Aeronautical Information Manual*. The AIM also includes a Pilot/Controller Glossary, so that you will know exactly what the controller means when instructions are given (controllers have an identical glossary in the Air Traffic Control Handbook). The AIM is updated every two years, with changes every six months, and is available by subscription from the Government Printing Office. You will also find it for sale by ASA, combined with

Section 3. AIRPORT OPERATIONS

4–3–1. GENERAL

Increased traffic congestion, aircraft in climb and descent attitudes, and pilot preoccupation with cockpit duties are some factors that increase the hazardous accident potential near the airport. The situation is further compounded when the weather is marginal– that is, just meeting VFR requirements. Pilots must be particularly alert when operating in the vicinity of an airport. This section defines some rules, practices, and procedures that pilots should be familiar with and adhere to for safe airport operations.

4–3–2. AIRPORTS WITH AN OPERATING CONTROL TOWER

a. When operating at an airport where traffic control is being exercised by a control tower, pilots are required to maintain two-way radio contact with the tower while operating within the Class B, Class C, and Class D surface area unless the tower authorizes otherwise. Initial callup should be made about 15 miles from the airport. Unless there is a good reason to leave the tower frequency before exiting the Class B, Class C, and Class D surface areas, it is a good operating practice to remain on the tower frequency for the purpose of receiving traffic information. In the interest of reducing tower frequency congestion, pilots are reminded that it is not necessary to request permission to leave the tower frequency once outside of Class B, Class C, and Class D surface areas. Not all airports with an operating control tower will have Class D airspace. These airports do not have weather reporting which is a requirement for surface based controlled airspace, previously known as a control zone. The controlled airspace over these airports will normally begin at 700 feet or 1,200 feet above ground level and can be determined from the visual aeronautical charts. Pilots are expected to use good operating practices and communicate with the control tower as described in this section.

b. When necessary, the tower controller will issue clearances or other information for aircraft to generally follow the desired flight path (traffic patterns) when flying in Class B, Class C, and Class D surface areas and the proper taxi routes when operating on the ground. If not otherwise authorized or directed by the tower, pilots of fixed-wing aircraft approaching to land must circle the airport to the left. Pilots approaching to land in a helicopter must avoid the flow of fixed-wing traffic.

However, in all instances, an appropriate clearance must be received from the tower before landing.

Components of a Traffic Pattern

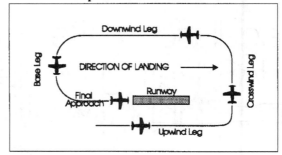

FIG 4–3–1

NOTE–
THIS DIAGRAM IS INTENDED ONLY TO ILLUSTRATE TERMINOLOGY USED IN IDENTIFYING VARIOUS COMPONENTS OF A TRAFFIC PATTERN. IT SHOULD NOT BE USED AS A REFERENCE OR GUIDE ON HOW TO ENTER A TRAFFIC PATTERN.

c. The following terminology for the various components of a traffic pattern has been adopted as standard for use by control towers and pilots (See FIG 4–3–1):

1. *Upwind leg:* A flight path parallel to the landing runway in the direction of landing.

2. *Crosswind leg:* A flight path at right angles to the landing runway off its takeoff end.

3. *Downwind leg:* A flight path parallel to the landing runway in the opposite direction of landing.

4. *Base leg:* A flight path at right angles to the landing runway off its approach end and extending from the downwind leg to the intersection of the extended runway centerline.

5. *Final approach:* A flight path in the direction of landing along the extended runway centerline from the base leg to the runway.

d. Many towers are equipped with a tower radar display. The radar uses are intended to enhance the effectiveness and efficiency of the local control, or tower, position. They are not intended to provide radar services or benefits to pilots except as they may accrue through a more efficient tower operation. The four basic uses are:

1. *To determine an aircraft's exact location:* This is accomplished by radar identifying the VFR aircraft through any of the techniques available to a radar

Figure 2-1. Example from a page of the AIM.

Figure 2-2. Federal Aviation Regulations in ASA's FAR/AIM series.

the Federal Aviation Regulations, at your pilot supply store (Figure 2-2). ASA provides a free online Update (www.asa2fly.com/farupdate) to keep pilots current on changes in regulations and procedures.

Every new edition of the AIM contains a list of changes since the previous edition, and there are always many. Be very suspicious of information from a copy of the AIM that is more than a year old, unless it contains at least one change. The AIM may be viewed online at www.faa.gov/air_traffic/publications.

/ Federal Aviation Regulations

The FAA expects you to be familiar with all of the Federal Aviation Regulations that apply to your flight operations, but as you read through the regulations you should be able to distinguish between those that are nice to know but do not affect your day-to-day flying, and those which you simply *must* know (e.g., basic weather requirements or right-of-way rules). This lesson will discuss those regulations that require explanation or illustration for full understanding, but all of Part 107 of the regulations apply to you when acting as a certified remote pilot of sUAS. If you are operating as a hobbyist, Part 101 would be applicable, as well as FAA Advisory Circular (AC) 91-57A, *Model Aircraft Operating Standards*. Note that Part 101 also applies to moored balloons, kites, amateur rockets, and unmanned free balloons. Before you say "I can't find it in the regs," be sure that you have checked all sources. Note also that the regulations list things that you cannot do—if something is not prohibited by a

___
[1] www.faa.gov/regulations_policies

regulation, it is permitted. A searchable version of all of the regulations can be found on the FAA's website.[1]

Prior to flying, you must determine the purpose of your planned activity. Simply, are you going to be using the sUAS as a certificated remote pilot (i.e., commercial or other non-recreational use), or are you going to fly as a hobbyist (i.e., for recreational use)? If you are planning to fly under the auspice of recreational use, be sure that you will comply with the requirements of Title 14 of the Code of Federal Regulations (CFR) Part 101, Subpart E, "Special Rule for Model Aircraft." This distinguishes between a model aircraft and an sUAS governed by Part 107.

Model Aircraft—Recreational Flying

In order to be considered a model aircraft, per 14 CFR §101.41, an aircraft must:

- Be flown strictly for hobby or recreational use;
- Be operated in accordance with a community-based set of safety guidelines and within the programming of a nationwide community-based organization;
- Not weigh more than 55 pounds (unless certified through a design, construction, inspection, flight test, and operational safety program administrated by a community-based organization);
- Be operated in a manner that does not interfere with and gives way to any manned aircraft; and
- Not be flown within 5 miles of an airport unless the operator provides prior notice to the airport operator and airport air traffic control tower (if applicable).

TFR= temporary flight restriction

An additional catch-all is added under 14 CFR §101.43, which states that no one may operate a model aircraft in a way that endangers the safety of the National Airspace System. So what exactly does this mean? Well, if you are flying as a hobbyist, you and your aircraft must comply with the requirements of 14 CFR Part 101. The "community-based" organization/safety guidelines refers to an entity such as the Academy of Model Aeronautics (AMA). AMA has very organized operations guidance and safety procedures, which is why the FAA wants you to use them. Any model aircraft flier would be wise to become a member of AMA due to its plethora of resources as well as insurance that comes with membership. By subscribing to AMA's policies and procedures, you are demonstrating your compliance with Part 101. Additionally, working with AMA can allow you to fly model aircraft larger than 55 pounds. Yes, there are models that big; in fact, some model aircraft, such as replica commercial aircraft, are as complex and sophisticated as their much larger counterparts.

Lastly, be sure to notify nearby airports (within 5 miles) prior to beginning operations. You can do this via phone, email, mail, or aircraft radio.[2] Airport manager and air traffic control tower phone numbers and frequencies (if applicable) are available in the *Chart Supplement* published by the FAA (available in print or digital formats).

How do you know if you are within 5 miles of an airport? Probably the easiest way is to use the FAA's B4UFLY application for smartphones. You can also refer to aeronautical charts, although pinpointing your exact location on them may be difficult. Using mapping websites or applications can also work well, but be sure you are accurately plotting your position and distance from all airports. Having an old-school road map or topographic map is another great option (as long as you can read them!). Keep in mind that the FAA's use of the term "airport" includes not only regular airports, but also heliports, seaplane bases, and private airports. If you live in a city, you're unlikely to be able to find a location anywhere in town that is more than 5 miles away from all of these places.

Model aircraft pilots must also operate in accordance with Advisory Circular 91-57A. This document specifies that model aircraft operators must comply with any Temporary Flight Restrictions (TFRs). TFRs are issued for disasters, national security, or to protect special events (e.g., airshows, sporting events). Do not operate any model aircraft within the confines of an active TFR. You may access current TFRs from the FAA's TFR website (tfr.faa.gov) as well as through Notices to Airmen (NOTAMs). AC 91-57A also states that model aircraft cannot operate within prohibited areas (i.e., places such as the White House), Special Flight Rule Areas, or within the Washington, D.C., area (referred to as the Washington National Capital Region Flight Restricted Zone). You should also be aware of additional NOTAMs cautioning against flying over or near stadiums, power plants, dams, oil refineries, and emergency services. This document states that model aircraft fliers should conform to the altitude restriction of 400 feet above ground level (AGL).

Lastly, there are some restrictions that aren't well broadcast to the public. For example, UAS operations in National Parks, National Monuments, National Seashores, and other sites run by the National Park Service are prohibited. Penalties can be as high as $5,000 and up to six months in jail. Some local governments have issued ordinances or restrictions on UAS flight. Although a variety of legal battles have occurred (and will continue to occur) over the ability of local governments to pass laws on UAS, which are covered by federal law, it is best not to attract any unwarranted attention from local law enforcement. Moreover, you do not want to have to spend lots of time and money defending yourself from something that isn't within local jurisdiction. Be sure to stay abreast of changes to rules governing the way you fly.

Non-Recreational Flying—Operation of sUAS Requiring a Remote Pilot Certificate

While the previous section outlines what you can and cannot do as a recreational, model aircraft pilot, you probably did not buy this book and become determined to become a certificated remote pilot simply to fly models around in a park. To use sUAS for commercial or other non-recreational missions and serve as the remote pilot-in-command (remote PIC), you must gain your Remote Pilot certification, which requires a fair amount of aeronautical knowledge that, unless you are already a manned aircraft pilot, will likely not be very familiar to you. Further, in order to safely fly

---

[2] To transmit on aviation frequencies, you need to ensure you comply with Federal Communications Commission (FCC) licensure requirements. See 47 CFR Part 87.

in the same skies as manned aircraft (ranging from general aviation up to airliners), you will need more subject matter proficiency than just the minimum required to pass the written Remote Pilot Knowledge Exam. So welcome aspiring remote pilot (or curious current remote pilot)! The first task at hand, as is almost always the case in anything related to aviation, is to understand all the regulations associated with sUAS and your intended use for them.

Regulations covering non-recreational sUAS flying can be found in 14 CFR Part 107. Part 107 is divided into four subparts: (A) General, (B) Operating Rules, (C) Remote Pilot Certification, and (D) Waivers.

Part 107, Subpart A—General

14 CFR 107.1 Applicability. This part of the regulations sets the stage as to what is covered by Part 107. Except for air carrier operations, model aircraft (subject to Part 101), or any operation conducted under a Section 333 of Public Law 112-95 exemption, Part 107 applies. If you don't know what Section 333 exemptions are, then they most likely don't apply to your operations.

14 CFR 107.3 Definitions. This section makes official the definitions of certain terms that are used in the rest of the regulations. It is important to note that if anything in this section conflicts with definitions in 14 CFR §1.1 (general definitions for all regulations), those found in Part 107 are "controlling"—i.e., the ones you should use.

- *Control station* means an interface used by the remote pilot to control the flight path of the small unmanned aircraft.
- *Corrective lenses* mean spectacles or contact lenses.
- *Small unmanned aircraft* means an unmanned aircraft weighing less than 55 pounds on takeoff, including everything that is on board or otherwise attached to the aircraft.
- *Small unmanned aircraft system* (*small UAS*) means a small unmanned aircraft and its associated elements (including communication links and the components that control the small unmanned aircraft) that are required for the safe and efficient operation of the small unmanned aircraft in the national airspace system.
- *Unmanned aircraft* means an aircraft operated without the possibility of direct human intervention from within or on the aircraft.

- *Visual observer* means a person who is designated by the remote PIC to assist the remote PIC and the person manipulating the flight controls of the small UAS to see and avoid other air traffic or objects aloft or on the ground.

14 CFR 107.5 Falsification, reproduction, or alteration. To summarize this section: Don't mess with the FAA. Any fraudulent or intentional false reports/records to show compliance with Part 107, as well as any reproduction or alteration of certificates, ratings, authorizations, or reports under Part 107, can land you in hot water. If you do any of the aforementioned, you can be denied from applying for a Remote Pilot certificate or a certificate of waiver, have your certificate or waiver suspended or revoked, or face civil penalty.

14 CFR 107.7 Inspection, testing, and demonstration of compliance. Any remote PIC (a remote pilot certificate holder responsible for and the final authority as to the operation of the sUAS), owner, or person manipulating the controls of an sUAS must, if asked by the Administrator (i.e., the FAA), present their remote pilot certificate with sUAS rating and any other document, record, or report required under Part 107. These same individuals are required, upon request, to allow the Administrator to make any test or inspection to determine compliance with Part 107. This part includes the requirement to allow the FAA to inspect the sUAS.

14 CFR 107.9 Accident reporting. In order for the FAA to get a better sense of the actual level of safety that exists within sUAS flying, rather than relying only on forecasts and projections, it is important to report any accidents, per this regulation. It may sound scary to report an accident to the federal government, but such reports are not intended to be a means of enforcement or penalty, but for information purposes. (That said, you should not be doing anything contrary to regulations, as you may be penalized.) So if something bad happens, the remote PIC has 10 calendar days after the event to file a report to the FAA. Not every little thing has to be reported; in fact, only two conditions require such a report: (1) if someone received serious injury or anyone is knocked unconscious, and/or (2) there is damage to property (other than the sUAS), unless the cost of repair (including labor and materials) does not exceed $500 or the fair market value to replace the property does not exceed $500 (if determined to be a total loss). For example, let's say you're out flying your

$1,000 sUAS at a park and you fly it into someone's car. It causes around $500 in paint damage. Do you have to report this as an accident? It depends. If the total cost of repair including labor is $500 or less, no report is required. But if there were labor costs on top of the $500 in damages, then yes, it would need to be reported. You may be asking, "Wait, but my drone is $1,000 and it's ruined!" Remember that the cost of or damage to the sUAS is not a factor in accident reporting. The FAA's sUAS accident reporting system can be found at www.faa.gov/uas/report_accident.

Although the FAA does not specifically describe it in Part 107, the term "serious injury" does appear in other regulations and documents. This level of injury is defined as "any injury which: (1) requires hospitalization for more than 48 hours, commencing within 7 days from the date an injury was received; (2) results in a fracture of any bone (except simple fractures of fingers, toes, or nose); (3) causes severe hemorrhages, or nerve, muscle, or tendon damage; (4) involves any internal organ; or (5) involves second- or third-degree burns, or any burns affecting more than 5 percent of the body surface" (FAA Order 8020.16 and 49 CFR §830.2).

It is critical to note that while the FAA requires accident reports under the aforementioned circumstances, additional reporting may also be required. Just like in manned aircraft accidents, the National Transportation Safety Board (NTSB), which is charged with investigating transportation accidents, may need to be involved: FAA reports are not a substitute for separate accident/incident reporting required by the NTSB under 49 CFR §830.5." According to the NTSB,

> an unmanned aircraft accident is defined in 49 C.F.R. § 830.2 as an occurrence associated with the operation of any public or civil unmanned aircraft system that takes place between the time that the system is activated with the purpose of flight and the time that the system is deactivated at the conclusion of its mission, in which: (1) Any person suffers death or serious injury; or (2) The aircraft has a maximum gross takeoff weight of 300 pounds or greater and sustains substantial damage.[3]

An example of a public sUAS is one operated by a government agency, while a civil sUAS is one operated by a private individual or entity (used for non-hobby/non-recreational purposes). The official definition of substantial damage, as provided in 49 CFR §830.2, is

> damage or failure which adversely affects the structural strength, performance, or flight characteristics of the aircraft, and which would normally require major repair or replacement of the affected component. Engine failure or damage limited to an engine if only one engine fails or is damaged, bent fairings or cowling, dented skin, small punctured holes in the skin or fabric, ground damage to rotor or propeller blades, and damage to landing gear, wheels, tires, flaps, engine accessories, brakes, or wingtips are not considered 'substantial damage' for the purpose of this part.

Immediate notification of the NTSB is required upon the occurrence of an accident, with a formal report being filed no later than 10 days after the event.

So let's say you're flying your quadcopter sUAS to photograph the scenery at a beachfront location when one of the propellers shatters for no apparent reason. Does this require NTSB notification? Technically the answer is no, because an sUAS is less than 300 pounds. If you were flying a 300-pound UAS and this type of propeller failure occurred, it would require notification. The NTSB does have the discretion to investigate what it views as non-safety critical occurrences. What if your sUAS suffers an uncontrolled fly-away and crashes into a bystander, breaking the person's arm. Do you have to tell the NTSB? Yes, this meets the definition of a serious injury, so you would need to make the report.

Additional parts of 49 CFR §830.5 apply to UAS operations, including the following occurrences which require notification of the NTSB:[4]

- Flight control system malfunction or failure: For an unmanned aircraft, a true "fly-away" would qualify. A lost link that behaves as expected does not qualify.

---

[3] National Transportation Safety Board (NTSB), Office of Aviation Safety, "Advisory to Operators of Civil Unmanned Aircraft Systems in the United States" (2016). Retrieved from www.ntsb.gov/investigations/process/Documents/NTSB-Advisory-Drones.pdf

[4] NTSB, "Advisory to Operators of Civil Unmanned Aircraft Systems in the United States."

- Inability of any required flight crewmember to perform normal flight duties as a result of injury or illness. Examples of required flight crewmembers include the remote pilot, or visual observer, if required by regulation. This does not include an optional payload operator.
- Inflight fire, which is generally associated with batteries.
- Aircraft collision in flight.
- More than $25,000 in damage to objects other than the aircraft.
- Damage to helicopter tail or main rotor blades, including ground damage, that requires major repair or replacement of the blade(s).
- An aircraft is overdue and is believed to have been involved in an accident.

It is important to note that no NTSB notification is required for occurrences involving hobby/recreational use of UAS.

Part 107, Subpart B—Operating Rules

14 CFR 107.11 Applicability. This part doesn't really tell us anything we don't already know, which is that the following operating rules apply to civil sUAS users covered under Part 107 (i.e., non-hobby/non-recreational users).

14 CFR 107.12 Requirement for a remote pilot certificate with a small UAS rating. In order to manipulate the controls of a sUAS, a person must have a remote pilot certificate with a small UAS rating issued under Part 107 and be compliant with the requirements under this part, or the person at the controls of the sUAS must be under the supervision of the aforementioned certificated pilot who has the ability to immediately take over control as necessary. The Administrator (i.e., FAA) may allow an airman to operate a civil foreign sUAS, consistent with the appropriate international standards, without an FAA-issued remote pilot certificate.

14 CFR 107.13 Registration. This section discusses the requirement to comply with 14 CFR §91.203 (a)(2), which refers to the requirement to register your sUAS. Regardless of your purpose of flying (recreational or not), any sUAS over 0.55 pounds must be registered. You can register online at: https://registermyuas.faa.gov/

14 CFR 107.15 Condition for safe operation. The FAA does not want remote pilots flying sUAS that are not in a safe condition to fly. Before each flight, the remote PIC must check/inspect the sUAS to ensure it is fit to fly.

14 CFR 107.17 Medical condition. Although no medical exam is required to be a remote pilot, such as is required to be a manned pilot, the person who is manipulating the controls of an sUAS cannot have (or have reason to believe that they have) a physical or mental condition that would interfere with the safe operation of the sUAS. The same standard applies to the remote PIC, visual observer, or direct participant in the operation.

14 CFR 107.19 Remote Pilot in Command. The person designated as the remote PIC before and during the flight of an sUAS is directly responsible for and is the final authority as to the operation. Additionally, this individual is responsible for ensuring that the sUAS does not pose any hazard to people, aircraft, or property in the event of the loss of control of the aircraft; that the operation complies with all applicable regulations; and that they have the ability to direct (control) the sUAS to ensure it complies with the aforementioned and other parts of the regulations.

14 CFR 107.21 In-flight emergency. During an emergency (one that is urgent and requires immediate response), the remote PIC can deviate from any rule as needed to deal with the emergency. Anyone who deviates from regulations per the aforementioned caveat must, upon request, send a written report to the Administrator (FAA).

14 CFR 107.23 Hazardous operation. It should be no surprise that no person may operate a sUAS carelessly or recklessly in a way that could endanger people or property. Also, objects cannot be dropped from sUAS in a way that endangers people or property.

14 CFR 107.25 Operation from a moving vehicle or aircraft. I know it sounds crazy. That's why there is a regulation. No person can operate a sUAS from a moving aircraft. You cannot operate an sUAS from a moving land or water vehicle, unless you are in a sparsely populated area (e.g., the middle of nowhere) and the aircraft is not transporting property for compensation or hire.

14 CFR 107.27 Alcohol or drugs. The person manipulating the controls of an sUAS, the remote PIC, and/or the visual observer must comply with 14 CFR §91.17 and §91.19. While much of §91.17 relates specifically to manned aircraft, the following standards clearly also apply to sUAS: No person may act or attempt to act as any of the previously mentioned crewmembers within eight hours of drinking alcoholic beverages, while under the influence of alcohol, while using any drugs that may impair safe use of the aircraft, or while having a 0.04 or more blood or breath alcohol concentration. This rule also implies that law enforcement may be able to request a sobriety test similar to those issued to suspected drunk drivers. Not surprisingly, you cannot transport narcotic drugs, marihuana, and depressant or stimulant drugs/substances controlled in federal or state statutes via sUAS, as specified by 14 CFR §91.19 (unless, of course, you are authorized to do so per the rule, but I don't recommend asking for a waiver for that).

14 CFR 107.29 Daylight operation. In short, you cannot operate sUAS at night. You can operate during civil twilight as long as the sUAS is fitted with anti-collision lights that are visible to at least 3 statute miles. The definition of "civil twilight" can get tricky for Alaska (you will need to check *The Air Almanac*[5]), but elsewhere it is a period that begins 30 minutes prior to official sunrise to official sunrise and again between official sunset and 30 minutes after official sunset. You can apply for a waiver of this rule, and several operators have successfully received such approval from the FAA.

14 CFR 107.31 Visual line of sight aircraft operation. At all times during flight, the remote PIC and the person manipulating the controls of the sUAS (if not the same person) or the visual observer must be able to determine the location of the sUAS; determine its attitude, altitude, and direction of flight; and ensure it is not endangering persons or property. Also, the applicable individual(s) must be able to monitor the airspace for other air traffic or hazards. This situational awareness must be maintained through line-of-sight that is unaided by anything other than corrective lenses.

14 CFR 107.33 Visual observer. If used, the visual observer must be in communication with the remote PIC and the person manipulating the controls of the sUAS (if different). The remote PIC must ensure that the visual observer can see the sUAS and is able to determine the necessary flight status information required in Section 107.31. The key is that all participants are communicating to maintain awareness of the sUAS position via direct observation and to vigilantly monitor the local area for any and all hazards.

14 CFR 107.35 Operation of multiple small unmanned aircraft. No person can be a remote PIC or visual observer for more than one sUAS at any given time.

14 CFR 107.36 Carriage of hazardous material. The government does not want sUAS transporting hazardous material; thus, sUAS are prohibited from carrying things defined as hazardous in 49 CFR §171.8. The term hazardous material "includes hazardous substances, hazardous wastes, marine pollutants, elevated temperature materials, materials designated as hazardous in the Hazardous Materials Table (see 49 CFR 172.101), and materials that meet the defining criteria for hazard classes and divisions in part 173 of this subchapter."[6] Interestingly, lithium-type batteries, such as those used to power many sUAS, are considered hazardous material. However, if you're transporting an sUAS, the battery is part of the system, so you're not considered to technically be "carrying" it, as you would be if transporting a lithium battery for delivery to a customer or remote location.

14 CFR 107.37 Operation near aircraft; right-of-way rules. The simplest way to remember this rule is that sUAS must give way to any and all aircraft, airborne vehicle, and launch/recovery vehicles. Yielding right of way also means you cannot fly your sUAS over, under, or ahead of the aforementioned vehicles unless the sUAS is well clear of them. You may never operate an sUAS so close to another aircraft that it creates the potential for a collision. Considering it is hard to judge distances between sUAS and other objects that are aloft, it is best to remain well clear of any local traffic. As the regulation is written, this means you must also give way to other sUAS and avoid flying close enough to other sUAS to create a collision hazard.

---

[5] U.S. Naval Observatory, Astronomical Application Department. http://aa.usno.navy.mil/data/docs/RS_OneDay.php

[6] Definitions and Abbreviations, 49 CFR §171.8

14 CFR 107.39 Operation over human beings. sUAS are not permitted to be flown over human beings unless they are directly participating in the operation thereof (e.g., visual observer) or the person is located under a covered structure or enclosed in a stationary vehicle, either of which would provide protection from a falling sUAS. Keep in mind that while this rule implies you can fly over non-humans (i.e., animals), those lives may be property—such as a horse, cow, dog, etc.—to which you must avoid causing undue hazard during your operation. So it is best not to buzz your local sheep farm.

14 CFR 107.41 Operation in certain airspace. No person can operate an sUAS in what is referred to as a controlled airspace (Class B, C, D, or surface-based Class E) without prior authorization from air traffic control. It is unlikely you will be granted permission to operate in these types of airspace without going through a formal airspace waiver process. You can apply for an airspace waiver at www.faa.gov/uas/request_waiver. Thus, Part 107 users are essentially restricted to uncontrolled (Class G) airspace. There are some exceptions to this in which you may enter Class E airspace not associated with an airport (i.e., not surface-based Class E) without notifying air traffic control and, of course, users can petition for a waiver of this part of the rule.

14 CFR 107.43 Operation in the vicinity of airports. Remote pilots must avoid interfering with operations and traffic patterns at any airport, heliport, or seaplane base. In cities, heliports may be everywhere—on or near police buildings, at television stations, at hospitals, or at local businesses just for convenience. One of the best resources to determine what types of facilities are near your operation is the FAA's B4UFLY application, and you can also refer to local aviation charts.

14 CFR 107.45 Operation in prohibited or restricted areas. Remote pilots are not allowed to operate sUAS in prohibited or restricted airspace without permission from the "owner" of the airspace (i.e., the using or controlling agency). Prohibited areas are typically designated over very sensitive locations such as the White House and Camp David. Sorry, you're not likely to get permission from the government to snap photos of the president. Restricted areas usually have some sort of military activity or national security interest within them. Again, it's unlikely you will get permission to enter, but it is important to note that some locations are designated "restricted" only at specific days and times. When they are not active, you are permitted to enter without prior notification (although it is *very* wise to call anyway, in case the schedule has changed). For information about the dimensions, time frames (if applicable), and contact information for restricted airspace, refer to aeronautical charts or call Flight Service (FSS).

14 CFR 107.47 Flight restrictions in the proximity of certain areas designated by notice to airmen. This part states that the remote PIC must comply with 14 CFR §§91.137–145 and §99.7. Simply, sUAS operators must comply with restrictions put forth via notices to airmen (NOTAMs). These may be issued in the vicinity of disaster/hazard areas, in proximity to the president or other parties, and near space flight operations, aerial demonstrations, and major sporting events. Additionally, emergency traffic rules may be put into place, such as the grounding of all air traffic after the 9/11 attacks, or during extreme atmospheric pressure conditions (e.g., very high barometric pressure). Examples of where you will be restricted from operating per NOTAMs include the Super Bowl, forest fires, volcanic eruptions, air shows, and rocket launches. It is critical that remote pilots, just like manned pilots, check for all possible NOTAMs or any other flight restrictions prior to operations. There are also special security instructions for operations near what are called Air Defense Identification Zones (ADIZs) or Defense Areas. If you are operating near these areas, be sure to comply with any and all restrictions or instructions. ADIZ are located near the edge of U.S. airspace off the East and West Coasts as well as along the border with Mexico. ADIZs also surround coastal Alaska, Hawaii, and some other U.S. territories.

14 CFR 107.49 Preflight familiarization, inspection, and actions for aircraft operation. Before each flight, the remote PIC must evaluate the surface and air operating environments to include assessing them for potential risks to persons and property. The remote PIC must check local weather conditions (which requires more than simply looking out the window), local airspace (to determine the type of airspace operating in), any/all applicable flight restrictions (e.g., NOTAMs), location of persons or property on the surface (bystanders, cars, children, dogs, etc.), and any ground hazards (such as powerlines). The remote PIC must also ensure all persons participating in the operation of the sUAS are informed about operating conditions, emergency procedures, contingency procedures, roles and responsibilities, and hazards. The remote PIC must confirm that all control links between the ground control station and the sUAS are working adequately. Also, the sUAS should have enough power (electric or gas) for the intended length of operation. Lastly, the RPIC must ensure that any object that is attached or carried by the sUAS does not negatively affect the flight characteristics or controllability of the aircraft and that all items are securely connected so as to not inadvertently become a falling object.

14 CFR 107.51 Operating limitations for small unmanned aircraft. The remote PIC and the person manipulating the controls of an sUAS (if different) must comply with the following operational limitations: a maximum groundspeed of 87 knots (100 mph); a maximum altitude of 400 feet AGL (unless within 400 feet of a structure, then no higher than 400 feet above the structure's highest point); a minimum flight visibility of 3 statute miles as observed at the ground station; and operations closer than 500 feet below and 2,000 feet horizontally from any cloud. For the purposes of this rule, flight visibility is defined as the average slant distance from the control station (since the sUAS is most likely viewed from the ground) that prominent unlighted objects during the day and prominent lighted objects during the night may be seen and identified.

This rule creates some "interesting" situations that must be considered. For example, let's say that you have set up your ground station close to the top of a canyon ridge. If you fly your sUAS out over the canyon, you may suddenly be more than 400 feet AGL, but if you were to drop the aircraft to 400 feet AGL you may no longer have it in your line of sight. In another example, if you are operating within 400 feet of a structure and go up to 400 feet above the highest point on the structure, it is also possible that your sUAS could end up in Class E airspace (which usually starts at 700 or 1,200 feet AGL depending on the location). In addition, the further the sUAS gets from you and/or your visual observer (if applicable), it becomes increasingly tough to judge when you are 500 feet below or 2,000 feet horizontally from clouds. Use excess caution and stay well clear of all clouds and areas of reduced visibility. It is best to think these things through before going flying.

Part 107, Subpart C—Remote Pilot Certification

14 CFR 107.53 Applicability. This subpart of the rule applies to the requirements to be issued a remote pilot certificate with an sUAS rating.

14 CFR 107.57 Offenses involving alcohol or drugs. If you get convicted of any federal or state statute related to drug dealing, you may be subject to denial of an application for a remote pilot certificate with sUAS rating for up to one year after the date of the final conviction, and if you already have such certification, it may be suspended or revoked. If you are convicted of violating the regulations relating to drugs and alcohol spelled out in 14 CFR §91.17(a) or §91.19(a), you may be subject to the same aforementioned admonishments (see above description of 14 CFR §107.27).

14 CFR 107.59 Refusal to submit to an alcohol test or to furnish test results. If law enforcement or the administrator (FAA) want to test you for alcohol in your system and you refuse or will not release results to the asking party, you may be subject to losing your right to apply for a remote pilot certificate with sUAS rating. If you hold one already, the certificate may be suspended or revoked.

14 CFR 107.61 Eligibility. In order to be eligible for the remote pilot certificate, a person must be at least 16 years old; be able to read, speak, and understand English; not know or have reason to know that they have a physical or mental condition that would interfere with sUAS operations; and demonstrate aeronautical knowledge necessary to operate sUAS. The proficiency in aeronautical knowledge can be satisfied either by (1) taking the initial aeronautical knowledge test (Remote Pilot Knowledge Test [Unmanned Aircraft General, or UAG]), or (2) if you hold a pilot certificate (other than student pilot) issued under 14 CFR Part 61, by meeting the flight review requirements in 14 CFR §61.56 and completing an initial training course that is acceptable to the Administrator (currently offered by the FAA online: www.faasafety.gov).

14 CFR 107.63 Issuance of a remote pilot certificate with a small UAS rating. In order to get your remote pilot certificate with sUAS rating, you must submit an application that includes your passing airman knowledge test report, or if you already hold a pilot certificate, you must show evidence of meeting the requirements outlined in §107.61 to a Flight Standard District Office (FSDO), designated pilot examiner, an airman certification representative at a flight school, a certificated flight instructor, or other person authorized by the Administrator. Current pilots must present identification and a logbook endorsement showing compliance with the flight review requirements specified in 14 CFR §61.56.

The FAA has eliminated much of the paperwork in keeping track of pilots and flight time by instituting the Integrated Airman Certification and/or Rating Application (IACRA). This system has essentially all but replaced paper applications. You will need to sign up for an account and follow the instructions to secure your remote pilot certificate once you have completed the necessary test or training. You will receive an FAA Tracking Number; write it in your logbook or somewhere where it can't be lost—you will need it. The nice thing about this system is that, after passing the UAG test, you can link your score results to your IACRA application and immediately receive your temporary remote pilot certificate.

14 CFR 107.64 Temporary certificate. A temporary remote pilot certificate with sUAS rating is valid for up to 120 days. You should receive your permanent certificate within that time frame. The temporary certificate expires on the expiration date shown on the certificate, upon receipt of the permanent certificate, or upon notice of its denial or revocation.

14 CFR 107.65 Aeronautical knowledge recency. A remote pilot must complete recurrency training every 24 months in the form of a recurrent aeronautical knowledge test or by taking the initial remote pilot aeronautical knowledge (UAG) test. If you hold a manned pilot certification under Part 61, you can use a flight review, initial or recurrent training course, or other means acceptable to the Administrator in lieu of the aforementioned tests.

14 CFR 107.67 Knowledge tests: General procedures and passing grades. In order to take knowledge tests, you will need to submit proper identification, which must include a photograph, your signature, date of birth, and a permanent mailing address. Government-issued IDs are generally acceptable for the purposes of this rule. The minimum passing grade is specified by the Administrator; it is currently 70% for the UAG.

14 CFR 107.69 Knowledge tests: Cheating or other unauthorized conduct. In sum, this rule tells you not to cheat or participate in other unauthorized conduct while taking your UAG test. Specifically, you cannot: copy or remove any test; give a copy or receive a copy of a test; give or receive help during the test; take a test for someone else; pretend to be someone else when taking the test; use any unauthorized material or aid when taking the test; or intentionally participate or be associated with the previous activities. If you violate any of these prohibitions, you will be prohibited from applying for any certificate, rating, or authorization and from applying for or taking any tests for one year following the wrongful act. If you cheat, you may also have any certificate or rating you already hold suspended or revoked.

14 CFR 107.71 Retesting after failure. If you fail the UAG test, you have to wait 14 calendar days prior to retaking it. (But this shouldn't happen after reading this book, right?)

14 CFR 107.73 Initial and recurrent knowledge tests. Your initial test (UAG) will require you to know the ins and outs of the following subjects: regulations, airspace, weather, aircraft loading, emergency procedures, crew resource management (CRM), radio procedures, aircraft performance, effects of drugs and alcohol, aeronautical decision making (ADM), airport operations, and maintenance/inspection requirements. While some of these topics are intuitive even to the non-aviator, if you are not already a pilot, many of these details can be rather foreign concepts and thus some study is required. Do not underestimate the complexity of the UAG test. Moreover, in order to stay out of trouble with the FAA or local law enforcement, it is best to be well-versed in the knowledge relating to sUAS operations.

Recurrent tests will cover: regulations, airspace, emergency procedures, CRM, ADM, airport operations, and maintenance/inspection requirements. Although these tests have not yet been developed, you can expect them to ensure that you have kept up-to-date with any changes that have occurred within any of the mentioned topics as well as sUAS operations in general. As with manned aviation, learning should not end once you have the certificate.

14 CFR 107.74 Initial and recurrent training courses. Not surprisingly, initial training courses cover all the topic areas that are covered on the UAG test outlined in 14 CFR §107.73(a). The same applies to recurrent training courses, which need to cover the items relating to the recurrency test topics listed in 14 CFR §107.73(b).

14 CFR 107.77 Change of name or address. If you change your name (e.g., perhaps you get married or want to change your name to Wilbur Wright), you need to tell the FAA via an application to change the name on your certificate. This application should be accompanied by your certificate and a copy of the legal document authorizing the name change (court document or marriage certificate/license). If you change your address, you must let the FAA know within 30 days of the date of the change. The address and website portal information to make this change are found under paragraph (c) of this section of the rules.

14 CFR 107.79 Voluntary surrender of certificate. You may voluntarily surrender your remote pilot certificate for cancellation. Perhaps you never plan to use it again, or the FAA, after you do something you weren't supposed to, asks you to surrender it. The proper phraseology to communicate this to the FAA is in paragraph (b) of this rule. You can always get it back, but you will have to start over with the requirements of Part 107 (i.e., take the UAG test again).

Part 107, Subpart D—Waivers

The FAA will grant waivers to certain parts of the regulations on a case-by-case basis. Pilots must apply for such authorizations at www.faa.gov/uas/request_waiver. The FAA uses performance-based standards for determining if they will grant a waiver, so you are well advised to thoroughly read the instructions for completing such a request. When the ability to apply for waivers was announced, the FAA released an example of the information that would be needed in an appeal for night operations, which is as follows:

- Applicant must provide a method for the remote pilot to maintain visual line-of-sight during darkness.
- Applicant must provide a method for the remote pilot to see and avoid other aircraft, people on the ground, and ground-based structures and obstacles during darkness.
- Applicant must provide a method by which the remote pilot will be able to continuously know and determine the position, altitude, attitude, and movement of the small unmanned aircraft (sUA).
- Applicant must assure that all required persons participating in the sUA operation have knowledge to recognize and overcome visual illusions caused by darkness, and understand physiological conditions that may degrade night vision.

- Applicant must provide a method to increase conspicuity of the sUA to be seen at a distance of 3 statute miles unless a system is in place that can avoid all non-participating aircraft.

If the FAA requires additional information about your application, you will need to promptly respond. Cases in which no communication is received within 30 days will lead to the closing of the application.

/ State, County, and Local Aviation Regulations and Legislation

Time for a Latin lesson. Do you know what the phrase *ignorantia juris neminem excusat* means? This roughly translates to "ignorance of the law is not an excuse." This legal concept infers that just because you did not know there was a state or local law, ordinance, or other restriction against operating sUAS at your location does not mean you are excused of any crimes or violations. Cities, states, and counties are jumping on the regulation bandwagon and passing a variety of different types of rules, some rather strict (such as "No Drone Zones"), while others are aimed at law enforcement (e.g., no armed drones, or police need a search warrant to surveil an individual). For example, Berkley, California, passed an ordinance making the city a "No Drone Zone." In Indiana, a recent bill submitted to the local legislature for consideration put restrictions on the use of UAS to scout game for hunters. Such restrictions are truly all over the place both in terms of the subjects of the restrictions and the locations scattered across the country. For more information about state and local rules and legislation, visit the Association for Unmanned Vehicle Systems International (AUVSI) or National Conference of State Legislatures (NCSL) websites.

Just when you begin to understand the complexity of the airspace in which you may operate your system, it gets even more dizzying. If you aren't too familiar with how jurisdiction works in terms of the federal, state, and local governments, understanding the basics will be helpful. Essentially, federal trumps all others; this is known as the "Supremacy Clause" of the U.S. Constitution (Article VI, Clause 2). Likewise, if there is a disconnect between state and local laws, the same hierarchy often applies and the state law trumps the local laws—although this is not as absolute as at the federal level (i.e., there are exceptions). Interestingly, in 2015, the FAA released a document concerning non-federal regulations of airspace and UAS. The FAA stated that it has the authority to supercede any state or local rules, regulations, ordinances, etc.:

> A consistent regulatory system for aircraft and use of airspace has the broader effect of ensuring the highest level of safety for all aviation operations. To ensure the maintenance of a safe and sound air transportation system and of navigable airspace free from inconsistent restrictions, FAA has regulatory authority over matters pertaining to aviation safety.[7]

The administration goes on to explicitly note how it is that it has absolute statutory authority:

> Substantial air safety issues are raised when state or local governments attempt to regulate the operation or flight of aircraft. If one or two municipalities enacted ordinances regulating UAS in the navigable airspace and a significant number of municipalities followed suit, fractionalized control of the navigable airspace could result. In turn, this 'patchwork quilt' of differing restrictions could severely limit the flexibility of FAA in controlling the airspace and flight patterns, and ensuring safety and an efficient air traffic flow. A navigable airspace free from inconsistent state and local restrictions is essential to the maintenance of a safe and sound air transportation system.[8]

So what does this all mean? Technically, there are instances when state or local laws may conflict with the precedent of "unrestricted airspace" and thus would not likely stand up in court if challenged. But as you are likely aware, lawyers are very expensive to hire. So even if a local law may be subject to the Supremacy Clause, it is probably not in your best interest to test it yourself. Local law enforcement probably won't enjoy a law lesson from someone they think is committing a crime or violating an ordinance. It is best to comply with whatever exists until it is challenged. One way to deal with the inconvenience is to contact the FAA Office of the Chief Counsel or a FAA Regional Counsel office and let them know about the restriction. Additionally, it's not a bad idea to carbon copy the letter to your state and local representatives. We want to be good representatives of the growing sUAS market.

/ Privacy Issues

One of the biggest public concerns about sUAS relates to privacy. Many worry that drones will soon be flying all over the place, including hovering outside bedroom windows and intruding on backyard barbecues. The FAA has clearly stated that they do not regulate privacy in terms of sUAS use. However, they do advocate the adoption of voluntary privacy best practices, which can be found at https://www.ntia.doc.gov/files/ntia/publications/uas_privacy_best_practices_6-21-16.pdf.[9] The key takeaways from this document are (1) use your head and (2) be a good neighbor. If you wouldn't want someone doing what you're doing over or near you or your house, don't do it yourself. Also, don't harass your neighbors, their dogs, their kids, etc.

Although technically there is no regulatory height above property that one "owns," there is a lone court case that, for now, is about the only guidance we have on this issue. In *United States v. Causby*, it was determined that the magic cutoff was 83 feet. (The case involved claims that military aircraft flying low over Causby's farm made his chickens suicidal; Causby won). The FAA controls all navigable airspace, which in general refers to 500 AGL and above (49 U.S.C. 40103[b][1]). This is part of the logic behind the 400 AGL restriction on most UAS operations. An additional rule allows for the FAA to regulate certain operations below 500 AGL (49 U.S.C. 44701[a]). So for now, it is a grey area regarding who controls what, but people do not "own" as much airspace above their land as they probably think.

Again, be a good citizen. Typically neighbors can argue that you are trespassing or harassing them if you are causing them to lose the value or enjoyment of their property. Check local laws and ordinances about how these potential issues may be defined in your area of residence.

---

[7] Federal Aviation Administration (FAA), Office of the Chief Counsel, "State and Local Regulation of Unmanned Aircraft Systems (UAS) Fact Sheet" (2015). Retrieved at www.faa.gov/uas/resources/uas_regulations_policy/media/uas_fact_sheet_final.pdf

[8] FAA, "State and Local Regulation."

[9] Consensus, Stakeholder-Drafted Best Practices Created in the NTIA-Convened Multistakeholder Process, "Voluntary Best Practices for UAS Privacy, Transparency, and Accountability" (2016).

CHART SUPPLEMENTS

Before setting off on an sUAS mission, you are required to become familiar with all available information regarding the flight, and the *Chart Supplement U.S.* (CS, or the online version referred to as the Digital Chart Supplement, d-CS) is your source of information on nearby airports. Aeronautical charts show the elevation, runway length, and limited radio frequency information for an airport, but only in the *Chart Supplement* will you learn details about airports that may impact sUAS operations, such as the location of obstructions, powerlines in the area, or bird activity. The legend for individual airport listings is provided in Appendix B of this text. In addition to the individual airport listings, the CS contains:

- Special notices in regard to airports listed
- FSS and National Weather Service telephone numbers
- Frequencies of Air Route Traffic Control Centers
- FAA Flight Standards District Office (FSDO) telephone numbers
- Parachute jumping areas
- Aeronautical Chart Bulletin (contains information about obstacles and hazards that have been noted since the last chart was printed and which will be included in the next printing)
- Airport diagrams for all public airports; detailed airport diagrams for large airports; airport diagrams are also available at www.faa.gov/air_traffic/ flight_info/aeronav/digital_products/dtpp/

The *Chart Supplement* is published in nine volumes depending on geographic location and is revised every 56 days.

An online version is available by going to www.faa. gov/air_traffic/flight_info/aeronav/ and clicking on "Digital Products" in the left column. The resulting page offers a number of valuable products in addition to the CS. The CS and its online counterpart are the only *official* sources of airport information. Do not rely on commercial publications.

Appendix B reprints the CS Legend. Read it thoroughly. An amazing number of "where does it say…?" or "where can I find out?" questions can be answered by reading the Legend. This is especially true of communications questions. The ability to interpret the airport listings is only part of what you need to know.

Much of the information contained in the CS (but not the Aeronautical Chart Bulletin) can be found at www.skyvector.com, www.airnav.com, www.landings. com, or www.1800wxbrief.com.

ADVISORY CIRCULARS

The Federal Aviation Regulations are brief and concise, written by and for lawyers, not pilots. There are many situations in which a regulation or a procedure needs to be explained in detail so that the flying public can understand exactly what is required. This is the function of Advisory Circulars (ACs). ACs are non-regulatory in nature, serving only to explain the actual regulation or provide additional useful information to aid in compliance; however, the government expects every pilot to be aware of information published only in Advisory Circulars! Unfortunately, many pilots are unaware of their existence.

Advisory Circulars are numbered to correspond with the regulations. To give three examples: 14 CFR Part 61 deals with airman and flight instructor certification, while Advisory Circular 61-65 explains flight instructor duties and responsibilities; 14 CFR Part 91 is General Operating Rules, and Advisory Circular 91-13 deals with cold-weather operations of aircraft; the 70 series deals with airspace. Most pilots are only aware of those Advisory Circulars that are published in book form, such as *Aviation Weather* (AC 00-6) or the *Airplane Flying Handbook* (FAA-H-8083-3), but you should investigate whether the FAA publishes an AC on any subject you may be curious about. You can access Advisory Circulars at the www.faa.gov home page, although they are also available through the Government Printing Office. Guess which is more convenient?

QR CODES

If you have a smartphone, all Aeronautical Information Services products now have QR codes on their covers. For sectional charts, the QR will take you to any of these sites:

- *Aeronautical Chart User's Guide*
- *Chart Supplement*
- NOTAMs and TFRs
- Safety alerts
- VFR chart update bulletins
- VFR Class B enhancement graphics
- Weather cameras

The QR code on the *Chart Supplement* will take you to:

- *Aeronautical Chart User's Guide*
- Digital CS
- NOTAMs and TFRs
- Safety alerts
- Weather cameras

The QR codes provide the opportunity to get the absolute latest information available.

NOTICES TO AIRMEN (NOTAMS)

Information that might affect the safety of a flight—such as an airport closure, Temporary Flight Restriction (TFR), communication frequency change, etc.—is available from your Flight Service Station (FSS) briefer.

Your briefer has access to NOTAMs. So do you, at pilotweb.nas.faa.gov/distribution/atcscc.html. If you use one of the computer flight planning products such as DUATS or the AOPA flight planner, you will also receive current NOTAMS—but be aware that TFRs can pop up without warning. Always check for them with flight service before takeoff to avoid being greeted by law enforcement or even the military.

To make it easier for pilots to scan through a list of NOTAMs for information specific to their flight, the FAA uses "key words" in the first line of text. See Figure 2-3 (although this FAA document does not include recent additions). Every 28 days the FAA releases the *Notices to Airmen* publication that contains all current NOTAM (D)s (these are "big deal" issues like runway or airport closures), except for Temporary Flight Restrictions. When a NOTAM is published here (or in the CS) it no longer shows up on the briefer's screen; if you don't *ask* the briefer for any published NOTAMs that will affect your flight, you will never find out about them. You can get this publication online at pilotweb.nas.faa.gov/PilotWeb/.

AVIATION MEDIA

All pilots are expected to stay abreast of changes in regulations and procedures, but advancing technology is teaching new ways of navigating and of solving some of the mysteries of weather, and pilots cannot expect today's methods to apply forever. It is a good idea to pay attention to any newly proposed regulations. You can see what may be implemented in the near future at the FAA's Notice of Proposed Rulemaking (NPRM) website. You can even subscribe for email updates at www.faa.gov/regulations_policies/rulemaking/recently_published/. The aviation press is the best source of information on the changing world of flight, and we recommend that you read aviation newspapers and magazines. The FAA's *Aviation Safety Briefing*, published six times a year, is available from the FAA home page, and you will find a wealth of information on the Academy of Model Aeronautics (AMA) website, www.modelaircraft.org. Another good resource for changes in sUAS regulations or other pertinent data can be found by becoming a member of the Association for Unmanned Vehicle Systems International (AUVSI), although non-members can still view recent events and some news features. Visit www.auvsi.org for more information. As with everything in aviation, remember the FAA is the official source of regulations, policies, and requirements.

The "D" NOTAM

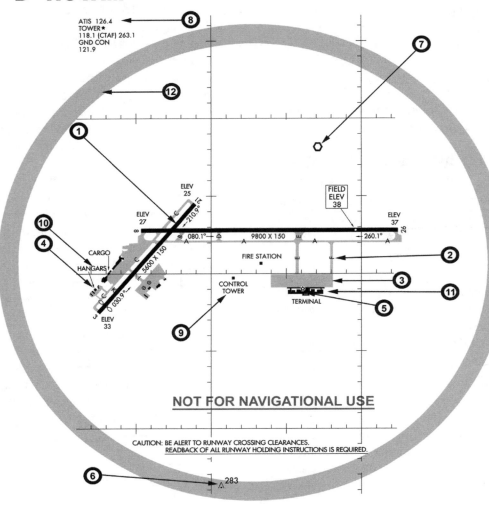

Figure 2-3. Example of FAA NOTAM "key words" (see AIM Table 5-1-1 for more keywords and definitions).

Key Words		NOTAM Examples
RWY	1	**RWY 3/21 CLSD** Runways 3 and 21 are closed to aircraft.
TWY	2	**TWY F LGTS OTS** Taxiway F lights are out of service.
RAMP	3	**RAMP TERMINAL EAST SIDE CONSTRUCTION** The ramp in front of the east side of the terminal has ongoing construction.
APRON	4	**APRON SW TWY C NEAR HANGARS CLSD** The apron near the southwest taxiway C in front of the hangars is closed.
AD	5	**AD ABN OTS** Aerodrome's airport beacon is out of service
OBST	6	**OBST TOWER 283 (246 AGL) 2.2 S LGTS OTS (ASR 1065881) TIL 0807272300** Obstruction. The lights are out of service on a tower that is 283 feet above mean sea level (MSL) or 246 feet above ground level (AGL) 2.2 statute miles south of the field. The FCC antenna structure registration (ASR) number is 1065881. The lights will be returned to service 2300 UTC (Coordinated Universal Time) on July 27, 2008.

Key Words		NOTAM Examples
NAV	7	**NAV VOR OTS** Navigation. The VOR located on this airport is out of service.
COM	8	**COM ATIS 126.4 OTS** Communications. The Automatic Terminal Information Service (ATIS) frequency 126.4 is out of service.
SVC	9	**SVC TWR 1215-0359 MON-FRI/1430-2300 SAT/1600-2200 SUN TIL 0809212200** Service. The control tower has new operating hours, 1215-2359 UTC Monday Thru Friday, 1430-2300 UTC on Saturday, and 1600-2200 UTC on Sunday until 2200 UTC on August 21, 2008.
	10	**SVC FUEL UNAVBL TIL 0807291600** Service. All fuel for this airport is unavailable until July 29, 2008 at 1600 UTC.
	11	**SVC CUSTOMS UNAVBL TIL 0808150800** Service. United States Customs service for this airport will not be available until August 15, 2008 at 0800 UTC.
AIRSPACE	12	**AIRSPACE AIRSHOW ACFT 5000/BLW 5 NMR AIRPORT AVOIDANCE ADZD WEF 0807152000-0807152200** Airspace. There is an airshow being held at this airport with aircraft flying 5000 feet and below within a 5 nautical mile radius. Avoidance is advised from 2000 UTC on July 15, 2008 until 2200 UTC on July 15, 2008.

NOTE: All "D" NOTAMs will have a key word at the beginning of the text of each NOTAM

Effective: JAN 2008 thru AUG 2009   FAA ATO AJR AIM #071307

REVIEW QUESTIONS

Lesson 2 — Regulations: Remote Pilot Certificate sUAS Rating Privileges, Limitations, and Flight Operations

1. In which publication can pilots find information about air traffic control procedures?

   A — Air Traffic Control Trainee Handbook

   B — *Pilot's Handbook of Aeronautical Knowledge*

   C — *Aeronautical Information Manual*

2. The part of 14 CFR that covers recreational use of sUAS is

   A — Part 91

   B — Part 101

   C — Part 107

3. The part of 14 CFR that covers non-recreational use of sUAS is

   A — Part 91

   B — Part 101

   C — Part 107

4. Without proper notification of the airport operator and air traffic control (if applicable), a recreational sUAS operator cannot fly within _____ miles of an airport.

   A — 3

   B — 5

   C — recreational pilots are not required to maintain separation from airports

5. You experience a fly-away during which your sUAS crashes through a storefront window, causing $800 in damages. By when must you report this accident to the FAA?

   A — immediately

   B — within 3 calendar days

   C — within 10 calendar days

6. You experience a fly-away during which your sUAS crashes into a person, knocking them unconscious. They are transported to the hospital for care. Who must you report this event to?

   A — No report is required.

   B — Only the FAA.

   C — Both the FAA and the NTSB.

7. You experience a fly-away during which your sUAS hits a house, causing $500 in damage to the garage door. Additionally, your sUAS, valued at $1,200 is destroyed. By when must you report this accident to the FAA?

   A — No report is required.

   B — Within 3 calendar days.

   C — Within 10 calendar days.

8. Which of the following operations is not covered by 14 CFR Part 107?

   A — Flying an sUAS to take pictures of a house for personal use.

   B — Flying an sUAS to take pictures of a house for business use.

   C — Flying an sUAS to survey a farm to provide precision agricultural services.

9. Which of the following UAS do not need to be registered with the FAA?

   A — Model aircraft used recreationally weighing 3 pounds.

   B — sUAS used recreationally weighing 0.50 pounds.

   C — sUAS used for business weighing 5 pounds.

10. How is a remote pilot medically certified to be authorized to fly sUAS under 14 CFR Part 107?

    A — The remote pilot is responsible for determining fitness to fly.

    B — The remote pilot must receive a physical from a FAA medical examiner.

    C — The remote pilot must receive a physical from their primary care physician.

11. Which of the following is not true regarding the responsibilities of the remote pilot-in-command during an emergency?

    A — The remote PIC may disregard any regulation if such deviation is required to respond to the emergency.

    B — The remote PIC may disregard any regulation regardless of circumstances.

    C — The remote PIC must send a report to the Administrator, if requested.

12. Which of the following would not be covered by 14 CFR Part 107?

    A — Flying your sUAS for hobby purposes.

    B — Flying your sUAS for business purposes.

    C — Flying your sUAS in exchange for a gift.

13. What length of time must a visual observer wait between having an alcoholic drink and helping with an sUAS mission?

    A — None; the remote pilot-in-command is the only person subject to restrictions.

    B — Eight hours.

    C — Four hours.

14. If you are convicted of any offenses related to alcohol or drugs, what may the FAA do to you as a remote pilot?

    A — Revoke your certificate.

    B — Revoke your certificate and deny application for a certificate for up to one year.

    C — The FAA does not have jurisdiction over local violations; therefore, they cannot take any action.

15. Which of the following fulfills the requirement for maintaining visual line-of-sight?

    A — The visual observer uses binoculars to monitor the status of the sUAS.

    B — The remote pilot-in-command uses binoculars to monitor the status of the sUAS.

    C — The remote pilot-in-command uses corrective lenses to monitor the status of the sUAS.

16. You wish to fly your sUAS during civil twilight. What special authorization is required?

    A — No special authorization is needed if the aircraft if fitted with the proper lighting system.

    B — No special authorization is needed, since twilight is considered daytime.

    C — Such operations are prohibited, unless you have a waiver, as twilight is considered nighttime.

17. While you are flying a mission with your sUAS, you notice a manned aircraft approaching. How do you determine who has the right of way?

    A — The lowest aircraft has the right of way.

    B — Manned aircraft generally have the right of way.

    C — Since the manned aircraft is approaching from the left, it must give way to you.

18. A friend asks you to help video-record their wedding from an aerial perspective. Which of the following would you be able to provide to remain in compliance with regulatory restrictions?

    A — Imagery shot from an area to the side of the guests.

    B — Imagery from directly above the guests, but high enough to be able to maneuver to safety in an emergency.

    C — Any video recording is legal as long as the sUAS remains in VLOS.

19. You are planning to photograph some real estate just outside the property line of a local airport that has a control tower. What action must be taken by the remote pilot-in-command prior to sUAS operations in the area?

 A — No action is required, as Part 107 does not specify a distance sUAS must remain away from airports.

 B — The sUAS must remain clear of all traffic patterns and operations at the airport.

 C — The remote pilot-in-command must receive authorization to conduct operations in the area.

20. You are planning to photograph some real estate just outside the property line of a remote, non-towered airport. What action must be taken by the remote pilot-in-command prior to sUAS operations in the area?

 A — No action is required, as Part 107 does not specify a distance sUAS must remain away from airports.

 B — The sUAS must remain clear of all traffic patterns and operations at the airport.

 C — The remote pilot-in-command must receive authorization to conduct operations in the area.

21. A Notice to Airmen (NOTAM) has been issued stating that flight operations are prohibited within 5 NM of a local football stadium. What precautions should you take when operating in the area?

 A — As a courtesy, you should avoid flying near or over the area.

 B — No precaution is required, as NOTAMs apply only to manned aircraft.

 C — Avoid the area, as sUAS operations are not permitted in the area.

22. The local news channel is reporting foggy conditions in the area. What is the minimum visibility required to permit non-recreational sUAS operations?

 A — 3 SM

 B — 3 NM

 C — 5 NM

23. In order to act as remote pilot-in-command, you must be at least _____ years old.

 A — 15

 B — 16

 C — 18

24. For persons not certificated as a pilot (other than student pilot) under 14 CFR Part 61, which of the following is not a requirement to receive a remote pilot-in-command?

 A — Take the FAA Knowledge Test.

 B — Be able to read, speak, and understand English.

 C — Hold a FAA medical certificate.

25. In order to act as remote pilot-in-command, you must have completed recurrent training or retake the UAG FAA Written Test every

 A — 12 months.

 B — 24 months.

 C — Not applicable; currency never expires.

26. How long do you have to notify the FAA of any change in your name or address?

 A — 14 days

 B — 30 days

 C — 120 days

27. If you discover that the city in which you are planning to fly has an ordinance against the operation of sUAS within its borders, which is the best option for your mission?

A — Cancel the mission.

B — Notify local law enforcement and carry out the mission as planned.

C — Federal law supersedes local law; therefore, you can fly without restriction or prior notification.

28. Where can you find phone numbers of FAA Flight Standards offices?

A — On aviation maps.

B — You cannot; they are not published for security purposes.

C — Within the *Chart Supplement*.

29. What is the best source of NOTAMs for remote pilots?

A — Employees at a nearby control tower.

B — Flight Service Station briefers.

C — Local law enforcement officials.

30. How long do you have to wait after failing the FAA Written Test before taking it again?

A — 7 days

B — 14 days

C — 30 days

air traffic control procedures = in Aeronautical Information Manual

Airspace and Navigation

At first glance, the National Airspace System (NAS) of the United States is a complex web of different types of airspace, each with their own restrictions, limitations, and unique requirements. For remote PICs to safely and legally operate in the NAS, they need to become intimately familiar with the various different airspace categories, including which ones to avoid, which are open for use, and the specifics for those that fall somewhere in between. Aeronautical charts are probably the best source of airspace information. You can access them online or through phone/tablet applications as well as have hard copies in hand. The key is to have current, up-to-date charts so you're not missing any recent changes. In addition, you will need to check all pertinent Notices to Airmen (NOTAMs) prior to each operation.

AERONAUTICAL CHARTS

You will use two types of charts as a remote pilot. The sectional chart is the one used most frequently because at roughly 8 nautical miles per inch, it affords sufficient detail for navigation by landmarks while retaining a manageable size. There are 38 sectionals covering the continental United States, plus three Canadian provinces in the Northeast, 16 more for Alaska, and one for Hawaii. New charts are published every six months. Before using an expired chart, consider that an average of 128 changes are made per charting cycle.

Sectionals show roads, freeways, railroads, power lines, lakes, rivers, terrain contours, and populated areas. Airports shown on sectional charts include public, private, military, and those to be used only in an emergency. Boundaries of controlled airspace are indicated by color tint and a variety of symbols. Before you take your written test, become familiar with the sectional chart legend, because knowing your way around a sectional will play a major role in the exam.

Terminal area charts are published for the busiest airports (those with Class B airspace, discussed later in this lesson). Their 4-miles-per-inch scale makes them quite detailed, and properly so: you must know where you are when flying in congested airspace. Revised charts are issued every six months.

The *Chart Supplement* (CS) is issued every 56 days and includes information not found in any other publication. It's important to note that the CS includes an Aeronautical Chart Bulletin. Now look at the chart revision frequencies mentioned above—the shortest is six months. What if a cell tower has been erected since the last issuance of the sectional chart you are using? What if an airport shown as uncontrolled on your chart now has an operating control tower? What if the control tower is shown on your chart, but the tower frequency has changed? Unless you refer to the CS's Aeronautical Chart Bulletin, you will be flying blind. Every year, pilots get themselves into trouble by using out-of-date charts. Don't be one of them.

Having said that, there is no provision in Parts 101 or 107 that requires you to carry any charts at all, recent or outdated. There are some online sources that you can refer to. Keeping in mind that web addresses come and go without notice, here are some useful URLs: www.faa.gov/air_traffic/flight_info/aeronav/digital_products is the official FAA source. Unfortunately, because sectionals are vast and consumer-level printers are small, you have to print out several individual charts

make sure you're using up to date charts!
new charts every 6 months

and tape them together. Among unofficial sources are www.skyvector.com and www.1800wxbrief.com. You can "fly" your proposed trip using Google Earth, checking out visual checkpoints along the way, and you can look at the area around your destination by using the "Airports" page under www.1800wxbrief.com.

GEOGRAPHICAL COORDINATES

To be able to better use navigation charts, you should be familiar with latitude and longitude. You will also use latitude-longitude coordinates with some advanced radio navigation systems such as GPS, so a brief explanation is in order.

Figure 3-1 shows parallels of latitude marching upward from the Equator (0° latitude) to the Poles (90° North or South latitude). If you slice a globe along lines of latitude, the slices get progressively smaller toward the poles, so distance measurements along latitude lines are useless.

Lines of longitude are called meridians and divide the earth from pole to pole, with the 0° meridian passing through Greenwich, England. Meridians are numbered eastward across Europe and Asia and westward across the Atlantic Ocean and the Americas until the 180° meridian is reached in mid-Pacific. The continental United States lies roughly between 70° and 125° West longitude and between 26° and 49° North latitude. Meridians are Great Circles: if you slice a globe along meridians, all of the slices will be the same size. All meridians are the same length: 10,600 nautical miles from pole to pole, and 60 nautical miles per degree.

Figure 3-1. Meridians and parallels

Each degree is further divided into 60 minutes, and this makes it possible to measure distance accurately: one minute of latitude equals one nautical mile when measured along a line of longitude toward either pole. Minutes are identified by a single tick—for example, 25' represents 25 minutes. Minutes are divided further into 60 seconds, which are shown by a double tick (e.g., 25").

As you look at your aeronautical chart, lines of longitude and latitude are at right angles. As you look at a globe, however, lines of longitude converge toward the poles. Because there is some unavoidable distortion of scale between the bottom and the top of an aeronautical chart, you should make course measurements as close as possible to the mid-latitude portion of the chart.

On the excerpt of the Seattle sectional chart (see Appendix D), find the Easton State airport (**A**). Count up (north) 15 minutes from the latitude line marked 47° to find the latitude of Easton State. Each little tick mark moving upward is a minute, with the larger tick indicating 10 minutes. Count left (west) 11 minutes from the longitude line marked 121° to find the longitude of Easton State. Its geographic position is 47° 15' 15" north, 121° 11' 15" west. You do not need to be any more accurate than the nearest minute to locate an airport using latitude and longitude. The geographic position of all airports is found in the CS.

TIME

The measurement of time is an integral part of air navigation. Before leaving the discussion of longitude and the 0° meridian, the subject of time zones and time conversions should be covered. The only rational way to have flight times and weather information apply across the country and around the world is to have a single time reference. That reference is the time at Greenwich, England (on the 0° line of longitude). Once referred to as Greenwich Mean Time, the time standard is now called Universal Time Coordinated (UTC). Each 15° of longitude east or west of Greenwich marks a one-hour time difference. Figure 3-2 shows the time differences across the United States with a legend for time conversion to and from Universal Time Coordinated, or Zulu time. Zulu is the phonetic identifier for the letter Z; in the 24-hour clock system, UTC is shown as 0800Z, 2200Z, etc. You should become familiar with time zone conversions for your area of operations.

Air traffic control and flight service station personnel use Zulu time and will be reluctant to do time conversions for you. If you are planning a departure for 1800 local time and there is a forecast for thunderstorms after 2100Z at your mission location, you will have to know time conversion to be able to relate that to your estimated time of flight. As a new pilot, you will probably stay within one time zone or possibly travel between two time zones. Just remember that, for example, you live in the "plus 5" time zone (plus 4 in the summer), and conversions will come easily to you.

STATUTE AND NAUTICAL MILE SCALE

Navigators on the sea or in the air find the use of nautical miles for distance measurement convenient, because a nautical mile is 6,000 feet (really 6,080, but that complicates things) and is also one minute of latitude. When you counted up 15 minutes to locate the latitude of Easton State airport, you counted up 15

nautical miles. You will find mileage scales for both nautical and statute miles on aeronautical charts. The FAA uses nautical miles for all distance measurements except visibility, which is measured in statute miles. Airspeed is usually referred to in knots (nautical miles per hour) only or in knots and miles per hour (MPH); you can find conversion calculators online or via various applications (or you can buy a flight computer). Winds are always given in knots, so you must be sure that you are dealing with like units when flight planning.

MAGNETIC VARIATION

Aviation has often followed the nautical path on a range of things but most notably in navigation. One such borrowed tool that has been used for aerial navigation for some time is the magnetic compass. It is a very effective means for determining which way is north and how to navigate from point A to point B, at least in most places on Earth. However, remote PICs must become aware that compasses and magnetic headings (used by

1 NM ≈ 6,000 feet = 1 minute of Latitude

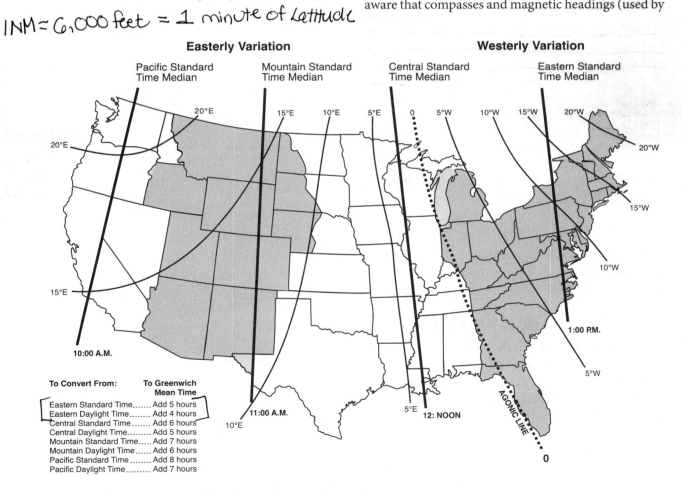

Figure 3-2. Time conversion (also showing magnetic variation)

EST = +5 hours
EDT = +4 hours

manned pilots) align with the Magnetic North Pole, which is in Northern Canada (and moves over time; see Figure 3-3). Thus, you should be aware that lines of latitude and longitude on charts are neatly perpendicular and relate to the True North Pole. The easiest way to keep these apart in your mind is to think of the True North Pole as where Santa lives, while the Magnetic North Pole is where your compass points.

You must take the variation between true north and magnetic north into account when interpreting air traffic headings and directions as well as things such as airport runway numbers. Additionally, when you receive aviation weather products, you need to realize that headings of winds are in reference to true north. However, winds provided directly from an air traffic control tower are in magnetic. In much of the United States, the difference between true and magnetic is not significant, but in certain areas it is huge (e.g., in Alaska).

Figure 3-4 shows isogonic lines, or lines of equal magnetic variation, across the continent. Along the line that passes through Chicago and Key West, a pilot looking toward the True North Pole will also be looking toward the magnetic North Pole, and there will be no variation. That line of zero variation is called the agonic line. East or west of that line, the angle between true and magnetic north increases. A pilot in Los Angeles who measures a course line on an aeronautical chart in relation to the longitude lines (or true north) must subtract 14° from that true course to get a magnetic course (*"East is least"*), while a pilot in Philadelphia will add 10° (*"West is best"*). You can determine the true course by using your navigation plotter.

The variation on your sectional chart is almost certainly out-of-date. The isogonic lines are only updated every three years or so. The next best source for variation is a current CS.

CORRECTING FOR WIND DRIFT

Figure 3-5 shows the effect of wind drift on an aircraft's flight path if no corrective action is taken. The wind correction angle necessary to offset the wind drift will allow the aircraft's track over the ground to agree with the planned course. Determining wind correction angle with a known wind direction, wind velocity, true course and true airspeed is a trigonometry problem. Because sUAS operations currently must be within visual line-of-sight (VLOS), wind correction will be

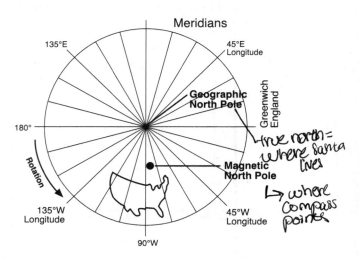

Figure 3-3. Magnetic and True North Poles

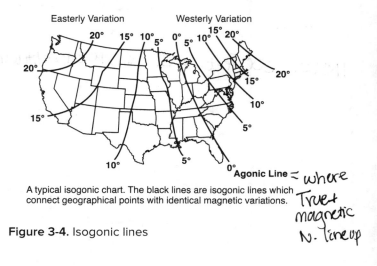

A typical isogonic chart. The black lines are isogonic lines which connect geographical points with identical magnetic variations.

Figure 3-4. Isogonic lines

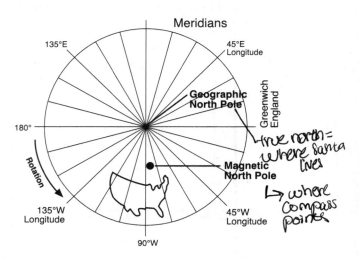

Figure 3-5. The effect of wind

made visually; thus, the calculations made by manned pilots for long-range flights is generally unnecessary. Beyond VLOS flights (when they eventually are authorized to occur or for those with a waiver) will employ relatively sophisticated navigation systems that will assist in or deal with necessary wind corrections.

GROUND SPEED VS. AIRSPEED

When you drive your automobile for one hour at 60 miles per hour, you can be fairly certain that you will travel 60 miles during that hour. In flight, whether or not one hour at 60 miles per will cover 60 miles will be determined by the wind. If you somehow manage to get airborne under control and are flying into a 60 MPH headwind with an airspeed of 60 MPH, you are not going to make it out of sight of the launch site: your speed over the ground will be zero. This is an extreme example, although pilots in the Great Plains states have plenty of stories about airplanes "flying" in strong winds that prove that it can happen. You can actually "fly" backwards if the winds are stronger than your forward speed! Though these tales are certainly entertaining, you need to develop an understanding of the airspeed/ground speed relationship on a more normal basis.

First, forget the comparison with the automobile and standardize all speed measurements in knots: the National Weather Service provides wind velocity information in knots and confusion will result if you mix units of measurement. Although much of aviation has adopted knots for airspeed indication, that does not appear to be the case with many sUAS manufacturers who report capabilities in MPH or kilometers per hour (KPH). Often the telemetry provided to you via your ground controller will not be in knots either. Remember that your true airspeed will increase 2% per 1,000 feet of altitude increase. This means that the speed at which a sUAS moves through the air (and along the ground, in no wind conditions) increases as either the sUAS climbs or when you choose an area of operation at a higher altitude.

Keep in mind the effects of wind on speed when determining how far is too far in regards to the distance between your sUAS and the intended landing zone. In high wind conditions, it is possible for an aircraft to get far enough away that it will not have enough battery power to make it back to you. Pay careful attention to battery power levels throughout the flight.

CHART READING

In other lessons, you will learn how to look at your aeronautical chart to determine radio frequencies and airspace designations. Bookmark the Seattle sectional chart excerpt in Appendix D; refer to it and its legend as you read this section. The importance of knowing the height of terrain and obstructions is evident. Notice that in each rectangle formed by lines of latitude and longitude there is a large blue number with an adjacent smaller number. This represents the height above mean sea level of the highest terrain or man-made obstruction within that rectangle, in thousands and hundreds of feet plus a safety margin. 83, for instance, means that you will clear the highest obstacle if you fly at 8,300 feet or higher. The heights of specific terrain features are indicated by a dot and the measured altitude; the altitude of the highest terrain within a latitude-longitude block is in large print—note Mount Rainier at the bottom of the chart and Mount Stuart at 47° 28′ N 120° 54′ W (*see* letter "N" west of airport H). You will notice that the highest obstacle is at least 100 feet below the 83 if it's a man-made obstacle, and at least 300 feet below if it's a natural obstruction. This is for added safety.

AGL It is important to remember that most altitude information that is available via the flight controller is relative to where the sUAS took off, *not* in relation to mean sea level. Therefore, it is helpful to have an idea of the elevation of the location at which you are flying. This can be determined using aeronautical charts or online mapping applications.

Man-made obstructions such as radio and television towers have two numbers adjacent to them. The top number (in bold italics) is the height of the top of the obstruction above mean sea level, and is the most meaningful number to you in choosing an altitude in that area. The number in parentheses is the actual height of the structure. Towers that are more than 1,000 feet in height (which usually require supporting guy wires that are virtually invisible) have a special symbol as shown in the chart legend. The dot at the base of the symbol represents the exact location of the obstruction. The group obstruction symbol (two symbols close together) means that there are two *or more* towers. There are several obstruction symbols, both single and group, north and west of Seattle-Tacoma airport.

Freeways, highways, and railroads are excellent references. Notice that major freeways are identified with their route numbers—Interstate 90 crosses the chart from Seattle to the lower right corner. You can often orient yourself by noticing an interchange or an obvious jog in a road, or by the relationship between a road and some other physical feature. Because power lines are centered in large right-of-way areas, they are just as useful as highways—you can see the cleared right-of-way much further than you can see the power lines themselves.

Do not rely on the city limits depicted so clearly in yellow on sectional charts; from the air, city limits are impossible to identify. This is particularly important if the city in question has restrictions on sUAS use (e.g., No Drone Zones).

Changes in elevation are depicted with contour lines. On the sectional chart excerpt, you can see how tightly packed the contour lines are in the Cascade Mountains. Notice the interval between contour lines. The lines are every 500 feet on sectionals. Mountain passes are indicated by a pair of back-to-back parentheses—for example, look about an inch to the left of airport **A** on the sectional chart excerpt to find Stampede Pass.

Always check your chart for markings that indicate parachute jumping areas (airport **G**), wind turbines, and low-lying cables across rivers and ravines. (Running into a skydiver or a power cable can ruin your whole day!) Where jumping is indicated, check the CS for details; the operators will usually announce the position of the jump aircraft and when jumpers begin their dive.

/ Airport and Navigation Aid (NAVAID) Identification

Aeronautical charts, as well as other sources, utilize an identification paradigm that can be thought of as a short name or abbreviation for a particular airport or NAVAID. This naming convention entails three letters (or four letters when using the international version [for airports only]; for most locations in the U.S., this comprises the regular three-letter abbreviation with a "K" prefix, which denotes that the location is within the lower 48 U.S. states).[1] Many of these identifiers will make sense to the non-aviator. For example, San Diego International Airport is denoted by the letters SAN (or KSAN internationally). Some other identifiers, however, are not as obvious—the Auburn, Washington, airport is identified as S50 (no K is required for these odd arrangements of letters and numbers). The same abbreviation system is used for NAVAIDs.[2] The main reason the four-letter arrangement exists is

to distinguish between airports and NAVAIDs, which, in theory, could use the same letters although each was in a different geographic location. An example of this is in Billings, Montana, where both the NAVAID and the airport use the identifier BIL, but the NAVAID is 4 miles west of the airport. In this case, using the four-letter identifier allows you to be clear which you are referring to: BIL (the NAVAID) or KBIL (the airport). For more information about the different kinds of navigation facilities, refer to the AIM. These do not mean much to sUAS operations other than that manned aircraft and ATC may use them in their communications, and they may be useful in relating information about aircraft location.

AIRSPACE

As you plan a flight, you know that the ability to maneuver in three dimensions makes you responsible for being aware at all times of your position, both geographic and vertical. You must ensure that you are always in compliance with the airspace regulations. These regulations are intended to keep airplanes safely separated. "See and be seen" is the basis of safe operations in the National Airspace System.

/ Controlled vs. Uncontrolled Airspace

You will encounter the terms "controlled airspace" and "uncontrolled airspace" frequently, and you must not assume that flight in controlled airspace means that Big Brother will be watching you to detect violations, or that uncontrolled airspace is the Wild West for flight. For the remote pilot, controlled and uncontrolled airspace refer to the possibility of being subject to air traffic control. (For manned aircraft, the difference is in minimum weather requirements, but for sUAS such requirements are currently the same regardless of airspace type). Controlled airspace is where aircraft of all types may be subject to ATC. For example, in Class E airspace, manned aircraft are not required to contact ATC or be subject to its control unless the aircraft is on an instrument (IFR) flight plan. However, all aircraft in Class D must communicate with ATC. In uncontrolled airspace—referred to as Class G airspace—no one is subject to ATC.

---

[1] Airports in Hawaii and Alaska use the prefix "P," while Puerto Rico uses "T."

[2] A NAVAID is a radio navigation facility that provides guidance to manned aircraft and that is used to define routes of flight. If flying from Columbus, Georgia, to Montgomery, Alabama, the route could be stated as KCSG-CSG-V20-MGM-KMGM (Columbus airport to Columbus NAVAID via Victor Airway 20 to Montgomery NAVAID to Montgomery airport).

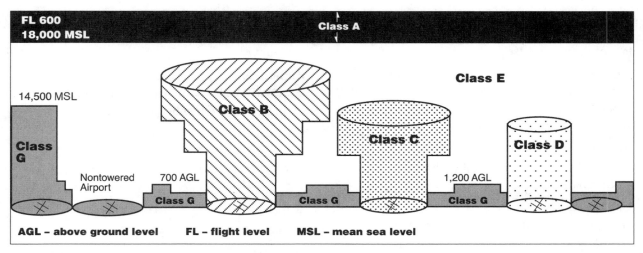

Figure 3-6. Airspace classification

Controlled airspace includes Class A, B, C, D, and E airspace (Figure 3-6). Look at the sectional chart excerpts in Appendix D and notice the blue and magenta tints—they represent the horizontal boundaries of controlled airspace (Class A airspace begins at 18,000 feet MSL and that is as high as a sectional chart goes). Blue is only used where it abuts Class G airspace, however.

At airports with instrument approach procedures (a means to permit manned aircraft to land in bad weather), controlled airspace can start at the surface—each of these situations will be covered in detail later. Figure 3-6 will give you an idea of what to expect. As you can see, most controlled airspace is Class E.

On the Seattle sectional chart excerpt (Appendix D), follow the 072 radial (the eastbound blue highlighted line) extending from the Seattle VORTAC (**C**) (a radio navigation aid used by manned aircraft); it is the V-120 airway (airways are "highways in the sky"—think of this airway as Interstate 120 for manned aircraft). Until you fly by the "powerhouse" depicted and cross the magenta line, you are in Class E airspace at or above 700 feet AGL. The fact that the magenta tint fades in the direction of Seattle indicates that this floor applies in the entire area surrounded by the tint.

Note that the floor of a Victor airway (V-120 in this example) is 1,200 feet above ground level (with some exceptions) and the ceiling is 18,000 feet above mean sea level.

After you pass the magenta line flying eastward along the 072-degree radial, the floor of Class E airspace becomes 1,200 feet above the ground (no shading) and that situation remains until you get to the magenta dashed line around the Wenatchee VORTAC.

Although you will not find any on the sectional chart excerpt, there are places where Class G airspace extends from the surface to 14,500 feet mean sea level (MSL). Look for the solid edge of a blue vignetted line—the floor of controlled airspace on the shaded side is 1,200 feet above the surface, but the airspace on the solid-edge side is uncontrolled all the way up to 14,500 MSL.

/ Class A Airspace

Class A airspace exists from 18,000 feet MSL to Flight Level 600 (all altitudes above 18,000 feet are called Flight Levels; FL230 is 23,000 feet, more or less). Not only are sUAS not permitted in Class A, they probably couldn't get up there even if they were allowed. Only large-scale UAS (e.g., military types) can fly that high.

/ Class B Airspace

Class B= cannot BE in w/o permission

The most important thing to remember about Class B airspace is that you cannot operate within its boundaries unless you have a specific authorization from ATC to do so. Class B airspace (Appendix D) is shown on sectional charts by solid blue circles or arcs; each segment within the airspace is identified with what looks like a fraction. On the sectional chart excerpt, the top of the fraction is 100, indicating that the top of Seattle's Class B airspace is 10,000 feet MSL.

The bottom of the fraction is the floor of the airspace in hundreds of feet. East of Bremerton National Airport (**D**) you can fly beneath the Class B airspace at 5,500 feet, and west of Bremerton the Class B airspace does not exist. Note that the floor of Class B airspace over Seattle-Tacoma International Airport is the surface of the airport itself.

Considering that manned student pilots are prohibited from operating to or from many of the following super-busy airports within Class B airspace, you probably won't be able to operate sUAS near them either:

Arizona:
- PHX / KPHX—Phoenix Sky Harbor International

California:
- LAX / KLAX—Los Angeles International
- NKX / KNKX—Marine Corps Air Station Miramar
- SAN / KSAN—San Diego International/Lindbergh Field
- SFO / KSFO—San Francisco International

Colorado:
- DEN / KDEN—Denver International

Florida:
- MCO / KMCO—Orlando International
- MIA / KMIA—Miami International
- TPA / KTPA—Tampa International

Georgia:
- ATL / KATL—Hartsfield–Jackson Atlanta International

Hawaii:
- HNL / PHNL—Daniel K. Inouye/Honolulu International

Illinois:
- ORD / KORD—Chicago O'Hare International

Kentucky:
- CVG / KCVG—Cincinnati/Northern Kentucky International

Louisiana:
- MSY / KMSY—Louis Armstrong New Orleans International

Maryland:
- ADW / KADW—Joint Base Andrews*
- BWI / KBWI—Baltimore/Washington International*

Massachusetts:
- BOS / KBOS—General Edward Lawrence Logan International

Michigan:
- DTW / KDTW—Detroit Metropolitan Wayne County

Minnesota:
- MSP / KMSP—Minneapolis–Saint Paul International/Wold–Chamberlain Field

Missouri:
- MCI / KMCI—Kansas City International
- STL / KSTL—St. Louis Lambert International

Nevada:
- LAS / KLAS—Las Vegas–McCarran International

New Jersey:
- EWR / KEWR—Newark Liberty International

New York:
- JFK / KJFK—New York–John F. Kennedy International
- LGA / KLGA—New York–LaGuardia

North Carolina:
- CLT / KCLT—Charlotte Douglas International

Ohio:
- CLE / KCLE—Cleveland Hopkins International

Pennsylvania:
- PHL / KPHL—Philadelphia International
- PIT / KPIT—Pittsburgh International

Tennessee:
- MEM / KMEM—Memphis International

Texas:
- DFW / KDFW—Dallas/Fort Worth International
- HOU / KHOU—Houston–William P. Hobby
- IAH/KIAH—Houston–George Bush Intercontinental

Utah:
- SLC / KSLC—Salt Lake City International

Virginia:
- DCA / KDCA—Ronald Reagan Washington National*
- IAD / KIAD—Washington Dulles International*

Washington:
- SEA / KSEA—Seattle-Tacoma International

*Note: The Washington, D.C., area is a "No Drone Zone." For more information, see: www.faa.gov/uas/where_to_fly/no_drone_zone/

Although all Class B primary airports have control towers, they do not have Class D airspace.

/ Class C Airspace

The Seattle sectional chart excerpt that has been included in Appendix D for your use does not contain any Class C airspace; however, Figures 3-7a and 3-7b show excerpts of the Spokane and Whidbey Island areas, where both Spokane International and Fairchild Air Force Base are in Class C airspace. Figure 3-7b shows the Class C airspace at the Whidbey Island Naval Air Station. Note how many satellite airports are located beneath the outer rings at both Spokane and Whidbey. The horizontal boundaries of Class C airspace are shown by solid magenta circles. Remember that you need authorization to fly sUAS in Class C airspace.

C= needs authorization

Many Class C areas do not operate 24 hours a day. Where operation is part-time, check the panel on the back of the sectional chart or, as advised by a chart notation near the airspace, check the CS for operating hours and the type of airspace the Class C reverts to when it is not in effect.

Each segment within the airspace is identified with what looks like a fraction. In Figure 3-7b, the top fraction is 40, indicating that the top of Whidbey Island's Class C airspace is 4,000 feet; you can fly over it at 4,500 feet without talking to anyone. The bottom of the fraction is the floor of the airspace in hundreds of feet—1,300 or 2,000. Note that the floor of Class C airspace over Whidbey Island Naval Air Station is the surface of the airport itself.

/ Class D Airspace

Class D airspace exists whenever a control tower is in operation, except for airports with Class B or C airspace (which include tower functions). Class D airspace imposes a requirement for ATC authorization for sUAS operations. What are the dimensions of Class D airspace? The horizontal boundary is shown on charts with a blue dashed line (the airport symbol is blue when there is a tower at the airport); the vertical extent is from the airport elevation to 2,500 feet above the airport (or the base of a different kind of airspace above). Figure 3-8 shows a nice cylindrical shape for clarity, but actual dimensions will vary widely. The elevation of the top of the airspace to the next highest hundred feet is shown in a little square box near the airport symbol. (Look at any tower-controlled airport

except Seattle-Tacoma to check this. Sea-Tac shows -30 because it sits on a plateau above Puget Sound and the top of its Class D airspace is the 3,000-foot floor of the associated Class B airspace.)

The shape of Class D airspace varies with local conditions. There will be extensions to provide protected airspace for incoming instrument flights, cutouts to exempt satellite airports from the communication requirements, or shelves to allow pilots to fly into and out of airports beneath the edges of the airspace (Figure 3-9). If an extension is 2 miles or less (still shown with blue dashed lines), you need tower permission to fly in that airspace; if the extension is more than 2 miles (shown with magenta dashed lines) the communication requirement does not apply to the extension. The fact that these extensions exist to protect instrument pilots is a clue that you should be alert when flying in or across them. sUAS are required to be authorized to fly in both Class D and surface-based Class E airspace.

Look at Hoskins Airport (44T), just east of Olympia (airport **F** on the chart excerpt) inside its Class D airspace. A pilot taking off from or landing at Hoskins (44T) must communicate with Olympia Tower and advise the controller of his or her intentions. There are no examples of cutouts or shelves on the chart excerpt.

The existence of Class D airspace is dependent on an operating control tower. There are hundreds of control towers that operate part-time, and when the controller goes home, the Class D airspace requirements usually go, too—the airspace often becomes Class E airspace that extends all the way to the surface.

Class D= control tower in operation; can change over time

You have to look at the CS to be absolutely sure which classification of airspace is left behind when the controller at a part-time tower goes home. Look at the towered airports on the sectional excerpt for the Tacoma Narrows tower (**J**). It is a part-time tower, and if you look just below the "E" you will find "See NOTAMS/Directory for Class D/E (sfc) hrs." Olympia and Paine Field are also part-time with similar notations. What "Directory" are they referring you to? The CS, of course. When these airports shut down, their surface areas become Class E down to 700 feet above the surface. There are part-time tower-controlled airports that go from Class D to Class G (uncontrolled) when the tower closes, but there are none on this chart. There is no substitute for the CS in making this determination.

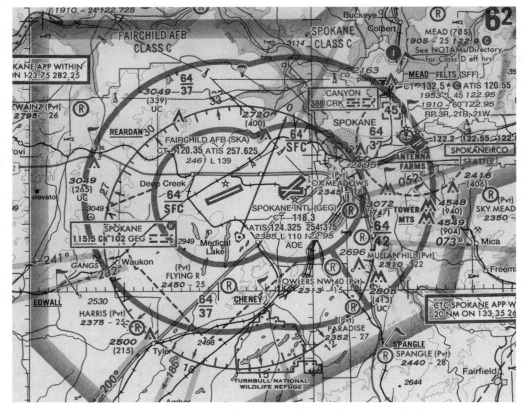

Figure 3-7a. Spokane International and Fairchild Air Force Base Class C airspace

SFC = surface

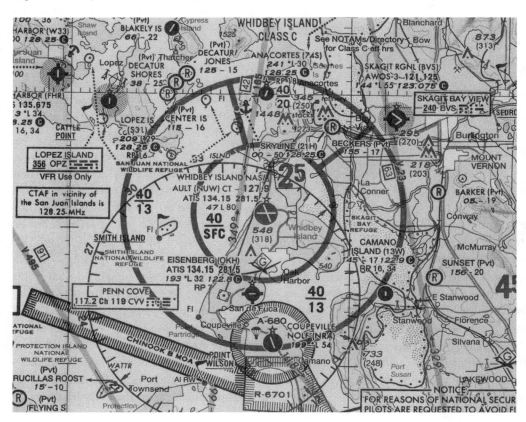

Figure 3-7b. Whidbey Island Class C airspace

/ Class E Airspace

This class of airspace has already been fairly well-defined; it exists above the floors defined by magenta dashed lines (the surface), the blue and magenta tints (700 or 1,200 AGL), and the MSL figures in mountainous areas (or 14,500 feet MSL). It extends upward to the floor of the overlying airspace (either Class A, B, or C).

Victor airways, the blue lines connecting NAVAIDs (VORs), are intended to be flown on their centerlines as accurately as possible. To allow for instrument errors, the airspace is protected from obstacles/terrain for four nautical miles on either side of the centerline. Victor airways extend upward from 1,200 feet above ground level (except in mountainous areas, where the floor of Class E airspace is designated on sectionals with a chain-link blue line) up to but not including 18,000 feet above sea level, and they do not lose their identity when passing through Class B, C, D, or E airspace. Because of their frequent use by

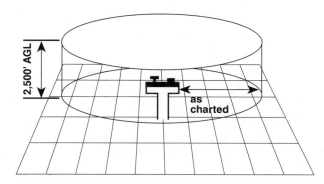

Figure 3-8. Class D airspace

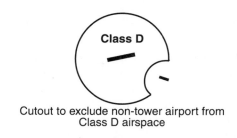

Cutout to exclude non-tower airport from Class D airspace

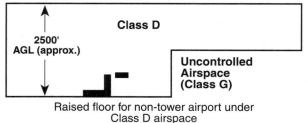

Raised floor for non-tower airport under Class D airspace

Figure 3-9. Class D, with cutouts or extensions

manned aircraft, sUAS operations near navigation aids and along Victor airways should be conducted with extreme caution.

The FAA is establishing Tango airways, to be navigated using GPS. They are also blue lines, but the airway identifier is T, as in T-139. They provide an easy way to circumnavigate congested and special use airspace without giving up the accuracy of GPS. T-routes are designated for low-altitude airspace (below 18,000 feet MSL).

Look at the airport data block for Paine Field (**B**), Tacoma Narrows (**J**), or Olympia (**F**). See the asterisk next to the tower frequency? That means that these are part-time towers, and you can find the actual operating hours on the back of the sectional chart or in the CS. When the tower is not in operation, the airspace reverts to Class E and thus the communication requirement goes away.

Look at the Bremerton National Airport (**D**) at the left edge of the chart excerpt or Wenatchee (**H**) airport at the right edge. The magenta dashed line indicates that Class E airspace extends from the floor of the overlying controlled airspace down to the surface. At Bremerton, the overlying airspace begins at either 18,000 MSL or 6,000 feet MSL if within the Seattle Class B airspace boundary. At Wenatchee (Pangborn Memorial), Class E airspace starts at the surface within the dashed, magenta line, and begins at 700 feet AGL within the magenta rectangle. In both areas, the top of Class E airspace is 18,000 feet MSL (Class A airspace).

Now look at the Ellensburg airport (**I**) at the lower right edge of the excerpt. There is no dashed line, but Ellensburg does have an instrument approach, although you can't tell that from the chart. An inbound instrument pilot's protection stops at 700 feet AGL at Ellensburg; below that altitude the pilot is in Class G (uncontrolled) airspace and must mix in with the other types of air traffic. *G = gets everything*

/ Class G Airspace *else*

An easy definition of Class G airspace is that it exists wherever other classes do not. Most of the Class G airspace lies beneath floors at 700 or 1,200 feet above the ground. Important note: Occasionally, the FAA establishes *temporary* control towers in Class G airspace for special functions such as fly-ins, Super Bowls, etc. As you might imagine, these towers do not show up on sectional charts (but they are announced by NOTAMs). Treat a temporary tower just as you would

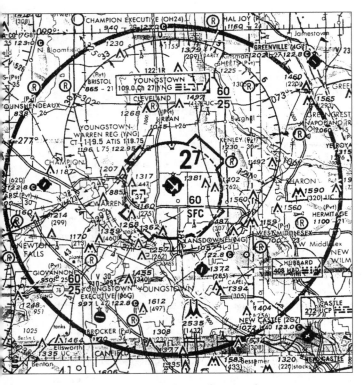

Figure 3-10. Terminal Radar Service Area

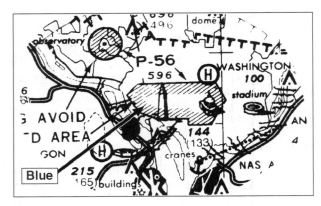

Figure 3-11. Prohibited Area

any operating control tower—mentally draw a five SM circle around the airport and get permission from the tower before entering its airspace.

Remember, it is paramount that remote pilots recognize that they need ATC permission to fly in Class B, C, D, and surface-based Class E airspace per Part 107. In general, ATC will deny these requests "on the spot." Instead, remote pilots should request access to such airspace using the airspace waiver form available from www.faa.gov/uas/request_waiver.

TERMINAL RADAR SERVICE AREA

A type of airspace that is rapidly disappearing is the Terminal Radar Service Area (TRSA, Figure 3-10). Indicated on charts by a solid black circle, a TRSA is a kind of voluntary Class C airspace. The only regulatory requirement for authorization for sUAS operations would be prior to entering Class D around the airport(s) centered within the TRSA.

SPECIAL USE AIRSPACE

Prohibited Areas. There are several types of special use airspace, but they are almost all indicated on charts with blue hatching. Look just to the right of the Olympia airport at the lower left corner of the chart excerpt. The most restrictive is a Prohibited Area, such as that

above the White House (Figure 3-11 is an example). Permission is required to enter a prohibited area and there is no way to get permission to fly a sUAS in a Prohibited Area. Getting caught in one is painful for both your pocketbook and remote pilot certificate.

Restricted Areas. The next step down is a Restricted Area (Figure 3-12). They are designated and controlled by the military and usually involve firing ranges, etc. A table on each sectional chart gives the operating hours and altitudes for each Restricted Area. The operating hours are not engraved in stone, however. During your preflight briefing, ask the FSS if a Restricted Area in the areas in which you plan to operate are "hot," or give the controlling agency a call (at Navy Whidbey, the status of their Restricted Area is on the ATIS). According to regulations, remote PICs must get permission to fly within restricted airspace. But don't expect to receive permission to fly in them unless you are part of what is going on inside of them.

Temporary Flight Restrictions. Because of the increased emphasis on security at places where large groups of people (or government bigwigs) are congregated, the FAA is issuing NOTAMs implementing Temporary Flight Restrictions (TFRs) over sporting events, political gatherings, etc. These areas do not appear on aeronautical charts, but their dimensions and locations are included in the NOTAM. It is incumbent on every pilot to make a last-minute check for such restrictions before taking off. Regulations specifically state that remote PICs are just as responsible as manned pilots to check for—and abide by—NOTAMs and TFRs.

Check for TFRs during flight planning by going to www.aopa.org and clicking on "TFRs" under the Go Fly menu. Check again with FSS on the phone to be sure that nothing new has come up.

NO.	NAME	ALTITUDE	TIME	APPROPRIATE AUTHORITY
632	Corpus Christi, Texas	From 6,000 but not incl. 11,000	SR-2400 Mon. Fri. 1400-2400 Sun	Chief Naval Air Training

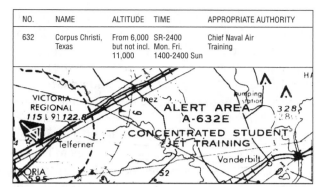

Figure 3-14. Alert Area

PROHIBITED, RESTRICTED, WARNING AND ALERT AREAS ON SEATTLE SECTIONAL CHART

NO.	NAME	ALTITUDE	TIME	APPROPRIATE AUTHORITY
R-6701	Admirality Inlet, Wash	to 5,000	Sunrise to sunset Mon. thru Fri. Sat. & Sun by NOTAM 24 hr. in advance	†FAA Seattle ARTC Center *Area FSS Comdr., Medium Attack Tactical Electronic Warfare Wing NAS Whidbey Island, Wash.

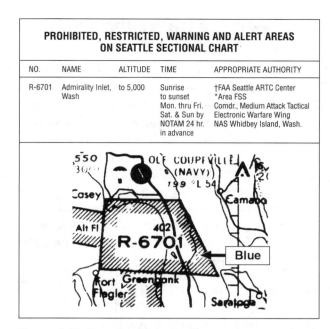

Figure 3-12. Restricted Area

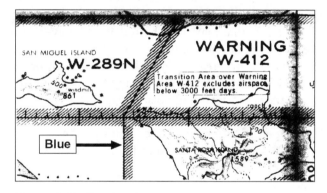

Figure 3-13. Warning Area

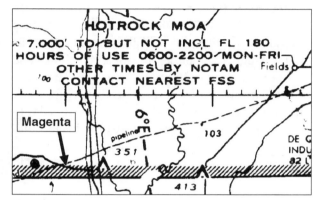

Figure 3-15. Military Operations Area

National Security Areas. The FAA has converted some TFRs to National Security Areas (NSAs), which are permanent but voluntary (pilots should avoid flying through NSAs, though). When it is deemed necessary, an NSA can be changed to prohibited airspace by NOTAM.

Warning Areas and Alert Areas. (Figures 3-13 and 3-14) These areas also involve the military. Warning Areas have the same kinds of hazards as Restricted Areas but are offshore in international waters. No specific permission is required, but keep your eyes open. Check their status with FSS. Alert Areas involve a high volume of training activity. Again, no clearance is required, but extreme vigilance (or avoidance) is. Altitude and hours of operation for alert areas are typically provided along the fringes of sectional charts.

Military Operations Areas (MOAs, Figure 3-15) are shown on charts with magenta hatching; again, look at the areas surrounding R-6703A, B, C, and D east of Olympia (that's the Army's Fort Lewis firing range, if you are curious). The altitude and hours of MOA operations are often included on sectional charts either adjacent to the airspace or along the edges of the chart. Always confirm times of operation with FSS or ATC. You do not need permission to fly in a MOA, but military airplanes operate in them without restriction—the regulations do not apply to them while flying in a MOA. Military pilots are not only flying at high speed, but they are not spending much time looking for hard-to-see sUAS. Your FSS can tell you the status of a MOA, of course, but the ATC Center (ARTCC) in whose airspace the MOA exists will be in direct contact with the military flights and can advise them of your presence. Your preflight planning should include getting Center frequencies from the CS. Extreme caution should be exercised when operating near MOAs.

Military Training Routes (MTRs) create a potential hazard for sUAS operators. The good news is that they are charted: see the gray lines that run from the top to the bottom of the chart excerpt west of Ellensburg? IR and VR mean instrument and visual routes, respectively, but there is more to it than that. Routes with 4-digit numbers are flown at or below 1,500 feet AGL, while routes with 3-number identifiers are flown above 1,500 feet AGL. Obviously, the 4-digit MTRs are the ones that most concern remote PICs. You can literally have fighter jets overhead at altitudes so low that you will feel the breeze from their displaced air as they pass by—definitely not good places to fly your sUAS.

"Hot" times for MTRs are available from the FSS, and you are foolish if you do not check on the status of any MTR that will cross your flight mission area. The military might schedule a route for several hours and only use it for a portion of that time, but you cannot afford to gamble. Military jet pilots fly very fast, with their heads in their cockpits, and they are painted with camouflage colors for a reason. Take note that the military is allowed to fly several miles off the centerline, so use caution when operating anywhere near an MTR.

AIR DEFENSE IDENTIFICATION ZONES

Air Defense Identification Zones exist along the Pacific, Gulf, and Atlantic coasts, and aircraft inbound to the United States from outside of the ADIZ whose place and time of arrival within the zone are unknown will be intercepted by armed military aircraft. Although the regulations do not stipulate the requirements for sUAS operations in or near ADIZ, it is wise to avoid these areas or seek notification of ATC facilities that handle aircraft in the applicable area. This discussion does not include the ADIZ that surrounds Washington, D.C. Special restrictions apply in that area. The FAA currently prohibits the flight of UAS within the District of Columbia and within a 30 NM radius of the Reagan Washington National Airport (DCA).

WILDLIFE REFUGE AREA

Along the bottom edge of the sectional chart excerpt, you will see Mount Rainier National Park. Note the line of dots that marks the boundary. Wherever you see those dots, they indicate a wildlife refuge area, and within this area you are asked, but not required, to stay at least 2,000 feet above the terrain to minimize the effect of aircraft noise on wildlife. Harassing, intentionally or not, certain types of wildlife can bring about penalties (monetary and/or prison). Remember that UAS are not permitted to fly in National Parks. Additional restrictions may exist for local and regional parks and similar land-use areas.

REVIEW QUESTIONS

Lesson 3 — Airspace and Navigation

For questions 1–30, refer to the Seattle sectional chart in Appendix D.

1. What are the latitude and longitude coordinates for the Easton State Airport (ESW) near letter "**A**" on the chart?

   A — 47° 15' N 121° 11' W

   B — 121° 11' N 47° 15' W

   C — 48° 45' N 122° 49' W

2. What is located at 47° 59' N 120° 17' W?

   A — a sawmill

   B — buildings

   C — a mountain peak

3. What frequency should you use for announcing your sUAS operation in the vicinity of Snohomish (near letter **G**)?

   A — 123.00

   B — 120.20

   C — 122.90

4. What is the Common Traffic Advisory Frequency (CTAF) for the Kenmore Inc. Seaplane Base just northwest of Kirkland (south of letter **B**)?

   A — 14.00

   B — 100.00

   C — 122.70

5. There are two Kenmore Seaplane Bases near Lake Washington (between letters **B** and **C**). What is the difference between the two locations (why do they have different symbols)?

   A — The north location has a control tower.

   B — The north location has services such as fuel.

   C — The south location has services such as fuel.

6. Which of the following is true about the Vashon (2S1) airport (between letters **C** and **E**)?

   A — It is a private airport.

   B — It has a runway that is 3,160 feet long.

   C — It has soft surface runways.

7. What kind of lighting is available at the Cashmere-Dryden airport (47° 30' 45" N, 120° 29' 15" W)?

   A — No runway lighting is available.

   B — Rotating beacon only.

   C — Pilot-controlled runway lighting (or on request).

8. How tall is the antenna about 8 miles south of the City of Wenatchee (near **H**)?

   A — 3327 feet

   B — 299 feet

   C — 2450 feet

9. Where would you look for information on how to contact an air traffic control center via a phone line?

   A — Sectional chart legend

   B — *Aeronautical Information Manual*

   C — *Chart Supplement*

10. How much magnetic variation exists in the area around Ellensburg (**I**)?

    A — 47° 30' North correction

    B — 15° 30' West correction

    C — 15° 30' East correction

11. You are flying in proximity to Port Ludlow (due west of **B**). What is the highest you can fly your sUAS while inspecting the tower just west of the city and south of DIGGN intersection?

A — 400 feet MSL

B — 400 feet AGL

C — 605 feet AGL

12. You are approaching an airport within Class C airspace. Which of these statements is true?

A — You must have authorization from ATC before entering the Class C airspace.

B — You must be in two-way communication with ATC before entering the Class C airspace.

C — Your airplane must be equipped with a transponder, two-way radio, and GPS to enter Class C airspace.

13. Under what conditions, if any, may remote pilots enter a restricted area?

A — With the controlling agency's authorization.

B — Following an ATC clearance.

C — Under no condition.

14. You have been asked to take photographs of the state capitol in Olympia, Washington (north of **F**). What type of airspace would you be in while flying around the building at 200 feet AGL?

A — Class E

B — Class D

C — Class G

15. What is the upper limit of Class D airspace?

A — 18,500 feet MSL.

B — The base of Class A airspace.

C — Usually 2,500 feet above the surface.

16. What are the horizontal limits of Class D airspace?

A — 5 NM from the airport boundary.

B — As indicated with blue dashed lines.

C — As indicated with magenta dashed lines.

17. Class D airspace is automatically in effect when

A — its associated control tower is in operation.

B — the weather is below VFR minimums.

C — radar service is available.

18. At what altitude does Class E airspace begin overhead Swanson airport (2W3) near Eatonville (between **F** and Mt. Rainier)?

A — 400 feet AGL

B — 700 feet AGL

C — 1,200 feet AGL

19. Unless otherwise specified, federal airways extend from

A — 1,200 feet above the surface upward to 14,500 feet MSL and are 16 NM wide.

B — 1,200 feet above the surface upward to 18,000 feet MSL and are 8 NM wide.

C — the surface upward to 18,000 feet MSL and are 4 NM wide.

20. What type of airspace is associated with VOR federal airways?

A — Class B, C, D, or E airspace.

B — Class E airspace.

C — Class D airspace.

21. Class E airspace in the conterminous United States extends to, but not including,

A — the base of Class B airspace.

B — 3,000 feet MSL.

C — 18,000 feet MSL.

22. You have been asked to photograph the outdoor theaters in the vicinity of Bremerton National Airport (PWT) (near **D**). What type of airspace would you be within and what type of permission, if any, would be required?

A — Class E, ATC authorization required.

B — Class E, ATC authorization not required.

C — Class D, ATC authorization required.

23. At what altitude does Class E airspace begin over Kachess Lake (near **A**)?

   A — 14,500 feet AGL

   B — 700 feet AGL

   C — 1,200 feet AGL

24. You are planning a mission to map a plot of land near Rosedale (northwest of **J**). Prior to launch, you listen to the Tacoma Narrows ATIS, which is reporting 2 SM visibility in mist. Can you fly the mission?

   A — Yes, if you have at least 3 SM ground visibility at your location.

   B — Yes, if you have at least 3 SM of flight visibility at your location.

   C — Yes, as visibility restrictions only apply if flying within Class D airspace.

25. You have been asked to inspect towers north of Bangor, which is north of area **D**. Which of the following is true about this mission?

   A — You can fly your sUAS up to 885 feet AGL.

   B — All towers at that location have anti-collision lights.

   C — The mission is not authorized.

26. Are you authorized to operate your sUAS over Yelm (East of **F** near Western airport)?

   A — No, you are in restricted airspace.

   B — No, you are in a Military Operations Area (MOA).

   C — Yes, there are no restrictions to operations.

27. What is the significance of the different colors of airports (for example, Snohomish County, near **B**, and Harvey, near **G**, are different colors)?

   A — Blue airports have a control tower.

   B — Magenta airports have a control tower.

   C — Blue airports always have surface-based Class E airspace.

28. Renton airport (RNT) (northeast of **C**) is surrounded by Class D airspace up to and including

   A — 2,500 feet MSL.

   B — 2,500 feet AGL.

   C — 3,000 feet MSL.

29. Would you expect to see aircraft flying in the traffic pattern north of Firstair airport (W16) (east of **G**)?

   A — No; the patterns for both runways are to the south of the airport.

   B — Yes; the traffic patterns for each runway are opposite of one another.

   C — Yes; the traffic pattern for runway 7 is to the right.

30. Which of the following hazards to flight exists north of the Sky Harbor airport (S86) (east of **G**)?

   A — A major road

   B — A railroad

   C — Powerlines

For questions 31–34, refer to the *Chart Supplement* excerpt in Appendix C.

31. When is the Olympia Regional Airport (OLM) control tower in operation in local time?

   A — 0800–2000 (0900–2100 during daylight savings)

   B — 0800–2000 all year

   C — 1600–0400 all year

32. Which is not a suitable means for receiving the weather conditions at Ellensburg Bowers Field airport (ELN)?

   A — Call 509-962-7523.

   B — Call 509-925-2040.

   C — Listen on frequency 118.375.

33. What type of airspace exists at the Olympia Regional Airport (OLM) when the tower is closed?

A — Surface-based Class D

B — Surface-based Class E

C — Surface-based Class G

34. Where is the control tower located on the Olympic Regional Airport (OLM)?

A — West of runway 35-17 and south of a ramp area.

B — On the far west end of the airport under the star symbol.

C — Just east of runway 35-17 indicated by the triangle shape.

For questions 35–40, refer to the North Alabama sectional chart excerpt in Appendix D.

35. You are planning to operate your sUAS just west of the Talladega airport (ASN). What factors may you want to consider before flying?

A — You need ATC authorization to fly in the vicinity of ASN.

B — You should avoid flight in the area due to national security.

C — You should check NOTAMs for sporting events.

36. What type of airspace exists at the surface on and around the Anniston Regional Airport (ANB)?

A — Class C

B — Class D

C — Class E

37. What type of airspace exists at the surface on and around the Birmingham Shuttlesworth International Airport (BHM)?

A — Class C

B — Class D

C — Class B

38. For a flight at 200 feet AGL over Trussville (just northeast of the BHM airport), what kind of ATC authorization is required?

A — No ATC authorization is required; Class G extends to 1,200 feet AGL.

B — ATC authorization is required; the area is within Class C airspace.

C — ATC authorization is required; the area is within Class E airspace.

39. The multiple (two or more) towers just north-northwest of and closest to the Anniston Regional Airport have tops that are _____ feet above the airport elevation.

A — 215

B — 1,305

C — 403

40. What frequency should you use for announcing flight activity in the vicinity of St. Clair County Airport (PLR)?

A — 119.625

B — 123.05

C — 123.80

Airport and Off-Airport Operations

Note: All discussions concerning the use of a radio (transceiver) in this lesson assume that the user is authorized and licensed to use such a system. Currently, handheld aviation radios require a FCC license for use. DO NOT use aviation transceivers if you are unlicensed. Instead, follow the guidance in this lesson about monitoring frequencies with an aviation band scanner. Also, if authorized to transmit, be aware that the FAA currently does not require remote pilots to communicate via radio to other aircraft and has not yet provided guidance on the proper terminology and procedures to be used by unmanned aircraft.

THE AIRPORT

For the most part, sUAS operators will remain clear of airports. However, remote pilots should be familiar with airports and how manned aircraft utilize them; thus, this section goes into such details.

At any airport, you will have to be able to identify the runway in use, stay clear of manned aircraft operations, be aware of wake turbulence hazards, deal with roaming persons and vehicles, know who (if anyone) controls your actions, interpret lights and markings, and more. This lesson will discuss general airport operations, differentiate between tower and non-tower airports, and provide guidance on what you should expect.

As your flying experience expands to include more airports, you will find some features that they all have in common. For instance, all runways are numbered according to their direction in relation to magnetic north, to the closest 10°. Magnetic headings are in degrees, like a geometric circle, from zero to 360 (0°

and 360° represent the same spot on the circle, i.e., north). A few key points on the compass circle are north (0°/360°, as just mentioned), east (090°), south (180°), and west (270°). The 45° increments are used for directions such as northeast (045°) and southwest (225°). A runway laid out 078° from magnetic north would be numbered 8 (078 is rounded to 080° and the zeros are dropped). The opposite end of the runway would be numbered 26, the reciprocal (Figure 4-1). Some large airports have parallel runways, which are identified as left, right, or center—e.g., runway 27R, runway 6L, etc. If you are heading or directionally "challenged," it may not be a bad idea to use a compass (the old-school, hiking kind or one on your smartphone) to help you get accustomed to this type of thinking. Also remember (this may sound silly, but some people forget) that the sun comes up in the east and goes down in the west. For example, when facing the sun in the morning, you'll be facing east, so to your right will be south and to your left will be north.

Figure 4-1. Runway numbering

Manned aircraft normally take off and land into the wind. (Operating into the wind is also a good idea for sUAS, as it makes maneuvering easier and generally increases performance.) The wind indicator tells the direction the wind is blowing from. Every airport should have some form of wind indicator or landing

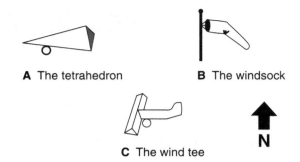

A The tetrahedron   **B** The windsock

C The wind tee

N

Figure 4-2. Wind indicators

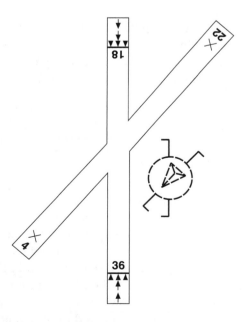

Figure 4-3. Landing strip and pattern indicators

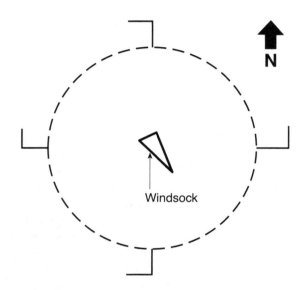

Figure 4-4. Pattern markings

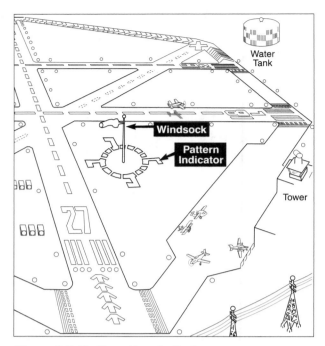

Figure 4-5. Traffic pattern indicators

direction indicator. Figure 4-2 shows several types of landing direction indicators: the tetrahedron, the windsock, and the wind tee. All of the indicators in the illustration indicate a wind from the west. Remote pilots must be especially sensitive to wind direction and velocity and the presence of gusts, because sUAS must be flown all the way to the ground, unlike large manned aircraft that are much more stable in windy conditions.

At some airports, the tetrahedron or wind tee may be tied down to show the favored runway and will not accurately reflect wind conditions. Always observe what pilots in the local area around the airport are doing and stay clear of the pattern in use; if there are no other airplanes in the area, you have a bit more operational flexibility. Figures 4-3 and 4-4 show landing strip indicators and landing pattern indicators—the landing strip indicators parallel the runways and the landing pattern indicators show the direction traffic flows to and from the runways.

Although the standard traffic pattern uses a left-hand pattern, terrain or the presence of a congested area frequently dictate the use of a right-hand pattern. Figure 4-5 shows pattern indicators that keep traffic from overflying the area northwest of the water tank. Where there are no pattern indicators, the regulations *left turns = the default*

require that all turns in the pattern be made to the left. When you fly at an unfamiliar airport and do not see a pattern indicator, you are safe in assuming a left-hand pattern. If an airport requires a right-hand pattern for any runway, the data block on the sectional chart will have a notation such as "RP 11 16," indicating that runways 11 and 16 have right-hand patterns. If the notation includes an asterisk: *RP 12, the right-hand pattern is in effect only during certain hours—check the *Chart Supplement* (CS) for details.

Figure 4-6 shows the FAA *recommended* standard left-hand traffic pattern with arrival and departure procedures (note the recommended—not required—45° entries to the downwind leg, but understand that almost everyone uses this entry). If the airport has an *FAA-required* traffic pattern, manned aircraft must use that pattern (few airports have such patterns; 14 CFR Part 93 lists them). This diagram can help the remote pilot become more aware of how manned aircraft approach and depart airports as well as how they maneuver in the immediate local area. Remote pilots should become well-versed in the terminology of the traffic pattern, with the ability to recognize if a pilot announces they are on left downwind for runway 18 where they are in the sky as well as in relation to the remote pilot's sUAS operations. In this case, the aircraft would be to the east of the airport (aircraft make all left turns and keep the runway to their left when using "left traffic," in this case on left downwind). This knowledge is critical for those operating

at or near airports of any size or type. Remember, it is your responsibility to remain well clear of all manned aircraft operations on or around airports and their associated traffic patterns!

Not illustrated but frequently used is the downwind departure. In the illustration in Figure 4-6, airplanes 5 and 6 are departing in the direction of takeoff; however, what if their destination is in the opposite direction? Then they perform (or ask the tower for) a downwind departure. To avoid conflict with airplanes entering the pattern on the 45, pilots performing downwind departures climb as indicated by plane #5 until well above pattern altitude before turning downwind.

Always be cautious of the rogue who does it their own unique way! It is an unfortunate fact of life that not all pilots observe recommended procedures. Listen carefully to the local radio frequencies and expect the unexpected.

Adjacent to every airport symbol on an aeronautical chart is an airport data block with the airport name and identifier, its elevation above sea level, the length of the longest runway in hundreds of feet, an "RP" to identify runways with right-hand patterns, an **R** if radar is available, a **C** indicating the Common Traffic Advisory Frequency (CTAF), the AWOS/ASOS frequency if available, the Automatic Terminal Information Service (ATIS) frequency for most tower-controlled airports, and information on runway lighting. The CTAF is the frequency manned pilots

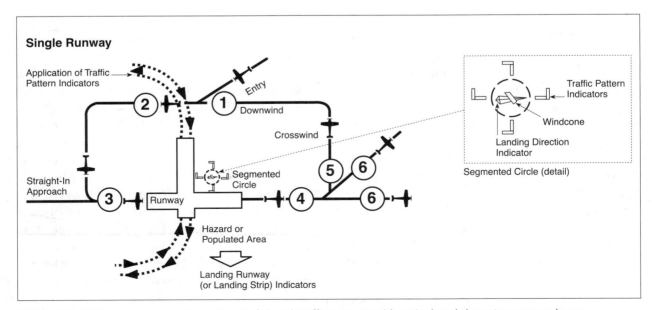

Figure 4-6. FAA recommended standard left-hand traffic pattern with arrival and departure procedures

should be using to announce their position, intentions, and operations in the local airport area. Remote pilots should monitor CTAF anytime when operating near an airport. For those individuals who have the required Federal Communications Commission (FCC) licensure,[1] they may want to announce similar information about their aircraft. All of the information in the airport data block can be deciphered by use of the sectional chart legend, but you should be able to get the essential information at a glance. A few pre-flight moments devoted to researching the CS for all local airports will be time well spent.

For example, look at the data block for Seattle-Tacoma International Airport on the sectional chart excerpt in Appendix D. The airport is 433 feet above sea level, the longest runway is 11,900 feet long, and runway lighting is available from sunset to sunrise. Radio frequencies for the control tower, Automatic Terminal Information Service, and Aeronautical Advisory Service (UNICOM) are also listed.

On the sectional chart you will notice many airports without runway symbols. These airports have unpaved runways or paved runways less than 1,500 feet in length. Airport symbols with little protrusions around their edges indicate that services (usually fuel) are available. You will also find airports with no radio service and airports without lighting. You should never be surprised by what you find at the end of a flight, because you should know all about your destination airport before you take off. Charts and the CS are the government's means of providing airport information; several private publishers also produce booklets with VFR airport information.

Airports can be divided into two categories: those with control towers and those without. Remote pilots need to be able to identify one from the other. You can get yourself into some real hot water if you fly around airports without notifying airport operators, but you will definitely cause yourself trouble if you fly around an airport with a control tower without contacting that control tower. On the sectional chart excerpt, you will see that airport symbols printed in blue represent airports with towers and those printed in magenta are airports with no towers. When the tower is not in operation, the airports with blue symbols are to be treated as non-tower airports. Part-time towers are

Airports w/o towers written in magenta

[1] Refer to 47 CFR Part 87.

indicated by an asterisk next to the control tower frequency. The CS also contains information on hours of operation.

You should always have an airport diagram, if one is available. The CS includes them with the airport listing for smaller airports and in the back for larger airports. Computer users can find diagrams for most large airports (which are the most confusing) by searching online for "airport diagrams," but be sure to only use up-to-date maps. For pilots without computer access, pilot supply stores carry several flight guides that include runway and taxiway layouts. Treat your ground operations as seriously as you treat flight planning.

Where runway markings are provided, you will find centerline marking, a threshold marking where the landing surface begins, and a "hold line" that separates the active runway from the taxiway (treat it like the lane separation on a two-lane highway—if the two solid lines are closest to you, do not let any portion of your airplane project past them; the solid lines are always on the taxiway side, and the broken lines are always on the runway side). For most sUAS, the use of runways won't be necessary; in fact, it is best to stay well clear of them. Do not cross the double solid yellow lines of the hold line unless authorized and no aircraft are in the area. An easy way to distinguish between taxiways and runways is that taxiways have yellow markings and runways have white markings. If you think your aircraft is on/over a taxiway but the lines on the pavement are white, you're actually operating on/over a runway.

Runways used for instrument approaches (procedures used by manned aircraft to land in poor weather) have fancier markings. If there are obstacles in the approach path, the threshold may be displaced; arrows will lead to the displaced threshold. Note that in the illustration (Figure 4-7) the threshold of runway 27 has been displaced because of the power lines. The existence of displaced thresholds can give remote pilots clues as to obstacles or other things to be aware of in the local airport environment. Any paved area that appears to be usable, but which is not usable for normal operations, is marked with yellow chevrons. Such areas may be used as overruns at the end of a runway. In Figure 4-7, the taxiway beyond the threshold of runway 18R is marked as unusable.

solid side = no movement

On taxiways, yellow lines—one solid and one dashed—separate movement areas (on the dashed side) from non-movement areas (on the solid side). The taxiway itself is a movement area, and the ground controller directs your movements; non-movement areas (usually called "the ramp") include aircraft parking, hangars, fuel facilities, etc. It is critical that remote pilots remain on the non-movement side—i.e., do not cross the solid yellow line without permission (towered airports) and with extreme caution, looking for any and all aircraft and vehicles in the area (at all airports).

A runway is closed when a yellow X is placed at its center. If there are multiple runways, a runway with an X at each end is closed, and an X at the center of the runway complex indicates that the whole airport is closed. The FAA does not close runways; they are closed by local authorities.

For night and low-light operations, taxiways are marked with omnidirectional blue lights, and the active runway is marked with omnidirectional white lights. Green lights mark the threshold from the landing direction, and red lights alert you to the end of the landing surface—these are directional lights, showing green in one direction and red in the other. Hazards, such as the water tank in Figure 4-5, are marked with red lights.

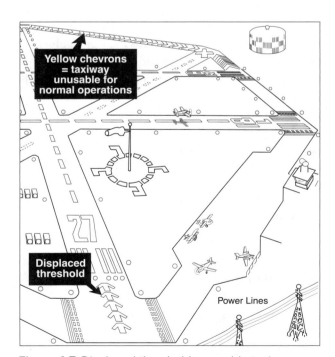

Figure 4-7. Displaced threshold; unusable taxiway

At many airports, the lighting is controlled by the pilot, who transmits on a specified frequency (usually the CTAF) and keys the microphone briefly to turn on the lights. At most airports with pilot-controlled lighting, the pilot can control the intensity of the lighting by varying the number of "clicks" on the microphone button. The lights turn off automatically after fifteen minutes. On aeronautical charts, airports with pilot-controlled lighting are indicated by *L; details on the frequency is found in the CS. If appropriately licensed by the FCC, remote pilots could activate the lights by clicking their microphone. (For more information about pilot-controlled lighting, refer to the AIM). Check the CS before the sun starts to go down (but don't forget to abide by the applicable rules about daylight-only operations, unless you have a waiver).

Rotating beacons are installed at all airports with towers and at many non-tower airports, and as they rotate the pilot sees a white flash followed by a single green flash. Military airports are identified at night by two white flashes between each green flash. When the rotating beacon is lighted in the daytime, it may mean that the weather is below the minimums required for manned visual flight operations. However, you should check the actual weather and not rely on the beacon, since many of these lighting systems are turned on by timers or photoelectric cells. You will need to find out more details about the weather conditions to determine if sUAS operations may be authorized.

/ Online Sources for Airport Information

Computer users can learn more than they need to know about any public airport by searching databases maintained by www.skyvector.com, www.landings.com, www.airnav.com, and www.aopa.org, among many others.

CROSSWIND OPERATIONS

Although airport designers try to align runways with the prevailing winds, there is always the possibility that the wind may not be blowing directly down the runway you intend to use. The manufacturer of your sUAS may have designated a maximum crosswind component or perhaps simply a recommended maximum wind speed for operations. Be sure to operate within the operational recommendations of the manufacturer. Also, you may not always be able to launch and recover your system into the wind, so care is required to ensure that adequate control is possible and maintained in windy and/or crosswind conditions. Always err on the side of caution, and if conditions are questionable, stay on the ground or recover the sUAS as soon as practical.

WAKE TURBULENCE

An important consideration for pilots at any airport is the avoidance of wake turbulence. Every airplane leaves behind it two twin tornadoes corkscrewing aft from the wing tips. As the high pressure air below the wing tries to travel around the wing tip to the low pressure area on the top surface and the airplane moves forward, the circulation is clockwise from the left wing tip and counterclockwise from the right wing tip as seen from behind. In the NASA photograph (Figure 4-8), the airplane has flown between two smoke generators and the vortices are clearly seen. Because these wing-tip vortices are a product of lift development, they are strongest and most hazardous behind airplanes that are heavy, slow, and with landing gear and flaps retracted: a takeoff situation. Second most hazardous is the heavy slow airplane in the landing configuration. Research has shown that wing-tip vortices descend 900 to 1,000 feet behind the generating airplane and then slowly dissipate. Crossing behind a heavy airplane and encountering both vortices can create destructive forces. These vortices can wreak havoc on sUAS. While you should always stay well clear of aircraft, this wake can last for some time after an aircraft passes and it can sink into your operation from well above, sneaking in for attack. The pattern and speed of the wake can easily overpower an sUAS, making it uncontrollable in an instant.

Any lifting surface creates tip vortices. As such, another dangerous wake situation can occur around helicopters. During and immediately after a helicopter is in a given location, airflow is severely disrupted in the local area. It is wise to keep sUAS well clear of any area or flight path of rotorcraft.

Operating at an airport with crossing runways requires special care. Avoid being airborne when crossing an area where a heavy airplane has just taken off or landed, and land short of the intersection if possible. *Remember that the heavy airplane creates vortices only when creating lift.* However, for the purposes of sUAS, even the airflow from engines and the displacement around aircraft fuselage may be enough to make any sUAS uncontrollable. In short, use extreme caution around other aircraft that are moving and/or have their engines operating, even other sUAS. Downwash from multicopters can disrupt airflow enough to cause control issues for closely following sUAS of any type, especially other multicopters.

OPERATIONS AT NON-TOWER AIRPORTS

There are approximately 19,299 landing facilities in the United States, and only 626 had towers in 2013 (the latest year for which statistics are available). Non-tower airports may have UNICOM (*see* Table 4-1), but many have no radio facility at all. Be aware that airplanes do not have to be radio-equipped to operate at these airports. Remember, even a tower-controlled airport becomes Class E or G airspace when the controller goes home; the airspace listing in the CS will tell you which applies at a given airport. Also, the sectional chart will have a note saying "See NOTAMS/Directory for D/E (or D/G) effective hours." Figure 4-9 shows a control tower and traffic pattern indicators around the windsock.

Figure 4-8. Wing-tip vortices

UNICOM Frequencies			
122.700	122.725	122.800	
122.975	123.00	123.050	123.075

Table 4-1. UNICOM

If a tower-controlled airport is the equivalent of an intersection with a traffic light, an uncontrolled airport is the equivalent of a four-way stop—don't move until you have looked in all directions for conflicting traffic, then proceed cautiously.

Most of the time, non-towered airports exist in Class G airspace and you will want to monitor the Common Traffic Advisory Frequency (CTAF) and other applicable frequencies with an aviation band scanner. If FCC licensed, you can broadcast information about your flight operations on a common frequency. This is often accomplished via UNICOM, an informal radio station that is not operated by the government but by a private business as a service to the flying public. The operator has many other duties, and may not always be able to answer your call. Information on runway in use received from a UNICOM is advisory only. If you are unable to communicate with UNICOM, the AIM suggests that you broadcast in the blind (no specific addressee: "Plant City traffic, DJI one two one four x-ray is about to depart ramp area adjacent to the airport beacon, Plant City") on the CTAF for that airport.

Some non-towered airports have surface-based Class E airspace associated with them. If you recall from the regulations governing sUAS under Part 107, you need permission to operate in this type of airspace. Remember, though, that "on the spot" authorizations to fly in this type of airspace may not be possible; instead, remote pilots should submit an airspace waiver form to the FAA well prior to any operations.

You will occasionally find runways at non-tower airports marked off with a large X at each end or in the center. An X-ed off *runway* is closed, and an X in the center of an airport indicates that the *airport* is closed. Do not use areas of pavement or runway with chevron markings upon them, as this indicates that the areas are unusable. Figure 4-9 includes a closed runway, an unusable taxiway, displaced thresholds, and parallel runways.

Because no clearance is required to operate at a non-tower airport, it is not required that you maintain continuous radio contact with the ground station or other aircraft. The AIM does recommend that you announce your position and intentions when within

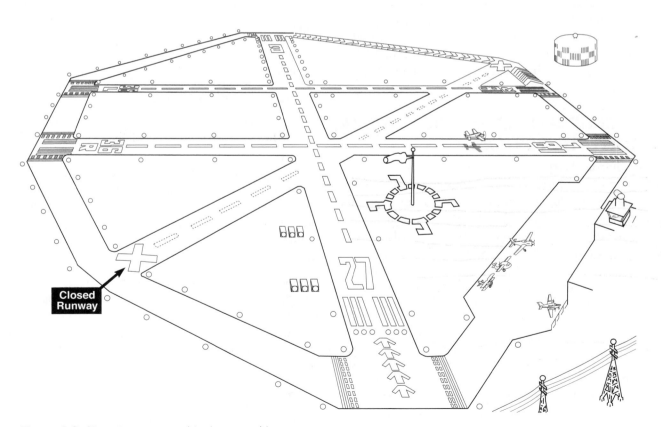

Figure 4-9. Airport runway and taxiway markings

10 miles as well as announce how you are operating or maneuvering in the area and around the airport so that other pilots in the area can coordinate their movements with yours. Also, because the CTAF may be shared by several airports, listen carefully for traffic that may be in your immediate area (i.e., they are using the name of the closest airport). If you have a FCC license and are transmitting information about your sUAS, be sure to include the name of the airport at which you are operating or closest to during flight. For example, "Denton Island Traffic, unmanned aircraft operations occurring at or below 400 AGL 2 statute miles south of the airport, Denton Island." Keep your transmissions brief and to the point so that others may use the frequency, and remember that there may be "no-radio" airplanes in the area. Do not use the blind call "Any traffic in the area please advise"—the AIM says that this phrase should not be used under any conditions.

There are applications and websites available that map aircraft location and altitude, which can be very helpful to keep track of aircraft in the local area (e.g., www.flightradar24.com). While this information is extremely helpful, it does not show all aircraft but only those that have special equipment that reports their position (called Automatic Dependent Surveillance–Broadcast [ADS-B]). More aircraft should become visible with these types of tools, as the FAA is requiring this system to be installed on almost all aircraft, big and small.

OPERATIONS AT AIRPORTS WITH CONTROL TOWERS

A controlled airport is one with an operating control tower. Control towers are commissioned at airports because the volume of traffic demands a high degree of coordination, so when you operate into, depart from, or operate near such an airport, you should expect your movements to be controlled by the tower. While control towers help keep aircraft apart from one another, never rely on a controller to keep you out of a potential collision. Additionally, the whole concept of having sUAS on or near their airport may be new to controllers, so be patient, proactive, and careful.

Many airports with control towers have an Automatic Terminal Information Service (ATIS), which continuously broadcasts non-control information on existing weather conditions, runway in use, and

applicable Notices to Airmen. Non-control means that the ATIS gives you the information necessary to plan your flight, but you still need to communicate with the tower or approach control to operate in Class B, C, and D airspace. (If you do not have a FCC license appropriate to your operation, this exchange will likely have to take place over the phone, or through prior authorization via other means of communication.) Your first action, whether arriving or departing, should be to monitor the ATIS broadcast. Each ATIS broadcast is identified with a letter of the phonetic alphabet. When contacting ground control, the tower controller, or an approach control facility, you should state in your initial contact that you have the ATIS information: "Brooksville Tower, Parrot eight eight four one uniform requesting permission to operate in Class D airspace, 3 statute miles southeast of the airport at and below 400 AGL, with DELTA." Federal Aviation Regulation Part 107 requires that you have ATC authorization before entering Class B, C, D, or surface-based E airspace.

Note: There are a rare few control towers in Class G airspace. At these airports, there is no dashed line denoting Class D airspace, only magenta tint denoting Class E beginning at 700 feet AGL. Manned aircraft are still required to talk to the tower within 4 nautical miles and below 2,500 AGL per 14 CFR Part 91. It would be wise for unmanned to do the same, even though not explicitly called for in Part 107.

/ Ground Operations

When instructions are received from the ground controller, they will be specific; you will be directed to hold short (i.e., stay clear) of any airport location as well as active, inactive, or closed runways. When in doubt, make no assumptions—stop and ask for clarification. Do not cross any runway without authorization that is crystal clear. To prevent misunderstanding, you are required to read back to the controller all "hold short" instructions.

Make it a point to have available an airport diagram for any airport you intend to use, and study it before you need it. Airport diagrams for large airports are included in the CS, and are available from www.faa.gov and many online sources. The ground controller's area of responsibility ends at the yellow hold lines, and the tower controller "owns" the runway and the airspace associated with the airport. Do not change radio frequencies without being instructed.

/ Pilot/Controller Phraseology

Controllers use an entire language of their own, as do pilots. It would be wise to get familiar with proper phraseology prior to operating anywhere near manned aircraft or controlled airports. The best way to learn is to read the AIM and to listen in on air traffic control frequencies (you can listen anytime on www.liveatc.net). Just as important as knowing what to say when (and if) you use the radio is understanding what ATC and other pilots in the area are talking about. This will help you recognize if another aircraft is getting close to your area of operation or may be in conflict with it in some form. If in doubt, notify ATC or pilots (if at a non-towered location) about the potential encounter.

/ Operations at Class C Airports

Hundreds of tower-controlled airports are protected by Class C airspace and more are being designated every year, so use current charts and check for NOTAMs. What you need to know in the context of operations at airports with control towers is that the controller at the radar facility that governs the airspace surrounding the airport serves as a sort of perimeter guard for the tower controller. You can't enter Class C airspace (shown on sectional charts with a solid magenta line) unless authorized by ATC. The most reliable way to gain such permission is to apply for an airspace authorization.

If you are operating outside the inner 5-mile ring of Class C airspace, you may be in contact with approach or departure control (rather than the control tower). The controller wants to know who you are, where you are, and your intentions. If the controller says to remain clear of the Class C airspace, you must do just that. The approach controller will eventually hand you off to the tower controller if you are operating from outside 5 miles from the airport to within 5 miles. Keep a sharper-than-usual lookout, because if the area weren't congested, there would be no need to designate it as Class C airspace.

/ Operations at Class D Airports

Because it is always associated with an operating control tower, to enter Class D airspace, remote pilots require ATC authorization. This should be attained through the airspace waiver process. Yet, it is possible to operate in Class D airspace without a radio. The best thing to do is to apply for an airspace waiver on the FAA's website. Some information you will need is your type of aircraft (you may need to explain what a multicopter is), your estimated time of operation, and the location at which you will be operating in respect to the airport. When the tower controller goes home, most Class D airspace becomes Class E airspace (or Class G if there is no weather observer; check the CS).

/ Operations at Class E Airports

There are airports that are within controlled airspace just like Class D but with no control tower; at those airports, controlled airspace (Class E) extends down to the airport surface. These airports are shown with a dashed magenta line on sectional charts (an example from the sectional chart excerpt in Appendix D is Bremerton National [D]). When an airport has either Class B, C, D, or E airspace, the lighting of the rotating beacon during daylight hours is intended to indicate that the weather is below basic visual weather minimums for manned aircraft (1,000-foot ceiling and three statute miles visibility). In many cases, these beacons are controlled by automatic devices and your decision on whether or not basic VFR minimums exist should not depend on the beacon alone. If you notice the beacon on during the day, double-check that you are legal to conduct sUAS operations per Part 107.

/ "I'm a Stranger Here, Myself..."

Surely the most daunting task for a new pilot is going to a strange airport—"Who do I call?" "Where might I be able to launch my sUAS?" "Are there any facilities I can use?" You can eliminate all doubt by calling a fixed-base operator or airport operator/manager at your proposed airport of operation. Phone numbers are available in many places; www.airnav.com is one, www.1800wxbrief.com is best.

/ Part 139 Airports

Part 139 airports are those explicitly certified and normally served by the airlines and commuters. When you are planning your flight, check the CS to see if the airport used for your operation is a Part 139 airport (but it will say ARFF, not Part 139). There are about 700 of them, so the chances are pretty good that you will encounter one or more in your travels. Computer users can find airport diagrams for Part 139 airports at www.faa.gov; AOPA members can get them on the organization's website.

The FAA has instituted a program of signage at Part 139 airports to make them consistent with one another, and to make it easier for pilots to identify the location of taxiways, runways, or other points on the airport. There are six kinds of signs; examples of these are included in the full-color Appendix D (page D-8).

Mandatory Instruction Signs have white letters on a red background; they denote entrances to runways or areas where aircraft are prohibited. Figure A is a runway/hold position sign and would be placed where a taxiway intersects runway 15-33. Figure C would be placed at a more complex intersection where two runways cross.

You should be aware of two special mandatory instruction signs: First, a red sign with ILS in white (Figure D) indicates an area on a taxiway where airplanes can interfere with the ILS signal, and when you see that sign you will also see a special hold line that looks like railroad tracks.

The second important sign has, for example, a white 15-APCH on a red background (Figure E). This indicates that the approach path for runway 15 crosses the taxiway and that you should hold there until authorized to cross by the ground controller. It's another way of saying "DANGER—LOW FLYING AIRCRAFT." This sign does not mean that you are at the approach end of runway 15—that location is indicated by a simple white-on-red 15 (for example, Figure B would be at the takeoff end of runway 33). A white-on-red sign is always significant; if you have any doubts about its meaning, do not let your sUAS beyond it and ask ATC for permission or clarification.

Figure F is the "no entry" sign—the area beyond the sign is forbidden territory.

Location Signs have yellow inscriptions on a black background, with a yellow border. They tell you on which runway or taxiway your sUAS is located. You would see a sign like Figure G if you were turning from an intersection onto a runway where the proximity of another runway might be confusing. A taxiway location sign would have a letter instead of a number.

Direction Signs have black inscriptions on a yellow background (no border), and they are normally located on the left prior to an intersection. They are used to tell pilots which way to move your sUAS to get to a runway or to another taxiway, and are called, "outbound destination signs." You would see Figure I

where the taxi route leads to two runways, and Figure J where two different taxi routes exist. When the controller says "Turn right at taxiway Alfa," look for a sign like Figure H.

Destination Signs also have black inscriptions on a yellow background, and they tell you which way to maneuver your sUAS to get to the runway, the ramp, the terminal, the military area, or other key locations.

Information Signs also have black inscriptions on a yellow background; they are installed by the airport operator and include things like noise abatement procedures, density altitude reminders, radio frequencies, and other important details.

Runway Distance Remaining Signs have white numerals on a black background and are spaced 1,000 feet apart. Figure K tells you that the runway remaining is 3,000 feet.

At airports equipped for low-visibility takeoffs and landings, these signs and markings are backed up by lights and additional signage.

Stop Bar Lights are installed at intersections where a centerline-lighted taxiway meets an active runway. They are red until the controller clears the aircraft onto the runway, at which time green lead-on lights illuminate the path to the takeoff position.

Runway Guard Lights are flashing yellow lights that denote the presence of an active runway and identify the location of the hold line.

Taxiway Centerline Lighting consists of green in-pavement lights to guide ground traffic at night and during low-visibility operations.

Clearance Bar Lights are installed at holding positions on taxiways in order to increase the conspicuity of the holding position in low visibility conditions. They may also be installed to indicate the location of an intersecting taxiway during periods of darkness. Clearance bars consist of three in-pavement, steady-burning yellow lights.

Geographic Position Markings, so-called "pink spots" with an identifying letter or number. They can also be used for reporting one's position on the airport.

Taxiway Centerline Marking is a solid yellow line, outlined with black for emphasis on light colored pavement.

Note: A key point to keep in mind is that the markings on airports are color-coded. Markings are yellow for taxiways and are white for runways. If you notice your sUAS is over pavement with white markings but it is supposed to be over a taxiway, you are in the wrong place. Alert ATC (at controlled airports) and local traffic (at non-towered airports) of your mistake.

OFF-AIRPORT OPERATIONS

While some remote pilots will frequent airports and areas close to airports, a large percentage of sUAS users will be in remote locations far away from airports. It may seem like this will make the lives of remote pilots easier, but these types of locations come with their own requirements and challenges that must be considered to ensure safe and efficient operations.

/ Location Considerations

If you are under the impression that you can just show up to a location and launch, think again. Some serious evaluation of the local environment is necessary before sending your bird(s) into the air. An initial overview evaluation of the area of operation is needed to evaluate obstacles and other potential hazards. You should pick suitable launch and recovery points. Are these staging areas large enough to safely conduct takeoffs and landings? Are they subject to unexpected wind or other environmental conditions? For example, are the areas downwind of obstacles that may cause turbulence that could make operations difficult? Is the immediate area free of obstacles, and are you aware of any that do exist? What will the procedure be to avoid these obstacles? You will also need to consider the location(s) from which you will operate the ground control station. Is the location adequate to maintain a clear view of the sUAS in light of local terrain and obstacles? Will visual observers be required? Where will they be in relation to the ground station and what possible obstructions to vision do they need to know about and consider? You should also evaluate the local terrain, noting how it may impact visual line-of-sight, altitude operating restrictions, signal blockage, and other issues.

What other hazards exist? Those high-tension power lines adjacent to the place you'll be flying should not be a concern if all goes according to plan, but what if something unexpected happens? It's important to keep in mind what is adjacent to your proposed

flying site. You don't want to draw unwanted attention from prison guards suspicious that you may be up to no good as you fly nearby. Perhaps there is a forest fire in the area with firefighter aircraft operating in response, or disaster recovery efforts are in full swing; these types of operations can be disrupted by rogue drones. So don't become one of these costly and annoying rascals. While these may be extreme examples, you would be surprised what stupid tricks drone pilots have pulled.

Another consideration is people. As you may recall, you are not allowed to fly over non-participating people. So to comply with this restriction, extensive forethought is needed. If you're planning to take pictures at a wedding, how do you get the right shots while avoiding being overhead of the crowd? What if you're at a festival shooting video for the organizer—how will you avoid obstacles and people all at the same time? Even something as innocuous as flying over a beach or in a park, you must always be aware of non-participants wandering into the area or transgressing below the flight path of your sUAS. Contingency planning is a must to avoid people who unexpectedly show up in the wrong places.

What about property rights and ownership? Clearly, you should not trespass on someone's property. You can avoid this faux pas by picking public land from which to operate or gaining the proper permissions to fly from private land. What may be less obvious is who owns the property over which you will be flying. Even more muddy is how high the owner's privacy and property rights extend. This argument goes well beyond the confines of this book, and you can expect that these issues will become frequent headlines and subjects of court cases as the number of drones flying around increases. For now, be respectful of other people's property. Ask permission and if denied, avoid overflight of the party's land. Also fly well clear of houses and other property to ensure your sUAS will not be a source of tension or involve local law enforcement. Remember that animals such as dogs and horses are considered property, so be sure not to disturb or harass them. Be aware of state (and sometimes local) privacy and trespass laws. You may want to at least read them over for familiarity. Essentially anything that is considered harassment (affecting one's enjoyment of life or property) can lead to some sort of enforcement action. In sum, it is best to be a proactive and respectful operator to avoid such issues.

Of course, Part 107 and local regulations (and ordinances, rules, or restrictions) must be considered. Other lessons outline the procedures and requirements for operating in different types of airspace as well as near airports. Be sure to check for any local limitations and abide by them to avoid unwanted visits from law enforcement. Remember that while some local laws may not be valid due to federal supremacy, unless you're a lawyer, or want to spend lots of money on one, it's best to let all of the regulatory dust settle as sUAS become more popular prior to challenging city, county, and state rules. If you are confronted by law enforcement, remain calm and ask for specifics in terms of what they are enforcing. If they are uncooperative, it is best to pack up and deal with the situation later through a discussion with police supervisors or city, county, or state personnel rather than ending up in handcuffs for failing to comply with police instructions. There are many videos online showing remote pilots interacting with police; some of these videos are good and others not so good, but they can be helpful to you as examples.

Considering the issues in the preceding paragraphs, you may want to designate certain areas in the local area as "off limits," and brief all participating parties of this. Don't forget to check NOTAMs and TFRs for your location. Again, you don't want to push the limits by operating near the borders of areas in which sUAS operations are not allowed. You may even be able to program geofences (operational restrictions that are followed by your autopilot/flight controller) to avoid transgressing into areas or up to altitudes you need to avoid.

Another issue worthy of your attention relates to wildlife. Use caution when operating in areas of bird activity, particularly territorial types of birds or birds of prey, as they very well may attack your aircraft (check out the Internet for some video examples). But the harm can also go the other way—a number of studies have shown that various types of wildlife can be disturbed or agitated by sUAS and the noise they produce. If you think that such disturbances are no big deal, think again. The Endangered Species Act protects a variety of animals that may be impacted by sUAS operations; specifically, the Act does not allow anyone "to harass, harm, pursue, hunt, shoot, wound, kill, trap, capture, or collect or attempt to engage in any such conduct." The term "harm" includes causing a mother animal to stay away from its nest of babies: "such an act may include significant habitat modification or degradation where it actually kills or injures wildlife by significantly impairing essential behavioral patterns, including breeding, feeding, or sheltering."[2] Offenses come with stiff penalties. Additional restrictions pertain to migratory birds under the Migratory Bird Treaty Act and marine mammals under the Marine Mammal Protection Act. Perhaps you're thinking to yourself: whatever, I don't need to worry about such nonsense. Well, two drone pilots who thought that way ended up being fined $1,000 for flying too close to Orca whales in the state of Washington. Just as you have to respect your neighbors and non-participant humans, do the same for the environment in which you operate.

Lastly, you will want to consider if there are any other oddities about where you want to fly. Do military helicopters fly close by at low altitude? Is the site next to the Super Bowl (which, of course, would be off limits)? Is there interference with the frequency spectrum used for sUAS control? Are there numerous other sUAS in operation in the vicinity? Try to consider every possible impact on your location and ensuing operation before starting to fly—plan ahead. Ideally, this will prevent you from coming across any unwanted surprises. Having a checklist or plan for evaluating any location is extremely helpful to ensure you're not missing anything when getting ready to go fly at new or regularly used locales.

/ Communications

It is important that remote pilots-in-command have a sound communication plan not only for people participating in the sUAS operation, but also with air traffic controllers, land owners, or other applicable stakeholders. Remote PICs should have access to a cell phone or satellite phone (as necessary) so they can communicate with emergency personnel, air traffic control (when out of radio range), and participants who may not be within radio range. Cell phones serve as a great communications backup to handheld radios. Remote PICs should also have handheld radios (walkie-talkies) to communicate to sUAS operations personnel such as visual observers. Ideally, team members would use

---

[2] U.S. Fish and Wildlife Service, Endangered Species Program, "ESA Basics: 40 Years of Conserving Endangered Species" (2013). Retrieved from https://www.fws.gov/endangered/esa-library/pdf/ESA_basics.pdf

headsets or ear pieces, because it is sometimes very difficult to hear in the field (e.g., due to windy conditions or other ambient noise). Additionally, Remote PICs will want to have a VHF aviation-band radio for monitoring aircraft and/or ATC (when within range). At the very least, this VHF radio can be used to monitor the emergency frequency (121.50) to keep abreast of local traffic and any potential urgent messages. As a good rule of thumb, the RPIC should be capable of instant contact with key participants (such as visual observers) and ATC (if applicable) at all times during sUAS operations. It is possible to transmit on aviation frequencies if the radio user has the appropriate FCC license.

ADS-B receivers can be purchased to show local traffic, and applications are available for use on smart phones, tablets, or computers to view ADS-B feeds. These utilities can dramatically improve situational awareness, but remember that not all aircraft have ADS-B or may be in range of the receiver. Moreover, few (if any) UAS have ADS-B. Depending upon your type of operation, you may want or need to file NOTAMs for your sUAS flights—don't forget to take this step, as necessary.

The key is to ensure that the communications plan is established prior to beginning your mission. In fact, it is a good idea to have a checklist or template to follow prior to each flight. Batteries can get weak or die. People can move out of range. Weather can impact radio waves. There are numerous variables. It is good to check the communication capabilities of your team regularly until the close of business for the day.

/ Contingency Planning

Flight operations rarely go exactly as planned. An unexpected aircraft may show up in the area. Weather conditions may change, or equipment might fail. You just never know what might catch you off guard. It is best to have backup plans for as many potential events as possible. Just as manned pilots do, remote PICs should use checklists or contingency plans in case of such occurrences. For example, what is the procedure you want your team (or just yourself) to use in case of a communication failure? How will you even know if you have a communication failure (i.e., how do you test, maintain, and update your communication links)?

FLYING AT NIGHT

Although most sUAS operations at night are prohibited, it is possible to receive a waiver to fly from sunset to sunrise. In fact, numerous operators have already received such waivers. However, the ground references you used for orientation and geolocation will be invisible, as will the terrain. A good policy is to do a survey of the area of proposed night operations during the day to evaluate obstacles and other nuances of the operational area. This orientation can save you the trouble of finding out the hard way where there are wires, towers, and other pesky structures or challenges. Stars can merge with ground lighting, making it difficult to maintain control, and you will not be able to see those clouds you are supposed to avoid. Don't fly at night if low clouds are forecast. Additionally, it may be hard to distinguish the lights on your sUAS from building, street, airport, and other lights, resulting in all them blending together. It is best to do some "test" flights under more controlled conditions until you get comfortable with keeping track of your system in a sea of lights at night.

REVIEW QUESTIONS

Lesson 4 — Airport and Off-Airport Operations

1. An air traffic control clearance provides

   A — priority over all other traffic.

   B — adequate separation from all traffic.

   C — authorization to proceed under specified traffic conditions in controlled airspace.

2. Which type of traffic pattern departure can manned aircraft be expected to use at an airport without a control tower?

   A — Depart in any direction consistent with safety, after crossing the airport boundary.

   B — Make all turns to the left.

   C — Comply with any FAA traffic pattern established for the airport.

3. When operating in the vicinity of an airport, remote pilots should

   A — conform with the established traffic pattern procedures used by manned aircraft.

   B — make all turns opposite that of the established traffic pattern procedures used by manned aircraft.

   C — remain clear of all manned aircraft traffic patterns and operations.

4. If instructed by ground control to maneuver/taxi to runway 9, the pilot may proceed

   A — via taxiways and across runways to, but not onto, runway 9.

   B — to the next intersecting runway where further clearance is required.

   C — via any route at the pilot's discretion onto runway 9 and hold until cleared for takeoff.

5. The numbers 9 and 27 on a runway indicate that the runway is oriented approximately

   A — 090° and 270° magnetic.

   B — 090° and 270° true.

   C — 009° and 027° magnetic.

6. Manned aircraft generally try to operate takeoff and landing operations

   A — facing into the wind.

   B — facing so that the wind is from behind.

   C — facing so that the wind is directly from the left or right.

7. Airport taxiways are identified by

   A — white pavement markings.

   B — yellow pavement markings.

   C — green pavement markings.

8. Unless otherwise noted, manned aircraft should enter the airport traffic pattern

   A — to intercept the downwind leg at a 90-degree angle.

   B — to intercept the downwind leg at a 30-degree angle.

   C — to intercept the downwind leg at a 45-degree angle.

9. How is a runway recognized as being closed?

   A — Red lights are placed at the approach end of the runway.

   B — Yellow chevrons are painted on the runway beyond the threshold.

   C — An X is displayed on the runway.

10. An aircraft reports that it is on a left downwind for runway 36. Where will the aircraft be in relation to the airport?

   A — West

   B — East

   C — North

11. An aircraft reports that it is on a right crosswind for runway 27. Where will the aircraft be in relation to the airport?

   A — Northwest

   B — Northeast

   C — Southwest

12. ATC has instructed you to remain clear of all runways during your sUAS operations on the airport property. Which sign color scheme warns you that you are approaching a runway from a taxiway?

   A — Red background, white lettering

   B — Black background, yellow lettering

   C — Yellow background, black lettering

13. ATC has instructed you to remain clear of all runways during your sUAS operations on the airport property. Which pavement marking color scheme warns you of approaching a runway from a taxiway?

   A — Approaching solid, double yellow lines, with dashed, double yellow lines beyond.

   B — Approaching dashed, double yellow lines, with solid, double yellow lines beyond.

   C — Approaching a solid yellow line, with a dashed yellow line beyond.

14. Which of the following would not be a significant concern for remote pilots in terms of encountering wake turbulence?

   A — Aircraft flying 1,000 feet overhead.

   B — Aircraft at idle thrust on the adjacent ramp area.

   C — A helicopter departing from a proximate location.

15. Pilots should monitor _____ at all times, if able.

   A — 122.95

   B — 243.50

   C — 121.50

LESSON 5

Radio Communication Procedures

Note: All discussions concerning the use of a radio (transceiver) in this lesson assume that the user is authorized and licensed to use such a system. Currently, handheld aviation radios require an FCC license for use. DO NOT use aviation transceivers if you are unlicensed. Instead, follow the guidance in this lesson about monitoring frequencies with an aviation band scanner. Also, if authorized to transmit, be aware that the FAA currently does not require remote pilots to communicate via radio to other aircraft and has not yet provided guidance on the proper terminology and procedures to be used by unmanned aircraft.

When you listen to an AM radio at night, and tune down toward the lower end of the dial, you can pick up stations hundreds and even thousands of miles away. Low frequencies can be received at long distances even in the daytime, because they are not weakened or attenuated as they travel through the air and over the ground as much as are higher frequencies, and low frequencies can even bounce off of the ionosphere (the charged layer of Earth's atmosphere). However, atmospheric interference, or static, is a problem with low-frequency transmissions. To avoid having critical aeronautical communications affected by static, frequencies in the very high frequency (VHF) range are used in aircraft radios. Radio transmissions in the VHF band are limited to line-of-sight (Figure 5-1) and that makes altitude an important factor—as you gain altitude the range of VHF is greatly increased.

The FAA has assigned the frequencies between 118.0 MHz (megahertz—millions of cycles per second) and 136.975 MHz for aviation radio communication.

The list below shows how they are allocated. Most modern aircraft radios are capable of transmitting and receiving on at least 720 frequencies, or channels.

The FAA spaces frequency assignments 25 kHz apart (kilohertz, or thousands of cycles per second—126.225, 126.275). If you are assigned a frequency which your radio cannot tune, just ask for an alternate frequency.

This is an all-inclusive list of frequency assignments, emphasizing those that you will probably be using most.

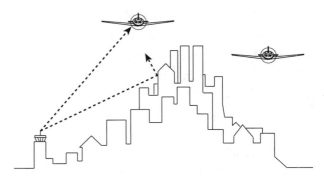

Figure 5-1. Line-of-sight radio limitations

/ Voice Communication Frequencies

118.0 to 121.4 MHz—Air Traffic Control

121.5 MHz—Emergency Frequency, ELT signals *(The FAA recommends that you monitor this frequency at all times, if possible, to listen for emergency Notices to Airmen or for being hailed by the FAA or other authorities if you are doing something you're not supposed to be doing.)*

121.6 to 121.9 MHz—Airport Ground Control

121.95 MHz—Flight Schools

121.975 MHz—Private Aircraft Advisory (FSS)

122.0 MHz—FSS

122.025 to 122.075 MHz—FSS

122.1 MHz—FSS receive only

122.125 to 122.175 MHz—FSS

122.2 MHz—FSS Common Enroute Simplex

122.225 to 122.675 MHz—FSS

122.7 MHz—Unicom, uncontrolled airports

122.725 MHz—Unicom, private airports not open to public

122.75 MHz—Unicom, air-to-air, private airports not open to public

122.775 MHz—Future Unicom or Multicom

122.8 MHz—Unicom, uncontrolled airports

122.825 MHz—Future Unicom or Multicom

122.85 MHz—Multicom

122.875 MHz—Future Unicom or Multicom

122.9 MHz—Multicom, airports with no tower, FSS or Unicom

122.925 MHz—Multicom, Natural Resources

122.95 MHz—Unicom, controlled airports

122.975 MHz—Unicom, high altitude

123.0 MHz—Unicom, uncontrolled airports

123.025 MHz—Future Unicom or Multicom

123.05 and 123.075 MHz—Unicom, heliports

123.1 MHz—Search and Rescue, temporary control towers

123.15 to 123.575 MHz—Flight Test

123.6 to 123.65 MHz—FSS or Air Traffic Control (note that 123.45 is *not* available to all users)

123.675 to 128.8 MHz—Air Traffic Control

128.825 to 132.0 MHz—Aeronautical Radio, Inc. (ARINC)

132.05 to 136.975 MHz—Air Traffic Control

When you select the proper communication frequency, you will be able to receive on that frequency. Modern radios have crystal-controlled frequency selection and require no tuning. Radio communication only allows for one user to transmit at a time, thus each party to the communication must finish transmitting before a reply can be received. You may hear loud squealing sounds on occasion, which is when two (or more) people try to talk at the same time. As a remote pilot-in-command, you will want to have a handheld or other type of radio capable of monitoring on the above frequency ranges. For those appropriately licensed, having a radio with transmission capabilities can be used to communicate with other users on the frequency.

The list above shows general frequency assignments, but you need to know how to contact a specific tower, UNICOM, or flight service station. The *Chart Supplement* (CS) lists all of the radio frequencies available at each airport and also includes a listing of all air route traffic control center frequencies; a ready reference for most frequencies is your sectional aeronautical chart. Another good source for frequencies is your local aviation chart. Refer to the Seattle sectional chart and the sectional chart legend in Appendix D. Airports with control towers have a blue airport symbol, and very close to the symbol you will find a data block with "CT"—such as the one near Seattle-Tacoma International Airport, where "CT 119.9" is the control tower frequency shown. If an asterisk (*) appears after the frequency, the tower does not operate continuously. If the chart says NFCT adjacent to the airport symbol, it is a non-federal control tower, operated by a private entity (which means nothing to you, as you still need permission from them if in their airspace!).

To get an idea what is going on at an airport, it is wise to tune into the Automatic Terminal Information Service (ATIS) frequency listed in the airport data block (where available). ATIS is a continuous taped broadcast of non-control information, such as ceiling and visibility, altimeter setting, wind (magnetic), runway in use, etc. The UNICOM (privately operated Aeronautical Advisory Service) frequency is listed at the end of the data block. Sectional charts also include a tabulation of all control tower and ATIS frequencies in the margin (Figure 5-2). Some airports, usually non-towered ones, have computer-reported weather. These frequencies are labeled as AWOS (Automated Weather Observing System) or ASOS (Automated

CONTROL TOWER FREQUENCIES
ON SEATTLE SECTIONAL CHART

Airports which have control towers are indicated on this chart by the letters CT followed by the primary VHF local control frequency. Selected transmitting frequencies for each control tower are tabulated in the adjoining spaces, the low or medium transmitting frequency is listed first followed by a VHF local control frequency and the primary VHF and UHF military frequencies, when these frequencies are available. An asterisk (*) follows the part time tower frequency remoted to the collocated full time FSS for use as Airport Advisory Service (AAS) during hours tower is closed. Receiving frequencies are shown thus: 122.5R. Hours shown are local time.

Automatic Terminal Information Service (ATIS) frequencies, shown on the face of the chart are normal arriving frequencies, all ATIS frequencies available are tabulated below.

ARS and/or PAR indicates Radar Instrument Approach available.

GRANT CO	Opr 0700-2300	118.1 124.2 247.8
GRAY AAF		126.2 248.2 ASR/PAR
LEWISTON-NEZ PERCE CO (Lewiston Twr)	Opr 0500-2200	119.4 318.8
McCHORD AFB	ATIS 109.6 270.1	124.8 259.3 ASR/PAR
McNARY (Salem Twr)	Opr 0700-2300	119.1 257.2
OLYMPIA	Opr 0800-2000	124.4 233.2
PENDLETON	Opr 0600-2200	118.7 257.8
PORTLAND HILLSBORO (Hillsboro Twr)	Opr 0700-2300	119.3* 239.3
PORTLAND INTL	ATIS 126.9 354.0	118.7 247.8 ASR

Figure 5-2. Tower and ATIS frequencies (example from sectional chart)

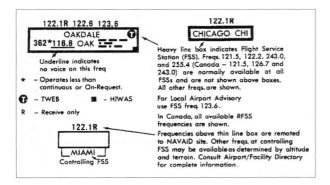

Figure 5-3. Communications boxes (from chart legend)

Surface Observing System). If you choose to tune in, Mr. Robot will read you the current weather conditions at the selected airport.

Figure 5-3 shows how flight service station frequencies are presented on the charts. Note that some frequencies are not listed directly: the heavy line box means that 121.5 and 122.2 are available (but not shown).

All other frequencies are listed above the box. If a frequency that is normally standard—such as 121.5 or 122.2—is not available, it will be listed above the box with a strike-through: ~~122.2~~.

RADIO PROCEDURES

The *Aeronautical Information Manual* (AIM) has a section on correct radio communications phraseology and technique, which contains a guide to the phonetic alphabet and pronunciation of numbers (this guide is also reproduced at the end of this lesson). The AIM also includes a Pilot/Controller Glossary of terms used in communication with air traffic controllers. You should become familiar with the contents of both. You might also want to look at www.aopa.org/training-and-safety/online-learning/ask-atc. This AOPA webpage offers video clips of answers to questions put to air traffic control (ATC) about communications and other pilot/controller topics. Knowledge of this "language" is necessary to understand what aircraft in the local area are doing and where they are going. This is essential for maintaining good situational awareness.

You may want to check out the book *Say Again, Please*, published by ASA. It includes a chapter for each class of airspace for pilots going, coming, or just passing through, using example pilot/controller transmissions plus lots of other information. Although these resources are geared towards manned aircraft, you will find it useful in crafting professional and proper communication transmissions with ATC and other aircraft.

You will learn a lot just by listening on aircraft frequencies to hear how other pilots communicate with each other and with ground personnel. Use a handheld radio to monitor frequencies you are likely to use during sUAS operations, or go to www.liveatc.com to listen to air traffic control from all over the country (and the world). Be warned, however, that you may hear pilots use poor techniques and phraseology; just because you have heard someone say something on the radio does not mean that it is correct usage. Check with the AIM or the aforementioned book for more details. A visit to a control tower or a radar facility will convince you that everyone on the ground is prepared to help you have a safe flight and that having "mic fright" will just keep you from taking advantage of the many services available.

For those with FCC licensure, be sure to listen before transmitting so that you do not interfere with a communication in progress, and listen to what is being said—in many cases you may hear information that makes your call unnecessary. Also make sure that you are on the correct frequency. Some airports have multiple approach, tower, and ground control frequencies based upon where you are in relation to or on the airport.

Always begin your initial transmission with the name of the station that you are calling: "Logan Tower," "Orlando Ground," "Dallas Radio," "Camano Island UNICOM," followed by your own identification (in full, if it is the initial contact): "Parrot two seven four four Zulu." Be sure to include your call sign, full or abbreviated, as part of every transmission. Be as brief as practicable without omitting necessary information, and always give your position when requesting a clearance from Air Traffic Control. Remember this sequence: WHO you are calling, WHO you are, WHERE you are, and WHAT your intentions are. Note: the FAA has not released guidance on sUAS communication procedures as of yet. This information is based upon manned aircraft operations.

If you have the ATIS information, you know which runway is being used by manned aircraft; giving the ground controller your location of operations might result in the assignment of a more convenient or expeditious instruction or help the local controller direct your flight more advantageously.

Your location of operation (e.g., the airport ramp) may have distractions and be loud. It may also be hard to hear transmissions over all the ruckus out in the field or on the ramp. You may want to consider a lightweight earphone or headset to make sure you can hear communications clearly.

Lastly, it is always in your best interest to monitor the emergency frequency of 121.50 at all times. This is the frequency that is most likely to be used to communicate to you that you are doing something you are not supposed to, such as entering restricted airspace, when you are not communicating with ATC or other controlling agencies.

RADIO USE AT NON-TOWER AIRPORTS

Unless an airport has an operating control tower, manned aircraft do not even need to have a radio to use that airport. For safety's sake, however, you should have a radio—but do not expect all airplanes in the area to have radios. Many airports have no radio facility. When operating in the vicinity of a non-radio airport, use the Common Traffic Advisory Frequency (CTAF, as shown on sectional charts) listed in the CS.

In most cases this will be the MULTICOM frequency 122.9 MHz, because you will hear manned aircraft broadcasting their position and intentions in the blind (no specific addressee): "Camano Island Traffic, Cessna five five one two Foxtrot, five miles southwest, inbound for landing, Camano Island."

At virtually every tower-controlled airport, the tower frequency becomes the CTAF when the tower is closed, so nothing changes after the controllers go home—except if the airspace reverts to Class G, no special approval would be required.

At most airports with a UNICOM (Aeronautical Advisory Service), the UNICOM frequency will be the CTAF. Don't be surprised if there is not much action on UNICOM—this is a non-governmental service provided by the local operator, and those busy people may not hear radio calls. UNICOM frequencies are shared by many uncontrolled airports, and some may be so close together that pilots at different airports will interfere with one another. To avoid confusion, listen closely for the name of the airport at which you are operating. Here is an example of a communication you may overhear at a non-towered airport: "Cle Elum traffic, Cessna eight eight one two Bravo, left downwind runway 25, touch and go, Cle Elum." UNICOM is used for many purposes and is quite informal, but you should not let this informality change your normal good communication habits. Be sure to use both your eyes and your radio at airports or in their vicinities at all times.

Some airports have installed new devices called SuperUnicoms®. They operate 24 hours a day and never take a coffee break. When you call in to an airport with a SuperUnicom®, your call will be answered by a computer-generated human voice giving temperature, dew point, wind direction and velocity, altimeter setting, and favored runway (based on calls from traffic in the pattern). Pilots can also get weather information with microphone clicks.

The FAA contracted Flight Service Station (FSS) duties to private industry. These duties have been consolidated and you will no longer find an FSS on the airport. Go to www.1800wxbrief.com or www.faa.gov/go/flightservice/ for more details. The radio frequencies in the CS and on sectional charts are remote communication outlets, and the controller you talk to might be hundreds of miles from your location. These individuals may or may not be familiar with the uniqueness of your location in terms of weather and terrain. Be sure to read the Communications section of the CS Legend pages in Appendix B; it makes clear how frequencies are to be used.

COMMUNICATION AT AIRPORTS WITH OPERATING TOWERS

Airspace around an airport with an operating control tower is Class D airspace (unless it is within Class B airspace). If you need to enter Class D airspace, you must have permission from the tower. If you are departing, you must first receive initial instructions from the ground controller, who directs all activity on the ramps and taxiways. With few exceptions, ground control operates on 121.6, 121.7, 121.8, or 121.9 MHz. Controllers will frequently shorten this by eliminating the 121: "Contact ground point seven leaving the runway."

The ground controller will authorize you to maneuver around the airport, but you must stop before crossing any taxiways or runways (active or not) and receive permission to cross. Think of it as a stoplight at every intersection that glows red until the controller turns it

to green. Figure 5-4 illustrates a situation where a pilot taxiing a larger UAS from the ramp to runway 9 would receive authorization for the whole route, but would be told to hold short of runway 27. With permission to cross, he or she would proceed to the unmarked intersection with the closed runway, stop, call for permission, and the procedure would be repeated at the hold lines for runways 36R and 36L. It is the controller's responsibility to issue precise instructions, but if you are getting close to any kind of intersection without having heard from the tower, stop and ask.

Note: Ground controllers do not use the word "cleared," because it might be misconstrued as a takeoff clearance...they say "taxi to" or "taxi across." If you are directed to "hold short" of a runway, you must read that instruction back to the controller verbatim—nothing else will suffice. To avoid a runway incursion, always stop and ask for clarification of any instruction you do not understand. "What do you want me to do?" works just fine. If you are at an unfamiliar airport, do not hesitate to ask for "progressive taxi instructions," and the controller will guide you to your destination on the field.

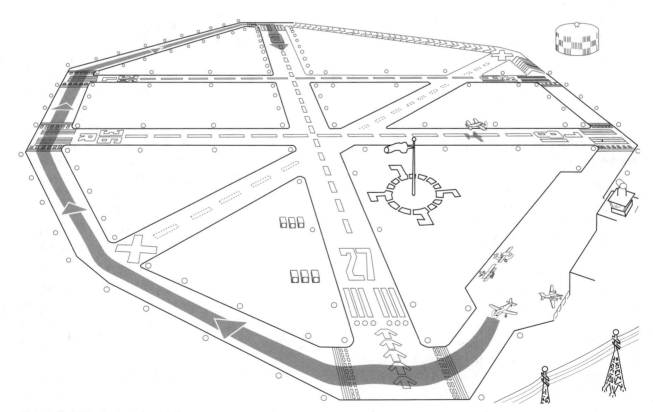

Figure 5-4. Taxiing to the active runway

ADS-B = Automatic Dependent Surveillance Broadcast

When you are ready for takeoff, contact the tower controller for takeoff clearance. The tower (or "local") controller is responsible for all aircraft in Class D airspace and on the active runway—don't cross onto the runway without a clearance. You must maintain communication with the tower controllers while you are in their airspace (Class D), but remember that separation from other airplanes is your responsibility; don't expect the controller to keep you from swapping paint. When you have departed Class D airspace, you are on your own (or you may request radar services). You do not have to ask the tower for permission to change frequencies after you have crossed the Class D airspace boundary.

On arrival, before you enter Class D airspace, you should listen to the ATIS (if there is one) and advise the tower controller on initial contact that you have the ATIS information. Where there is no ATIS, listen on the tower frequency and note the instructions given to other pilots. After landing, do not change to ground control until advised to do so by the tower. Some tower-controlled airports have UNICOM, but because you will get all of your weather information and clearances from the tower, your use of UNICOM at that tower-controlled airport will be limited to such things as calling for fuel, ordering rental cars, etc. Do not forget that in order to transmit on aviation frequencies, proper FCC credentials are needed. *Note:* Towers report wind direction relative to magnetic north. In fact, any wind direction you receive by radio is referenced to magnetic north; winds in written form, such as forecasts, are referenced to true north.

AIR TRAFFIC CONTROL RADAR SERVICES

In locations with dense air traffic, ATC will likely incorporate radar monitoring of aircraft movements. Additionally, such radar monitoring services is provided for enroute aircraft away from individual airports. ATC uses radar two different ways. Radar energy bounces off of the objects of ample size, such as a general aviation airplane, providing a rough "target" on the controller's screen (also referred to as a primary target). Manned aircraft are generally equipped with a transponder that communicates with air traffic control radar when within the range limits of the facility (this is referred to as a secondary target). This allows controllers to more easily track and separate (as applicable) aircraft. Because sUAS are so small,

it is unlikely they would show up on ATC radar as a primary target. One of these days, sUAS may have transponders or other reporting systems onboard (see the ADS-B discussion below). This will potentially make sUAS visible to ATC, manned pilots, and other users (like you), making sUAS much safer in terms of collision avoidance and situational awareness. For now, remote pilots will not be dealing much with radar control provided by ATC.

ADS-B

It's all good in big cities with their fancy ATC towers and radar systems, but what about the rest of the country (and world)? How do you get flight following in an area without radar service? Or how do you see aircraft that may be too small to generate a primary target or that don't have a transponder? The answer is Automatic Dependent Surveillance–Broadcast (ADS-B). Where it is available, and if your sUAS is properly equipped, it fills in the blanks where radar coverage is not available due to terrain or altitude. Your GPS continuously transmits your position, track, altitude, ground speed, and tail number to a ground-based transceiver (GBT), where it is relayed to an air traffic control facility, making it possible for controllers to know all about you without using radar (this is called ADS-B out). Controllers can also see returns from other similarly equipped aircraft in your vicinity and provide separation. This is the basic ADS-B function; for a few more bucks, you can enhance it by equipping your airplane to receive the information directly from nearby airplanes and have it available on a display, giving you real-time traffic positions (this is called ADS-B in). The equipment also provides for datalinked weather. This is not the end of the line for radar controllers, though; providing your own separation based on ADS-B is not in the cards (yet). You can check out ADS-B equipped air traffic by visiting www.liveatc.com. Using this site can greatly enhance situational awareness of local traffic. Remember, though, that not all aircraft have ADS-B out yet.

ADS-B is altitude-limited in that the transmission from an aircraft to the ground is line-of-sight and may be obstructed by terrain in some areas. Still, it is good down to 2,000 feet AGL or lower wherever it is available.

ADS-B has proved its worth in Alaska, where radar coverage is limited. The service is available along the east coast and in North Dakota as well as Alaska. The

FAA is installing GBTs across the continent, and has mandated that manned airplanes flying in airspace where a Mode C transponder is now required have ADS-B Out equipment installed by January 2020. Portable ADS-B does not comply with the mandate.

RADIO COMMUNICATION PHRASEOLOGY AND TECHNIQUE

Always use the phonetic alphabet when identifying your aircraft and to spell out groups of letters or unusual words under difficult communications conditions. Do not make up your own phonetic equivalents; this alphabet was developed internationally to be understandable by non-English speaking pilots and ground personnel.

/ Phonetic Alphabet

A ALFA . . . . . (ALFAH)
B BRAVO . . . . (BRAHVOH)
C CHARLIE . . . (CHAR-LEE OR SHAR-LEE)
D DELTA . . . . (DELL-TA)
E ECHO . . . . . (ECK-OH)
F FOXTROT . . (FOKS-TROT)
G GOLF . . . . . (GOLF)
H HOTEL . . . . (HOH-TEL)
I INDIA . . . . . (IN-DEE-AH)
J JULIETT . . . (JOO-LEE-ETT)
K KILO . . . . . (KEY-LOH)
L LIMA . . . . . (LEE-MAH)
M MIKE . . . . . (MIKE)
N NOVEMBER . (NO-VEM-BER)
O OSCAR . . . . (OSS-CAH)
P PAPA . . . . . (PAH-PAH)
Q QUEBEC . . . (KEH-BECK)
R ROMEO . . . . (ROW-ME-OH)
S SIERRA . . . . (SEE-AIR-AH)
T TANGO . . . . (TANG-GO)
U UNIFORM . . (YOU-NEE-FORM)
V VICTOR . . . (VIK-TAH)
W WHISKEY . . (WISS-KEY)
X XRAY . . . . . (ECKS-RAY)
Y YANKEE . . . (YANG-KEY)
Z ZULU . . . . . (ZOO-LOO)

1 ONE . . . . . . (WUN)
2 TWO . . . . . (TOO)
3 THREE . . . . (TREE)
4 FOUR . . . . . (FOW-ER)
5 FIVE . . . . . . (FIFE)
6 SIX . . . . (SIX)
7 SEVEN . . . . (SEVEN)
8 EIGHT . . . . (AIT)
9 NINER . . . . (NIN-ER*)
0 ZERO . . . . . (ZEE-RO)

* to avoid confusion with the German word "nein," which means "no"

/ Figures

Misunderstandings about altitude assignments can be hazardous. The examples below are taken from the AIM and demonstrate officially accepted techniques. However, as you monitor aviation frequencies, you will hear pilots use a decimal system—for example, TWO POINT FIVE for 2,500. The FAA has never commented on this practice and it is commonly accepted—don't try it in another country.

500: FIVE HUNDRED

3,000: THREE THOUSAND

13,500: ONE THREE THOUSAND FIVE HUNDRED

Pilots flying above 18,000 feet use flight levels when referring to altitude:

"CENTURION 45X LEAVING ONE SEVEN THOUSAND FOR FLIGHT LEVEL TWO THREE ZERO."

Bearings, courses, and radials are always spoken in three digits:

"CESSNA 38N TURN LEFT HEADING THREE ZERO ZERO, INTERCEPT THE DALLAS ZERO ONE FIVE RADIAL."

Address ground controllers as "SEATTLE GROUND CONTROL," control towers as "O'HARE TOWER," radar facilities as "MIAMI APPROACH," or "ATLANTA CENTER." When calling a flight service station, use radio: "PORTLAND RADIO."

When making the initial contact with a controller, use your full call sign, without the initial *November*: "BOISE GROUND, PARROT EIGHT EIGHT ZERO SEVEN DELTA, AT THE RAMP WITH INFORMATION GOLF, TAXI FOR TAKEOFF."

Use of the last three digits is acceptable for subsequent transmissions: "ROGER, TAXI TWO EIGHT RIGHT, PARROT ZERO SEVEN DELTA."

Many uncontrolled airports share UNICOM frequencies, and if you do not identify the airport at which you are operating, your transmissions may serve to confuse other pilots monitoring the frequency. Don't say, "STINSON FOUR SIX WHISKEY DOWNWIND FOR RUNWAY SIX," say "ARLINGTON TRAFFIC, STINSON FOUR SIX WHISKEY DOWNWIND FOR RUNWAY SIX, ARLINGTON." That way, pilots at other airports sharing Arlington's UNICOM frequency will not be nervously looking over their shoulders.

/ "Unable" and "Immediately"

The most valuable word in radio communication is "unable." It should be used whenever you are asked to do something you don't want to do or are prohibited from doing, like flying close to a cloud. An air traffic controller who hears "unable" will come up with an alternative plan. You are the remote pilot-in-command and the only person in position to determine the safety of a proposed action. The second most important word is "immediately." If a controller tells you to turn left immediately, or to climb immediately or to do anything else immediately, do not reach for the microphone—do it. One exception: If a controller says "Cleared for immediate takeoff" your response should be "Negative, I'll wait." You don't want something unexpected to happen when there is a plane on short final. The other side of the coin is when you need to cut corners to get on the ground in a hurry—your battery is getting low, for example. When you make your initial call, tell the controller that you need to land immediately.

/ Online Sources

The websites www.ourairports.com and https://skyvector.com are not official and they should be used only for planning and orientation. Aerial views are not current. Information from 1800wxbrief.com is official. You can find the frequencies to be used at any airport at www.airnav.com. An excellent resource for radio communication procedures is "Say It Right," produced by the Air Safety Foundation. It can be found at www.asf.org/courses.

REVIEW QUESTIONS

Lesson 5 — Radio Communication Procedures

Refer to the full-color Seattle sectional chart excerpt in Appendix D.

1. What UNICOM frequency, if any, is indicated for Seattle-Tacoma International Airport (near **C**)?

    A — None is listed

    B — 119.9 MHz

    C — 122.95 MHz

2. Approaching the Bowers airport (ELN) (near **I**), which frequency would you use to listen to traffic in the pattern and determining which runway they are using?

    A — 122.3 MHz

    B — 111.0 MHz

    C — 123.0 MHz

3. Which individuals are authorized to make transmissions on aviation frequencies using a handheld radio?

    A — All remote pilots are permitted to make such transmissions once they receive their certificate.

    B — Remote pilots with the necessary FCC license.

    C — Only manned aircraft pilots are permitted to use aviation frequencies.

4. The correct method for stating 4,500 feet MSL to ATC is

    A — "FORTY-FIVE HUNDRED FEET."

    B — "FOUR POINT FIVE."

    C — "FOUR THOUSAND FIVE HUNDRED."

5. When operating at an airport that does not have a tower, FSS, or UNICOM, broadcast your intentions in the blind on

    A — 123.0 MHz.

    B — 123.6 MHz.

    C — The Common Traffic Advisory Frequency.

6. ATIS is the continuous broadcast of recorded information

    A — concerning nonessential information to relieve frequency congestion.

    B — concerning non-control information in selected high-activity terminal areas.

    C — concerning sky conditions limited to ceilings below 1,000 feet and visibilities less than 3 miles.

7. What is the best resource for determining the correct phraseology to use on ATC and aviation radio frequencies?

    A — The AIM

    B — The *e*-CS

    C — The ICAO

8. What is meant by the "*" symbol adjacent to a communication frequency (e.g., Tacoma Narrows [TIW] airport tower frequency)?

    A — This notes that this is the Common Traffic Advisory Frequency.

    B — This notes that this is the preferred frequency for use to communicate with ATC.

    C — This notes that the facility is not open 24 hours/continuously.

9. Which is not part of the aviation phonetic alphabet?

    A — Zulu

    B — Cierra

    C — Mike

10. Which is true if the control tower reports that winds are 090 at 10?

A — The winds are blowing from 090 degrees magnetic at 10 knots.

B — The winds are blowing from 090 degrees true at 10 knots.

C — The winds are blowing from 090 degrees magnetic at 10 mph.

LESSON 6

Weather: General Weather Theory, Aviation Weather Sources, and Effects of Weather on sUAS Performance

As a remote pilot limited to flight under good weather conditions (also referred to as visual flight rules), your primary interest in weather and weather changes should be "How will this weather affect visibility for my flight or mission?" Your second area of concern will be clouds, because you must maintain separation from clouds at all times. You need to know whether clouds might form where none now exist or if scattered clouds might merge into an impenetrable overcast. You will want to avoid thunderstorms and other severe weather for safety reasons as well as because they may potentially cause loss of control of your sUAS. Flying is fun, but fighting the weather is not. Every remote pilot should be a student of the weather, and as the hours in your flight log accumulate, you should develop a "weather sense" to keep the fun in flying.

The primary source of all weather changes is the sun. It heats the surface of the earth at varying rates, depending not only on cloud cover and the angle at which the sun's rays strike the earth but on the type of surface being heated. For instance, land changes temperature far more rapidly than water; deserts, urban areas (i.e., concrete and asphalt), and barren areas change temperature faster than forested areas; and cloud cover affects the rate at which any surface gains and loses heat. Heated air, being less dense than cool air, rises and creates low-pressure areas. When the rising air has cooled, it descends and creates areas of high pressure. Air heated at the equator rises, cools, and moves toward the North and South Poles. Meteorologists have identified three loops of rising and descending air, as illustrated, with a net flow toward the poles at high altitude (Figure 6-1). The relatively weak cell over the mid-latitudes (including the United States) flows south-to-north. The moisture content of an air mass depends on its temperature and affects its density, and it is these variations in pressure, density, temperature, and moisture content that define air masses and weather systems. The earth, of course, rotates beneath these weather systems and their effects are felt many miles distant from where the sun's heat began the process. If the earth did not rotate, air descending from the poles would flow directly south to the equator, to be heated again to repeat the cycle.

Because of the earth's rotation, a phenomenon known as the Coriolis force deflects the moving air, so that in the latitudes of the United States the prevailing upper-level winds are westerly.

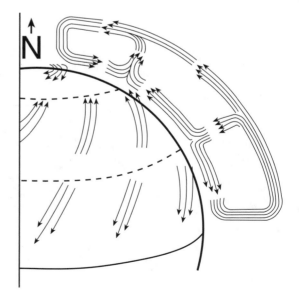

Figure 6-1. Three-cell circulation pattern and prevailing winds

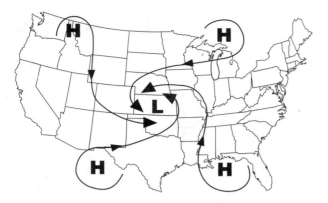

Figure 6-2. Circulation around pressure centers

Air rising in a low-pressure area draws air from outside the low into the center, and the general circulation pattern is counterclockwise (see Figure 6-2). Find the station models (Figure 6-3) around the highs and lows on a surface analysis chart (see later in this lesson) to see how actual winds follow this rule. An extreme example of this is the tornado or cyclone which, as it rotates, draws air, houses, trees, and other debris into its center and up, depositing them many miles away. As you can imagine, this incoming air contains moisture, and rising moisture means clouds, poor visibility, etc. When you are at your departure point, where is that wind coming from? A lake? A snowfield? Land soaked with rain?

Air descending in a high-pressure system circulates clockwise, and as the air reaches the surface, it travels away from the center. Descending air warms and dries. That is good news when you need to keep a good eye on your sUAS.

On the most basic aeronautical weather map, the surface weather analysis chart, you can see high- and low-pressure areas. These are defined by meteorologists who take barometric pressure readings at airports and National Weather Service offices across the country and plot their findings on a chart. By connecting the points of equal pressure (called isobars), they define pressure patterns. Where the isobars are tightly packed, pressure is changing rapidly, and strong winds should be expected. Isobars that are widely spaced indicate less force to drive the wind. As the air from high-pressure areas rushes to fill in the low-pressure areas, you would expect the wind to blow downhill—that is, directly outward from the center of a high to the center of a low.

The air tries to do exactly that, and the driving force is called the pressure gradient force. This force, combined with Coriolis force, deflects the wind so that the direction of air motion crosses the isobars at an angle (Figure 6-4). This figure describes how air moves from high pressure toward low pressure—you might call a high-pressure area a "pile of air," and a low-pressure area a "hole in the air" that the high-pressure air seeks to fill. If the earth did not rotate, the general circulation of air shown in Figure 6-1 would be from south to north over the United States, and it would be at 90° to the gradient wind. However, the earth does rotate, and that rotation causes the wind to veer to the right. The prevailing winds over the United States are from the west and weather systems tend to move across the country from west to east.

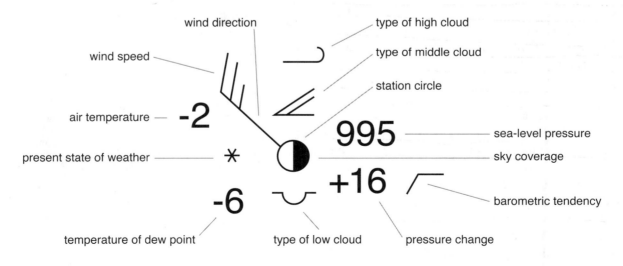

Figure 6-3. Station model example

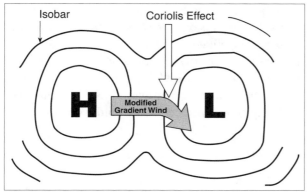

Figure 6-4. Coriolis effect

On the surface analysis chart, you will see wind arrows that do not seem to agree with any rule, because of the effects of local conditions or surface friction. Mountain ranges, passes, and valleys all have a local influence on the direction of air movement up to about 2,000 feet above ground level.

The National Weather Service (NWS) provides extensive weather resources at www.aviationweather. gov. Your first choice when looking for weather reports and forecasts should be the Aviation Digital Data Service (ADDS) website: www.aviationweather.gov/adds. Using the ADDS web page, you get more detail. On the winds page there you can select an altitude.

To understand and anticipate weather changes, you must be aware of pressure systems and their movement. To know what might happen with cloud formations and obstructions to visibility, you must consider the moisture content of the air. All air contains moisture in the form of water vapor; *the amount of water a given volume of air can hold is dependent on the temperature of the air*. As a volume of air is heated, the amount of moisture it can hold in invisible form increases: a temperature increase of 20°F (11°C) doubles the air's capacity to hold moisture. Conversely, cooling the air reduces the amount of water vapor that can be hidden from sight. When the air contains 100% of the moisture it can hold invisibly, the moisture becomes visible in the form of clouds, fog, or precipitation. The moisture condenses into droplets which can be seen, and which restrict your ability to see.

Moisture can be added to the atmosphere through evaporation or sublimation. Evaporation can be from a body of water, a field of snow, or from rainfall; sublimation occurs when water changes state from solid to vapor without a liquid phase.

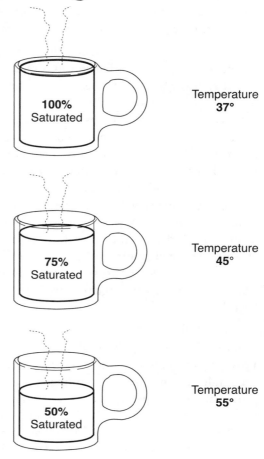

Dew Point 37°

Figure 6-5. Temperature vs. saturation

The temperature at which the air becomes saturated and can contain no more moisture, without that moisture getting you wet, is called the **dew point**. You have heard the television weather person report, "The temperature is 65°, the dew point is 48°." Under those conditions, if the air suddenly cools 17°, it will be saturated, and any further cooling or addition of moisture to the air will result in fog or rain. What the weather reporter calls relative humidity is simply how close the air is to being saturated. The illustration (Figure 6-5) uses a cup of liquid (representing the atmosphere) at different temperatures to show how the percentage of moisture content increases from 50% to 100%. A good example of high relative humidity is a hot July day when the air is full of moisture, but there isn't a cloud in the sky. You feel uncomfortable because perspiration on your body cannot evaporate into air already full of moisture. Take a cold can out of a soft drink dispenser on a clear July day and watch beads of water form on its sides. Where do you think that water comes from?

The measure of relative humidity is the spread between temperature and dew point. If that spread is reported to be less than 5°F, you should investigate further to determine the potential for a reduction in visibility. Is the sun rising, or setting? The answer can help you predict the temperature trend and whether the temperature/dew point spread will increase or decrease. Is the wind blowing from over water or from over land? Moisture can be added to the air by evaporation from rain or bodies of water. Moisture being added to the air can tip the balance toward saturation. If your investigation shows the potential for a decrease in the difference between temperature and dew point for any reason, you must consider the possibility that you will not be able to complete your flight or mission under visual conditions.

Knowledge of the temperature/dew point relationship is valuable in estimating the height of cloud bases. When rising air currents are evidenced by the formation of cumulus clouds, the air is cooling at the rate of approximately 4.4°F per 1,000 feet. For example, if the temperature at the surface is 78°F and the dew point is 62°F, the difference is 16° ÷ 4.4 x 1,000 = 3,600 feet above the surface. This is where you would expect cloud bases to be, under the conditions stated. For the height of cloud bases above sea level, you must add the elevation of the station at which the observations were made.

FRONTS

A weather front exists where air masses with different properties meet. The terms "warm" and "cold" are relative: 30°F air is warmer than 10°F air, but that "warm" air does not call for bathing suits. Cold air is denser than warm air, so where two dissimilar masses meet, the cold air stays near the surface. Figure 6-6 shows a cold front: cold air advancing from west to east and displacing warm air. Because the cold air is dense and relatively heavy, it moves rapidly across the surface, pushing the warm air up. Notice that in both cases the warm air is forced aloft and the cold air stays at the surface. When air is lifted, stuff happens. Just how bad that "stuff" might be is determined by the moisture content of the warm air and where that moisture is coming from.

Friction slows the cold air movement at the surface so that the front is quite vertical in cross-section and the band of frontal weather is narrow. Cold fronts can move as fast as 30 knots. Your awareness of this rapid movement, together with facts you already know about temperature and dew point, will allow you to make the following generalizations about **cold front** weather:

Visibility: Good behind the front. Warm air and pollutants rise rapidly because warm air is less dense than cold air.

Flight conditions: Bumpy as thermal currents rise. Also, depending on the location and time of year, windy conditions can occur at or after cold front passage, making flying conditions unfavorable for most sUAS.

Precipitation: Showery in the frontal area as the warm air is forced aloft and its moisture condenses. The ability of the air to hold moisture decreases as the air cools, and as the moisture contained in each column of rising air condenses into water droplets, showers result. The overwhelming majority of sUAS cannot (and should not) be flown in precipitation, although showers tend to be readily identifiable to see and avoid. The best source for local precipitation is your local weather radar facility (either NWS/ADDS or perhaps a local news channel's radar).

Cloud type: Cumulus, due to air being raised rapidly to the condensation level. Cumulus clouds are a sign of unstable air; the rising air columns are warmer than the surrounding air and continue to rise under their own power. Rising air currents can be very problematic for sUAS, making positive control difficult.

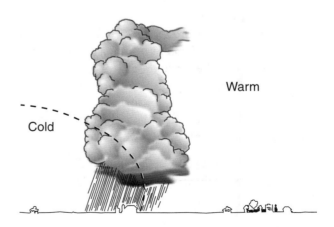

Figure 6-6. Cross-section of a typical cold front

Icing possibility: Clear ice. Cumulus clouds develop large water droplets that freeze into clear sheets of ice when they strike any surface on your sUAS. Due to the performance limitations of most sUAS, you should avoid flying in precipitation (check your sUAS manufacturer documentation for environmental constraints) and if icing conditions are suspected, land your sUAS.

A **warm front** exists when a warm air mass overtakes a slow-moving cold air mass; the lighter warm air cannot displace the heavier cold air, and the warm air is forced to rise as it moves forward (Figure 6-7). This slow upward movement combined with the slow forward movement characteristic of warm fronts allows the warm air to cool slowly. As it reaches the condensation level, stratiform clouds develop. While cold frontal conditions exist over a very short distance, warm fronts slope upward for many miles, and warm frontal weather may be extensive.

You may encounter warm front clouds 50 to 100 miles from where the front is depicted on the surface analysis chart. The following are the characteristics of warm frontal weather:

Visibility: Poor; pollutants trapped by warm air aloft. Air warmed at the surface can only rise until it reaches air at its own temperature.

Flight conditions: Smooth, little to no thermal activity.

Precipitation: Drizzle or continuous rain as moist air is slowly raised to the condensation level. Again, most sUAS need to avoid precipitation. With warm fronts, precipitation can be a factor over large areas or for long periods of time. The best sources for precipitation coverage are the aforementioned radar sources.

Cloud type: Stratus or layered, the result of slow cooling.

Icing possibility: Rime ice; small water droplets freeze instantly upon contact with an aircraft and form a rough, milky coating. Obviously, sUAS should not be flying in icing conditions. If they are suspected, you should land.

Occasionally, a fast-moving cold front will overtake a warm front (Figure 6-8) and lift the warm air away from the surface. This is called an *occlusion*, and occluded frontal weather contains the worst features of both warm and cold fronts: turbulent flying conditions, showers and/or continuous precipitation, poor visibility in precipitation, and broad geographic extent of frontal weather conditions.

Air masses can maintain their warm/cold identity and yet not exert any displacement force. When this happens, the front becomes stationary, and the associated weather covers a large geographic area. In your planning, what you see is probably what you will get during your sUAS operations.

When you look at a weather map that shows frontal positions, cold fronts will be marked in blue, warm fronts in red, occluded fronts in purple, and stationary fronts will alternate red and blue. You can identify fronts on black-and-white charts because the cold front symbols look like icicles and warm front symbols appear as blisters (Figure 6-9). Visualize the lifting process, and you will be on your way to being your own weather forecaster.

When a front passes your location, the most obvious change is the direction of the wind, but it may also be accompanied by a change in temperature, visibility, and/or cloud cover.

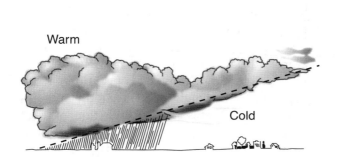

Figure 6-7. Cross-section of a typical warm front

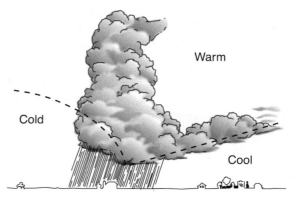

Figure 6-8. Occluded fronts

Occluded fronts show both icicles and blisters on the same side of the front in the direction of movement, and stationary fronts show the symbols on opposite sides of the frontal line, indicating opposing forces (Figure 6-9).

STABILITY

You need a general understanding of air mass stability to anticipate weather changes that might affect your flight. The amount of moisture in the air influences the rate at which the air cools with increasing altitude. The standard "lapse rate," or rate at which cooling takes place, is 2°C per 1,000 feet of altitude. An air mass that cools more rapidly than 2° per 1,000 feet is considered unstable. Any situation that has cool or cold air overlying warm air is a potentially unstable situation, because the warm air, being lighter, will rise and cool more slowly than the surrounding air. The column of rising air then has the impetus to continue to rise; this is the basis upon which thunderstorms develop.

An air mass with warm air overlying cold air is stable because the heavy, cold air cannot rise to displace the lighter warm air. When the temperature rises abruptly with altitude, a temperature inversion exists—this condition is marked by poor visibility because warm, polluted air cannot rise above the inversion level. This is the familiar smog or haze layer, and it usually takes the passage of a major system to clean it out. The possibility of turbulence always exists at the top of an inversion layer.

CLOUD FAMILIES

What you have learned about air movement and the relationship of temperature to moisture content leads right into the study of cloud formation, and by "reading" the clouds you will be able to anticipate the effects of weather changes on your flight.

Meteorologists divide clouds into four families: high clouds, middle clouds, low clouds, and clouds with extensive vertical development. The latter group signals the presence of strong columns of rising air (called convective air currents), which at the very least mean rough air, potentially having an adverse effect on the controllability of your sUAS, and may herald the onset of precipitation or a developing thunderstorm (Figure 6-10).

$$\frac{Dewpoint}{4.4} + 000 = AGL\ of\ Clouds$$

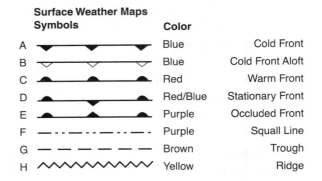

Surface Weather Maps Symbols   Color

	Symbol	Color	
A	▼▼▼	Blue	Cold Front
B	▽▽▽	Blue	Cold Front Aloft
C	⌒⌒⌒	Red	Warm Front
D	⌒▲⌒▲	Red/Blue	Stationary Front
E	▲⌒▲⌒	Purple	Occluded Front
F	– · – · – · –	Purple	Squall Line
G	– – – – –	Brown	Trough
H	∿∿∿∿	Yellow	Ridge

Figure 6-9. Surface analysis chart symbols

When a ground station reports a dew point more than 50°F, it is a sign of strong convective currents. Stay aware of your current surroundings and regularly check the local weather and radar, cutting your flight short if poor weather begins to develop.

Nice fluffy-looking clouds marking the tops of columns of rising air are called cumulus clouds because they are in a building or accumulating stage as the air rises to the condensation level—you can expect turbulence that may make your flying more challenging beneath them (Figure 6-11). Stratocumulus clouds are in the low family, altocumulus in the middle altitudes, and cirrocumulus are the fluffy clouds at high altitudes. Cumulus clouds are a sign of instability in the air mass because stable air has little tendency to move vertically.

You can calculate the approximate altitude of a cloud base above ground level by dividing the Fahrenheit temperature-dew point spread at the surface by 4.4 and adding three zeroes. For example, if the difference between the temperature and dew point is 9°F, the cloud bases are at 9 ÷ 4.4 = 2.05—or approximately 2,000 feet AGL. To convert this to "above mean sea level," you must add the field elevation of the reporting station.

Stratus or layered clouds indicate a stable air mass; they have little vertical development. Fog is defined as a stratus cloud at the surface. A stratus cloud deck may make the day dark and gloomy, but the air below should be smooth, making for a beautiful day for flying. Altostratus clouds are found in the mid-altitudes, and cirrostratus are very high, thin layers of ice crystals. Cloud names can be combinations: stratocumulus is a good example. Clouds with "nimbo" or "nimbus" in their names indicate the presence of

Cirro

Alto

Stratus

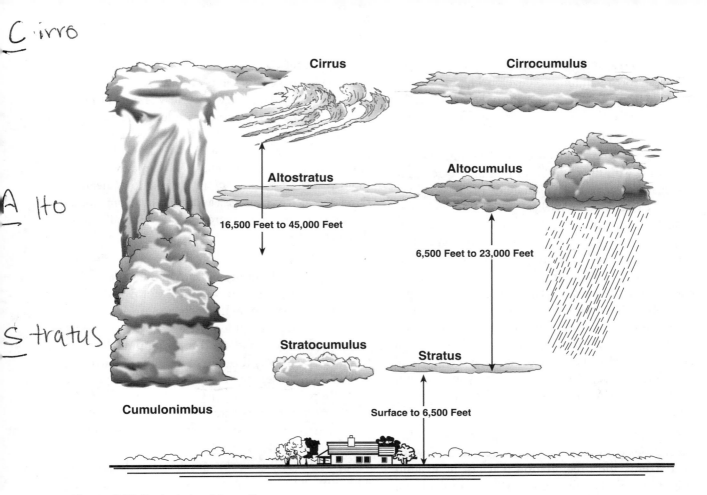

Cirrus

Cirrocumulus

Altostratus

Altocumulus

16,500 Feet to 45,000 Feet

6,500 Feet to 23,000 Feet

Stratocumulus

Stratus

Cumulonimbus

Surface to 6,500 Feet

Figure 6-10. Typical cloud formations

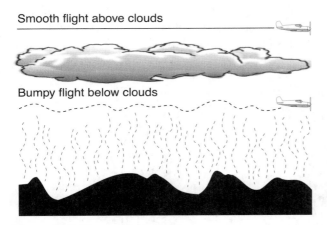

Smooth flight above clouds

Bumpy flight below clouds

Figure 6-11. Thermal turbulence

precipitation. "Virga" is the name for moisture that falls from a cloud but evaporates before reaching the surface. This phenomenon is common when the air near the ground is very dry (large temperature–dew point spreads), such as in desert areas. It is a visible indication of a downdraft and possible wind shear. Do not fly beneath or through virga.

THUNDERSTORMS

Thunderstorms deserve special treatment, and they even have a special cloud name: cumulonimbus, abbreviated as CB. When you hear pilots on the radio talking about "towering cues to the northwest" or "several CBs to the east," they are not talking about pool halls or CB radio but about clouds indicating dangerous weather. Three items must be present for thunderstorm development: sufficient water vapor, an unstable lapse rate, and a lifting force. With all three present, it takes very little to begin the process: the sun heating a parking lot or a plowed field, wind blowing up a mountain slope—these are typical of the things that can start a column of rising air.

Storms begun by the sun heating the surface are called air mass thunderstorms. They are usually localized, and you can fly around them. When warm, moist air moves up a mountain and a storm develops, it is called an orographic thunderstorm. A rapidly moving cold front forcing warm, unstable air to rise can result in the most hazardous of thunderstorms, the squall line thunderstorm. It is not unusual, especially in the Midwest, for squall lines to develop well in advance of a cold front. As you can see, the only variable is the force that starts the lifting process; after that, the storm grows on its own.

Figure 6-12 shows the life cycle of a thunderstorm, beginning with the cumulus or building stage as the warm, moist air rises. The instability of the air allows this process to feed on itself, as the air column—even though cooling with altitude—is warmer than the surrounding air. The moisture in the air condenses into water droplets, adding more heat to the rising air. The droplets do not fall out of the cloud initially but are carried to higher altitudes as they grow even larger through collision with other droplets in the turbulent air. These growing water droplets can even freeze into hail at the top of the cloud and be blown downwind to create a hazard well outside the cloud mass. Anytime thunderstorm activity encroaches on your location while flying sUAS, you should land the device and take cover.

A thunderstorm has reached maturity when the water droplets are big enough to overcome the upward air currents and precipitation reaches the ground (Figure 6-13). The falling rain creates downdrafts in opposition to the updrafts that began the whole process. This updraft/downdraft combination within a short distance makes penetrating a thunderstorm hazardous to sUAS operations, not to mention the potential for lightning, tornados, and hail—which can clearly ruin the day for remote pilots and those with them. The downdrafts soon overpower the updrafts, and the storm cell dissipates into heavy rain. The process just described is continuous as long as the conditions of warm, moist air, instability, and lifting force are present and as far as the pilot is concerned, the birth and death of individual cells are not apparent. The rapid vertical movement of air up and down nearby develops electrical charges, and lightning from cloud to cloud or from cloud to ground is a part of all thunderstorm activity.

The external appearance of cumulus clouds should never be used as an indicator of what might be found inside. As a remote pilot, you must not fly into any cloud, but a knowledge of thunderstorms may save you from encountering hail in clear air downwind from a cumulonimbus cloud or from being punished by turbulence as you fly through conflicting air currents beneath one. Severe turbulence should be expected up to 20 miles from a severe thunderstorm, and up to 10 miles from lesser storms. Remote pilots may also experience gusty winds and turbulence near the surface many miles around the actual location of a thunderstorm cell as the downdrafts strike the ground and move outward (Figure 6-13).

Weather associated with thunderstorms is more severe on the side toward which the storm is moving; you will see a dark column extending to the ground with occasional shafts of lightning. Surface winds will be gusting. Approached from the back, a thunderstorm

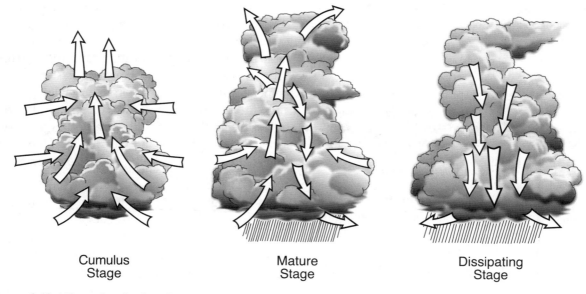

Cumulus
Stage

Mature
Stage

Dissipating
Stage

Figure 6-12. Life cycle of a thunderstorm

can be misleading—you do not realize what you have flown into until it is almost too late. You may see some scuddy clouds at middle altitudes, then low clouds as you get closer. In other words, if you see lowering clouds and decreasing visibility, don't go any farther.

"Microbursts" have recently been identified as small shafts of descending air associated with thunderstorms. Because of their small diameter, microbursts are not easily detected by weather instruments, making it even more important that pilots stay away from areas where thunderstorms are occuring or forecast.

WIND SHEAR

Wind shear is defined as a change in direction or speed of air movement, either horizontal or vertical, that takes place within a short distance. It can occur at any level in the atmosphere. It can be the result of mechanical forces such as turbulence around buildings or trees adjacent to your flying site, or it may be encountered when flying into the wind on the lee (downwind) side of a mountain ridge as well as near other types of terrain such as cliffs, hills, etc. (Figures 6-14 and 6-15). Caution is also advised when flying near solid objects such as towers, buildings, bridges, trees, and other structures, as turbulent airflow may be created downwind of these objects. In particular, an urban environment can generate winds that very rapidly and unexpectedly change when flying around and between buildings. Wind shear is most frequently related to a weather phenomenon such as a thunder-

storm. A rapid wind shift can wreak havoc on sUAS, and if a storm cell is within 15 miles, you should delay your mission to avoid such a shift.

The gust front associated with thunderstorm-generated downdrafts can create wind shear hazards 15 to 25 miles from the storm itself, and unless its presence is revealed by blowing dust, there will be no warning. Winds aloft blowing at 50 knots or more can create severe turbulence downwind from mountain ranges (Figure 6-16).

If there is sufficient moisture in the air for cloud formation, a lens-shaped cloud will form and remain stationary about the ground. This "standing lenticular"

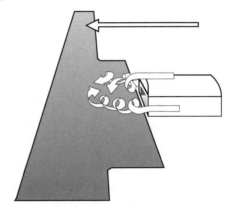

Figure 6-14. Turbulence near buildings

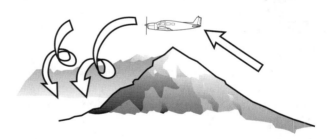

Figure 6-15. Turbulence near terrain

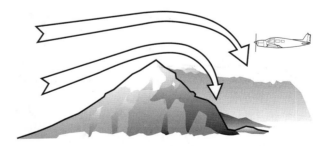

Figure 6-16. Turbulence flying into wind near terrain

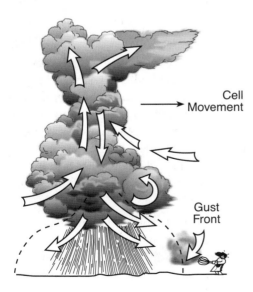

Cell Movement

Gust Front

Figure 6-13. Mature stage of a steady-state thunderstorm cell

(called an "altocumulus standing lenticular" or ACSL) is a signpost warning of turbulence (Figure 6-17). Note the rotor cloud; destructive turbulence can be present in and beneath rotor clouds. In your flight planning, be sure to check into the possibility of thunderstorm activity and/or strong winds near or at your area of operation. If you will be flying in mountainous terrain, wind shear and turbulence are almost always a possibility.

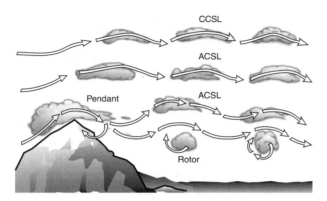

Figure 6-17. Standing lenticular wave pattern

FOG

Fog is probably the most deceptive hazard to safe flight that a remote pilot has to consider in flight planning. Fog can form or dissipate virtually instantaneously, and it can form under conditions that appear to be ideal for flight. Still, with your knowledge of the movement of air masses and the temperature/dew point relationship, you can guard against unpleasant surprises.

Radiation fog catches many pilots off guard. Calm winds and clear skies would seem to be the answers to a pilot's prayers, but when these conditions occur, and the temperature/dew point spread is small, radiation fog is a real possibility. The clear skies allow the land to radiate heat, cooling the air near the surface to the dew

Figure 6-18. Radiation (ground) fog

point and causing fog to form (Figure 6-18). Although this is often a night or early morning phenomenon (when most sUAS operations are not allowed) it is not uncommon for this type of fog to literally form at the blink of an eye just after sunrise. This is particularly the case in places like open fields (which radiate heat very efficiently) that are often the "airports" of remote pilots. The good news is that after a few hours of sunlight, the air temperature will rise above the dew point, "burning off" the fog.

When ground fog is predicted (or any time the temperature/dew point spread is less than 3°F), use extreme caution and be sure that your sUAS remains close by and in sight at all times. Even better, delay the flight until you are confident that fog will not form.

Advection fog results when moist air moves, and to anticipate it you must consider where the moist air is coming from and what it is moving toward. Typically, the moist air is moving from over water to over colder land; the moist air condenses into fog when cooled by the land (Figure 6-19). The process can be reversed when warm moist air from land moves over cold water.

Your key for planning purposes is knowing the wind direction, surface temperatures, and dew points, and whether the wind is coming from over land or water. What is the relative humidity at a reporting station upwind from you? Because advection fog is created by moving air, wind will not blow it away, and it will not burn off as readily as radiation fog; advection fog can be persistent and can form at any time. If the visibility makes it difficult for you to remain in VLOS with your sUAS, it is time to scrub the mission until the fog clears.

Upslope fog's name gives away its origin. As moist, stable air is moved toward higher terrain, it cools to its dew point and condenses as fog. While flying, you will see it first in valleys, filling them and obscuring as much of the high ground as the moisture content of the air allows and lasting as long as the upward force exists. Contrast this with the upward movement of moist, unstable air that can lead to thunderstorm formation.

While it is unlikely that most remote pilots will be flying when it is raining, what starts out as a simple rainy day flight can end up quite differently. When rain falls into cool, almost saturated air, the moisture it adds can result in what is called precipitation-induced fog, and can lower visibilities well below the minimums

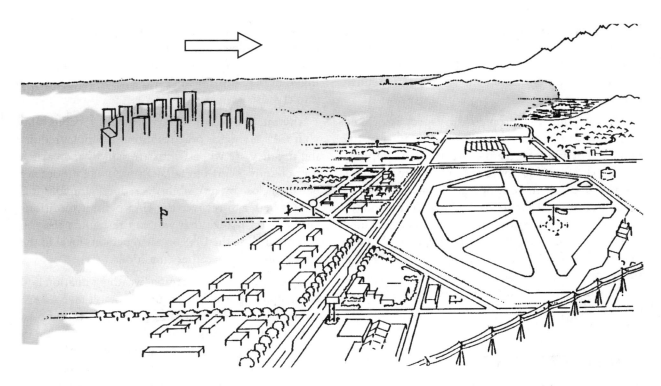

Figure 6-19. Advection fog

required for flight. Occluded fronts, warm fronts, slow-moving cold fronts and stationary fronts all have the ingredients necessary for the onset of precipitation-induced fog. When any of these conditions are forecast for your time of flight, you must consider the possibility of reduced visibility due to fog.

/ Condensation Nuclei

In industrial areas, or anywhere that pollutants might be found in the air, fog will form more readily and dissipate more slowly. When the water vapor has something to condense on, such as a pollutant particle, fog will be more persistent than when such nuclei are not present.

STRUCTURAL ICING AND FROST

Structural icing and frost adversely affect UAS performance. Whenever the air temperature is at or below freezing (32°F or 0°C) and visible moisture is present (rain, fog, etc.), icing is possible. Under such conditions, it is advisable to discontinue UAS operations.

When the surface temperature is below freezing, and the relative humidity is high, frost may form all over your UAS in a process called sublimation—the direct change from water vapor to solid form. Frost does not fall on your UAS; it forms on it. Frost does not weigh much, and it does not change the basic aerodynamic shape of the lifting surfaces; it does, however, create so much drag that it may be impossible to develop enough lift to support flight, either via a wing or propellers/rotors. UAS that do manage to get airborne with a coat of frost find that disruptions in lift (also known as a stall) may occur unexpectedly and/or they cannot climb.

Although most sUAS are stored indoors, if they are left outside or in an unheated area, there may be times when ice or frost accumulate on the vehicle. All ice and frost must be removed from the UAS before flight is attempted.

COLD WEATHER OPERATIONS

In addition to the hazards of icing, you must consider the effects of cold weather on UAS operations. It is best to store UAS, batteries, controllers, and other equipment related to operations indoors at room temperature. If the UAS and other components are subjected to extreme temperatures, they may not perform properly if used in such environments. Abnormal wear may occur if parts contract in cold or expand in heat. Battery performance may be reduced in cold temperatures. Always conform to the operating temperature restrictions published by the UAS manufacturer. If no such limits exist, use caution when operating at temperatures near or below freezing as well as very high temperatures. Lastly, if the UAS has been altered, upgraded, or customized, be sure to abide by battery, motor, and other component temperature limits, which may be different than published recommended temperature ranges.

In reality, the most problematic aspect associated with cold-weather operations is the comfort of the remote pilot and their team. Always be sure to properly prepare for cold flying days and be sure that your clothing does not impede operations in any way. For example, if it is extremely cold with a fair amount of wind, you will likely want to wear gloves. But how might this impact your ability to manipulate the controller as well as other types of equipment? How might snow-covered ground affect your ability to maintain VLOS with a white UAS? These are just some items to think about when operating in any situation, but particularly in cold weather.

LAKE EFFECT SNOW

If you plan to fly downwind of a large body of water during the winter (e.g., the Great Lakes), you should be aware of lake effect snow. Water temperature is warm compared to the overlying air, meaning that the air over the water surface picks up moisture. When the wind speed increases up to seven knots or more, it begins to pick up that moisture and carry it over the colder land downwind of the lake. This means snow and reduced visibility. The resulting clouds are layered; the tops basically depend on wind strength. Be alert to the possibility of lake effect snow.

USING YOUR WEATHER KNOWLEDGE

The greatest hazard you face as a remote pilot is if you lose contact with your UAS or become disoriented about its position due to reduced visibility or precipitation. Statistics show that a loss or a reduction in visibility is the most common factor in general aviation accidents—and the same can likely be said about UAS flying. Armed with the information in this lesson and a little common sense, you can avoid this hazard.

Obstructions to vision are related to moisture in the air. That moisture might take the form of a cloud, a rain shower, snow, or fog. Look at the big picture:

Is the wind coming from over a body of water toward rising terrain? (It does not have to be a lake or ocean. The rain-soaked ground can provide plenty of moisture.) Is a cooler air mass coming your way? Is the temperature-dew point spread decreasing? Will the air in your vicinity be cooled enough by the approach of nightfall that any moisture it contains will condense into clouds?

Anytime the weather becomes questionable, land your UAS as soon as practical. Some examples requiring urgency are when winds are rapidly increasing, rain or snow begins to fall, lightning or thunder are detected close by, or visibility is reducing rapidly. It is always better to recover the UAS before conditions get bad and realize that you can re-launch than to potentially lose the UAS or harm persons local to the operation due to weather conditions.

When looking at a marginal weather situation and contemplating whether or not to go and take a look, remember the old pilot's motto: It is better to be on the ground wishing you were flying than to be up in the air wishing you were on the ground. While many people think UAS are toys, you certainly don't want to risk losing your investment (which is sometimes significant) by flying in marginal conditions. Moreover, you put people and property at greater risk while flying in bad weather, as it may be harder to control the system, or you may totally lose control.

LEARNING MORE ABOUT WEATHER

The more you know about the physics of weather, the better off you will be as a remote pilot. The FAA's tried-and-true Advisory Circular 00-6A, *Aviation Weather*, is the source of all weather questions on the knowledge examinations, but there are dozens of other places for you to look and learn. FAA Advisory Circular 00-45, *Aviation Weather Services*, is your reference to all weather reports and weather charts. Be aware that you can go to www.faa.gov and read or download all of the government publications mentioned in this book. Excellent weather videos are available at www.aopa.org/asf/online_courses/. Go to www.asa2fly.com/reader/ppt to find a matrix of articles on various aspects of weather and weather forecasting.

Remote pilots should explore all potential sources of weather information. Because UAS operations will likely take place in locations with cell phone service, remote pilots should be able to access both FAA and third-party weather images and reports. There is a plethora of useful applications that provide aviation and general weather conditions and forecasts. It is advisable for remote pilots to always check current conditions and forecasts for the specific location at which they plan to operate and, when available, monitor local weather conditions as well as satellite and radar imagery.

/ Aviation Weather Sources

The regulations require that you obtain "all available information" regarding a proposed flight and that the information includes weather reports and forecasts. It is to your benefit if your briefing comes from a provider that maintains briefing records. That might prove valuable in the event of an incident. Many pilots get their weather briefings from an Automated Flight Service Station (1-800-WXBRIEF), which does keep records, but many self-brief using web tools and applications on tablets using services such as FltPlan.com and ForeFlight, which may not. Table 6-1 provides a list of helpful URLs. Note that the ADDS page, while an invaluable source for self-briefers, does not maintain a record of visits.

/ Weather Briefing Process

Self-brief first, to get the big picture before calling or logging onto the briefing site. Your first choice when looking for weather reports and forecasts should be the Aviation Digital Data Service (ADDS) web page (see Table 6-1). In the next few pages, I will walk you through the ADDS tabs and menus. The next best source is http://digital.weather.gov. It is loaded with information but in a different format than the ADDS page. In some cases, that ADDS page will refer you to this site.

To learn how to interpret the reports and forecasts, refer to FAA Advisory Circular 00-45, *Aviation Weather Services* (AWS). Ideally, you should have a copy of the AWS in your library, but it is available for reading and download at the FAA website (www.faa.gov). The advantage of the online publication over the book is that the online version includes changes and updates and is searchable. Still, it is the only place where you can find explanations for all of the online weather charts and graphics—and a list of abbreviations used in text products.

Because weather can significantly impact your ability to fly safely and efficiently, you want to get a weather briefing, and you want that briefing on record. The way to do this is to use a government-sponsored site such as DUATS or the Automated Flight Service Station system. Go to www.1800wxbrief.com and register. The Lockheed-Martin website www.1800wxbrief.com has a weather tab with a treasure trove of weather data. There is some duplication with the ADDS page, but there are also sites not covered by ADDS. You do not have to be registered to access the weather pages.

URL	NAME
aviationweather.gov/adds	Aviation Weather Center, Aviation Digital Data Service (ADDS) Page
http://digital.weather.gov	National Weather Service (NWS) Graphical Forecasts page
www.aviationweather.com	ASOS Information
www.accuweather.com	AccuWeather Website
www.weather.unisys.com	Unisys Weather
www.wunderground.com	Weather Underground
www.spc.noaa.gov	NOAA/NWS Storm Prediction Center
www.youtube.com/avwxworkshops	videos on weather subjects
www.weather.com/maps/severe/lightningstrikes	lightning = thunderstorm

Table 6-1. Weather URLs

Of course, if you want to talk to a human being, 1-800-WXBRIEF will do the trick. Three types of briefings are available: standard, abbreviated, and outlook. If you have not collected any weather information before calling the FSS, ask for the standard briefing—then you can be sure that nothing will be left out. Ask for an abbreviated briefing if you want to update an earlier standard briefing or add to information you have already received from other sources. In this situation, tell the briefer where you got the original information so that he or she can fill in any gaps. Request an outlook briefing when your proposed departure time will be more than six hours after the briefing, then back it up with a standard briefing closer to takeoff time.

/ Weather URLs

Members of the Aircraft Owners and Pilots Association have access to dozens of weather products at www.aopa.org. Internet users will find links to dozens of weather products, both textual and graphic, to be readily available (see Table 6-1). Search for "aviation weather" on the web and you will be overwhelmed. Place your faith in government sites, however; third parties can alter the data. Also, *Aviation Weather Services* (AC 00-45) includes several pages of weather URLs.

They tell us that one picture is worth a thousand words, so search the web for weather cams and road cams—in many areas you will be able to see the weather around your area of operation. Check the forecasts carefully, because what you see on your monitor will surely change.

OVERVIEW

Weather information can be divided into two categories: observations and forecasts. An observation is a snapshot of weather conditions at a stated time; its utility degrades over time. Some observations can be as much as an hour old when you first see them. Examples of observations are:

METARs (Aviation Routine Weather Reports): These answer the question "What's going on at the airport where I plan to operate?" or "What is the weather like at airports near me?" These will be discussed in detail in this lesson.

Satellite Images: Literally, snapshots of cloud cover.

Automated Weather Observations (AWOS/ASOS)

NEXRAD/Doppler Radar: Not to be taken at face value; can be misleading. I will explain later in this lesson.

THE AWC HOME PAGE

Figure 6-20 shows the Aviation Weather Center's home page. Right out of the box you have an overview of the weather. As you can see, you can choose which weather elements you want to be displayed.

Beneath the chart, "FltCat" gives you the colored dots indicating MVFR, IFR, and LIFR. Essentially, MVFR (marginal visual flight rules) means you probably need to pay extra attention to the weather. For remote PICs, MVFR means the weather will likely allow for sUAS flight but is poor enough to warrant extra caution. MVFR conditions are visibilities 3 to 5 statute miles and ceilings (cloud height of lowest broken or overcast layer) of 1,000 to 3,000 feet AGL. IFR (instrument flight rules) is when the weather is 1 to 3 statute miles visibility and ceilings of 500 to 1,000 feet AGL. Recall that when visibility is less than 3 statute miles, Part 107 operations are prohibited, unless you have a waiver. Also consider that because sUAS must fly 500 feet below clouds, a ceiling of 500 feet would essentially ground sUAS. Lastly, LIFR (low IFR) is when the weather is atrocious: less than 1 statute mile visibility and less than 500 feet AGL ceilings. As you go through the tabs and drop-down menus, look for INFO in the upper right corner of each chart; that is where you will find explanations, broadcast schedules, etc.

(The relevant AWC home page "tabs" are covered in the following individual sections.)

/ Forecasts—Prognostic (Prog) Charts

Under the Forecasts tab, "Prog Charts" appears in the drop-down menu (Figure 6-21). On this page, scroll down until you see side-by-side Low-Level SFC-240 charts; click to enlarge. The low-level (SFC-240) 12/24 hour prog chart is issued four times daily, at 0000, 0600, 1200, and 1800. Click on the INFO tab for more details. This is big-picture stuff, to be used in planning ahead.

Beneath the Prog Charts, you will find a Surface Analysis Chart. Once again, click to enlarge: On the resulting page, note the "Thumb" button. Click on it, and you will see thumbnail charts extending out to seven days (Figure 6-22). Precipitation intensity is indicated by shading. To interpret the shading on prog charts, the legend is shown in Figure 6-23.

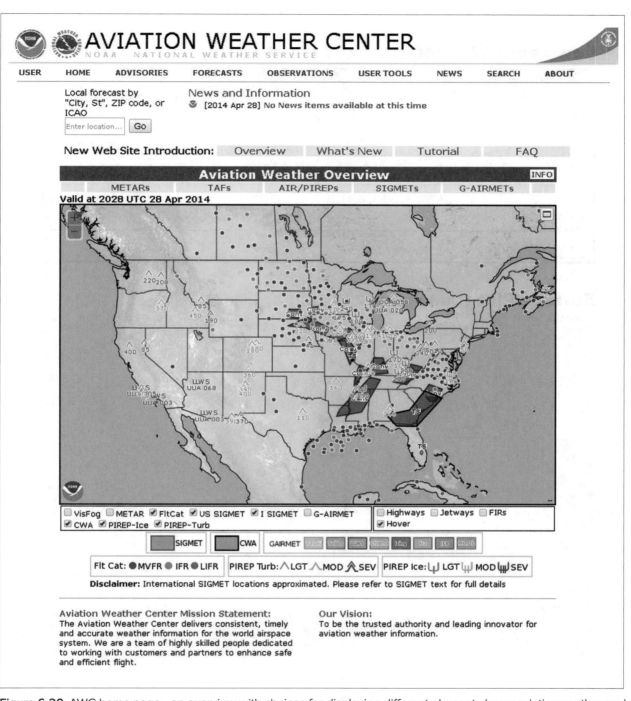

Figure 6-20. AWC home page—an overview with choices for displaying different elements (www.aviationweather.gov)

Low Level SFC-240 (Updated 12Z at 1604Z)   B&W

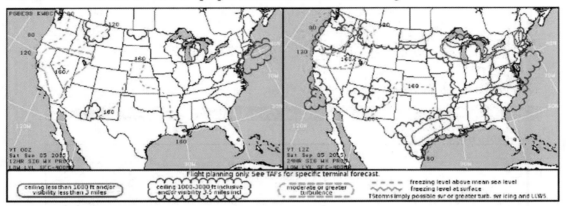

Surface Plot (Updated 16Z at 1626Z)

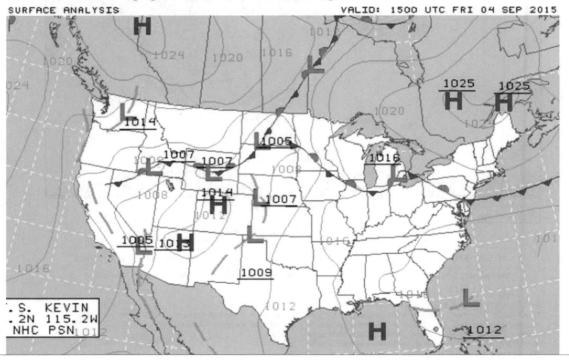

Figure 6-21. Low-level SFC-240 prog chart; surface analysis chart

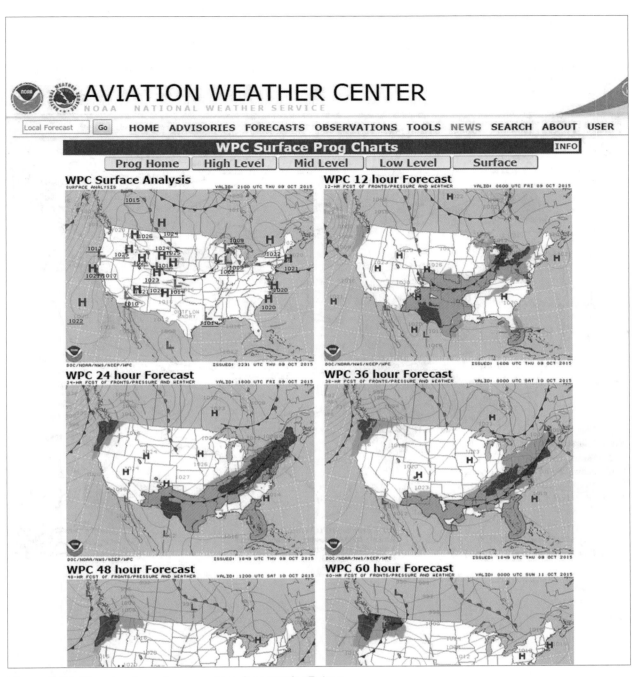

Figure 6-22. Thumbnail versions—surface forecast for 7 days

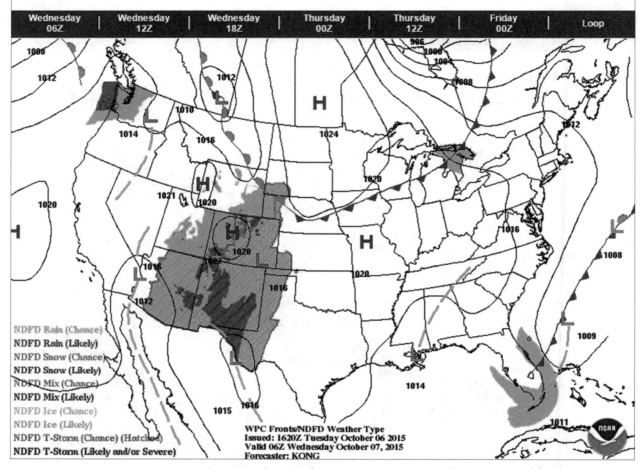

Short Range Forecasts (Days ½-2½)

The graphics on this page combine WPC forecasts of fronts, isobars and high/low pressure centers with the National Digital Forecast Database (NDFD) depiction of expected weather type.

Learn more about these NDFD graphics.

| Wednesday 06Z | Wednesday 12Z | Wednesday 18Z | Thursday 00Z | Thursday 12Z | Friday 00Z | Loop |

NDFD Rain (Chance)
NDFD Rain (Likely)
NDFD Snow (Chance)
NDFD Snow (Likely)
NDFD Mix (Chance)
NDFD Mix (Likely)
NDFD Ice (Chance)
NDFD Ice (Likely)
NDFD T-Storm (Chance) (Hatched)
NDFD T-Storm (Likely and/or Severe)

WPC Fronts/NDFD Weather Type
Issued: 1620Z Tuesday October 06 2015
Valid 06Z Wednesday October 07, 2015
Forecaster: KONG

Figure 6-23. Prog/surface chart legend

Prognostic charts help you determine if there may be weather that you will likely want to avoid. In your computer testing supplement, the prog chart's legend answers most knowledge test questions.

The National Digital Forecast Database or NDFD (http://digital.weather.gov) is a great tool to use while checking out the weather situation (Figure 6-24). It provides many choices of weather data overlays, and the time scale changes according to the product. For example, if you want to see a forecast of precipitation *probability*, the scale goes seven days out; if you look for the forecast *amount* of precipitation, the forecast goes out only three days. You have a slider with which to choose the time frame within those limits. It is a great tool—experiment with it. Click on the "Maximum Temperature" box on the main page and scroll through the drop-down list to see a partial list of what is available. To get aviation-specific details, you will want to visit www.aviationweather.gov.

/ TAFs and FAs

Terminal Area Forecasts, or "TAFs," is where you find pinpoint forecasts for specific airports: the forecast area is a five-mile circle around the primary airport. Many pilots mistakenly use the TAF as a source of weather information for a larger area around the airport—that is what the Area Forecast (also covered later on) provides. To view TAFs on the graphical page, simply click on the "TAF" button (you can also access this page via the "Forecasts" tab at the top of the webpage).

When you click on the TAF menu item, you will see Figure 6-25. You can add the number of stations displayed by going to "Data Density" and clicking on +1 or +2. Beneath the figure are boxes where you can enter the ID of a specific airport and get its TAF (if one is issued for that location). Check the Hover box in order to see specifics for each station as you "hover" the cursor over it. Many pilots are gun-shy about interpreting METARs, so check that box as well as "Decoded." If you check the "Tempo" box, you will see conditions that are forecast to be temporary when you hover your cursor over a station. Click on INFO in the upper right corner for details. Textual TAFs and METARs will be discussed later in this lesson.

When you select "GFA Tool" under the Tools tab, you will see the Graphical Forecasts for Aviation (GFA), which provide an overlay of reports, forecasts and observations into a graphical map. Click on the type of information you're interested in (TAF, ceilings/visibility, clouds, etc.) for the region in which you will be operating.

/ Observations Tab

The first menu item is Pilot Reports (PIREPs). In general, this will not be useful to remote pilots, as these reports typically refer to weather much higher than sUAS will operate. However, if there are reports of wind shear near the surface, it may provide some additional information to the remote pilot about whether or not to fly in a particular location.

Moving down the drop-down menu under Observations, the next item is METARs (Figure 6-26). In the screenshot, I left the data density at zero because the chart gets crowded when you select more reporting stations. I selected Hover for the usual reason and selected "Decoded" to make it easy on you. When we cover textual METARs, I will discuss decoding the reports as transmitted. METAR observations are taken hourly.

On the METARs page, beneath the map, you are given the opportunity to enter an airport designator and look back at METARs for that airport over the past several hours. This information is invaluable in determining if the weather is improving or going downhill.

The Ceiling and Visibility Analysis (Figure 6-27) is updated every five minutes; it is an automated observation. You can choose to display ceiling only or visibility only, but in my opinion, Flight Category (FltCat) is more meaningful for a quick-glance method of learning what is going on at stations around you. Click on INFO in the upper right for details.

Radar is another big-picture product (see Figure 6-28). Zoom in to examine your area of interest. Be sure to click on INFO for details. The Radar chart is important in flight planning because it shows the location of precipitation along with the type, intensity, and cell movement of precipitation. Note that radar does not show clouds, just precipitation. Remote pilots will typically want to avoid all types of precipitation, but the color coding of this map is meant to be intuitive in terms of determining what is light rain versus what is likely a dangerous storm. Green means lighter rain, yellow a bit heavier, and red is very heavy. In short, the hotter the colors, the worse the weather. For those flying in colder areas, it is important to note that dry snow does not always show up very well on radar, so use caution when forecasts are calling for snow.

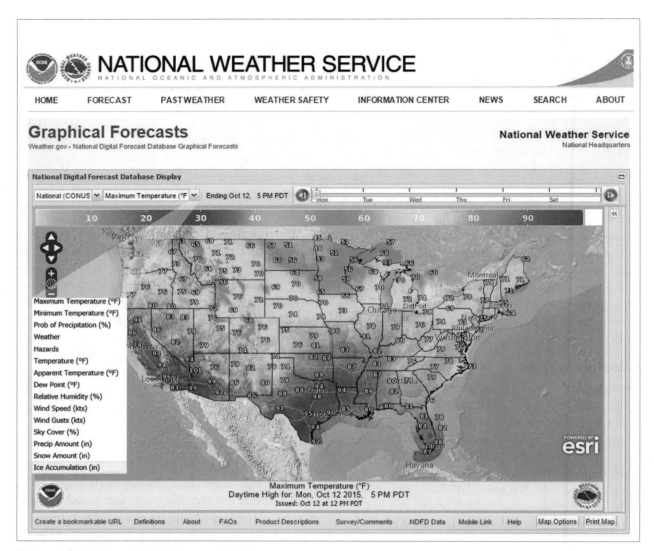

Figure 6-24. National Digital Forecast Database

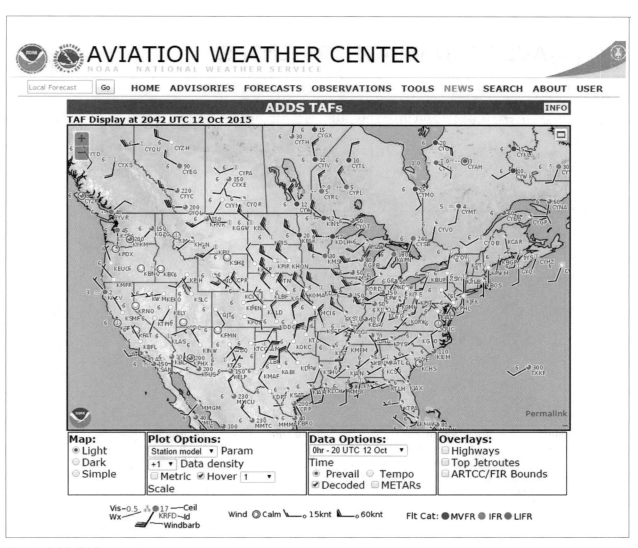

Figure 6-25. TAF example

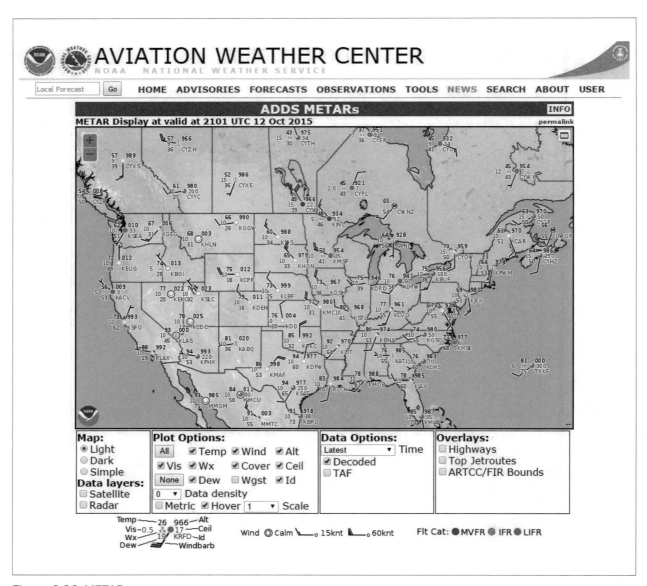

Figure 6-26. METAR

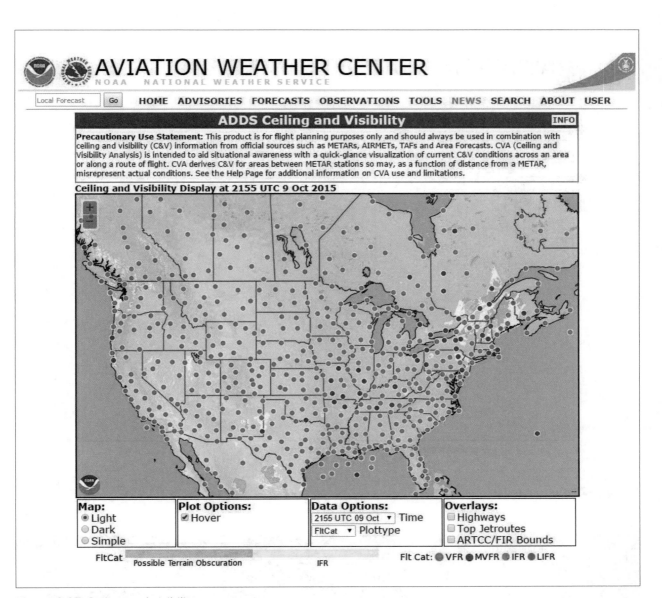

Figure 6-27. Ceiling and visibility

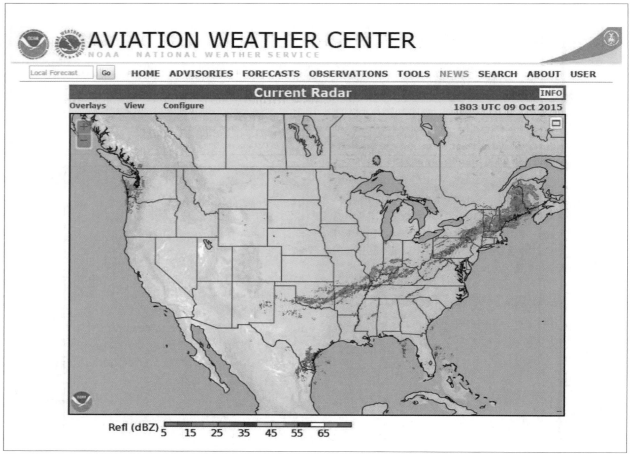

Figure 6-28. Current radar

Figure 6-29. ADDS satellite image

if you hear on radio = magnetic
if you read it, it's true

The "Satellite" view (Figure 6-29) offers a choice between visible, infrared, and water vapor observations; visible or infrared are what you are looking for. Click on "GOES Vis/Fog" and you will see not only cloud cover but the familiar-colored MVFR/IFR/LIFR symbols. Unfortunately, the satellite view does not tell you how high the clouds are or if there are layers. However, visible satellite images give hints at cloud type and height. Bright white colors mean high tops. You can often see the puffiness associated with cumulus clouds and can even see thunderstorms with their anvil clouds being blown downwind. On infrared imagery, the "hotter" the color, the higher the cloud is—giving you some indication of what's going on in a particular location. Dense clouds with high tops are often associated with poor weather.

BR = BRUME
haze/mist

TEXTUAL WEATHER PRODUCTS

The Knowledge Test contains quite a few textual weather questions, so be sure to spend some time learning how to read these versions of the various weather products. However, the National Weather Service and Aviation Weather Center are rapidly moving to graphics-only.

/ METAR (Text)

The Aviation Routine Weather Report (METAR) is the basis for all forecasts and warnings. Specialists at airports that report METARs make their observations at 55 minutes past the hour, but the coded time of the date-time-group uses the exact hour. As you saw in the discussion of Aviation Weather Center graphic presentations, some weather maps pop up a METAR when "Hover" is checked and you hover your cursor over a reporting station.

METAR KOKC 011955Z AUTO 22015G25KT 180V250 3/4SM R17L/2600FT +TSRA BR OVC10CB 18/16 A2992 RMK AO2 TSB25 TS ORD MOV E SLP132

This METAR from the Oklahoma City airport is for the first day of the month at 1955Z. It is an automated report (because it says "AUTO"); SPECI in this spot would mean a special report, issued between regular reports when a notable change in weather conditions has occurred.

The next group in the code is the Wind group: the observed wind is from 220 degrees about true north; if you asked the tower for a wind report on final, though, it would be given in degrees relative to magnetic north.

Observed wind velocity is 15 knots with gusts of 25 knots; the wind direction is variable between 180 and 250 degrees true. As a rule of thumb: If you hear a wind report over the radio, it will be magnetic; if you read it, it will be true.

The next group is Visibility: ¾ statute mile. Visibilities reported by automated stations will add an "M" to indicate "less than": M1/4SM means "less than one-quarter mile." The reported runway visible range (RVR) on Runway 17 Left is 2,600 feet; note that visibility from the cockpit (flight visibility) governs your actions unless ground visibility is reported at the airport. In this case, ground visibility is reported, and if it is less than 3 statute miles you cannot operate your sUAS.

+TSRA BR in the "Present Weather" group indicates thunderstorms and rain; the plus sign tells you that heavy rain along with the thunderstorm is occurring at the airport and that visibility is reduced due to mist. BR is one of those abbreviations that come to us from French by way of the International Civil Aviation Organization (ICAO) and stands for BRUME, meaning haze or mist. A key to decoding METARs is in Figure 6-30. If a weather phenomenon such as a thunderstorm is observed between 5 and 10 statute miles from the observer, the letters VC will indicate in the Vicinity.

The Sky Condition group is a description of the appearance of the sky. Cloud heights are reported in hundreds of feet: At KOKC the sky is overcast at 1,000 feet above ground level. OVC means that the entire sky is covered with clouds; BKN means that 5/8 to 7/8 of the sky is covered with clouds, and SCT means scattered clouds cover 3/8 to 4/8 of the sky. FEW would indicate 1/8 to 2/8 sky coverage. CLR is used by automated stations (clear below 12,000 feet), while SKC (sky clear) is used by human observers. Vertical Visibility, coded as VV, is how far a ceilometer can penetrate into clouds at ground level; human observers give it their best guess. No rational pilot, instrument-rated or not, will descend into an airport where VV is reported unless electronic guidance is available.

The Temperature/Dew point group is important in flight planning. These numbers are reported in degrees Celsius, and the closer they are together, the greater the possibility of obstructions to visibility. At KOKC the group is 18/16, only two degrees apart; remember that "BR" in the Present Weather group? Dead giveaway.

the closer temp + dewpoint = more likely to have obstructions

Key to Aerodrome Forecast (TAF) and Aviation Routine Weather Report (METAR) *Front*

TAF KPIT 091730Z 0918/1024 15005KT 5SM HZ FEW020 WS010/31022KT
FM091930 30015G25KT 3SM SHRA OVC015
TEMPO 0920/0922 1/2SM +TSRA OVC008CB
FM100100 27008KT 5SM SHRA BKN020 OVC040
PROB30 1004/1007 1SM -RA BR
FM101015 18005KT 6SM -SHRA OVC020
BECMG 1013/1015 P6SM NSW SKC

Note: Users are cautioned to confirm *DATE* and *TIME* of the TAF. For example FM100000 is 0000Z on the **10th**. Do not confuse with *1000Z!*

METAR KPIT 091955Z COR 22015G25KT 3/4SM R28L/2600FT TSRA OVC010CB 18/16 A2992 RMK SLP045 T01820159

Forecast	Report	Explanation
TAF	METAR	Message type: TAF: routine or TAF AMD: amended forecast; METAR: hourly; SPECI: special or TESTM: noncommissioned ASOS report
KPIT	KPIT	ICAO location indicator
091730Z	091955Z	Issuance time: ALL times in UTC "Z", 2-digit date, 4-digit time
0918/1024		Valid period: Either 24 hours or 30 hours. The first two digits of EACH four-digit number indicate the date of the valid period, the final two digits indicate the time (valid from 18Z on the 9th to 24Z on the 10th).
	COR	In U.S. METAR: CORrected ob; or AUTOmated ob for automated report with no human intervention; omitted when observer logs on.
15005KT	22015G25KT	Wind: 3-digit true-north direction, nearest 10 degrees (or VaRiaBle); next 2–3 digits for speed and unit, KT (KMH or MPS); as needed, Gust and maximum speed; 00000KT for calm; for METAR, if direction varies 60 degrees or more, Variability appended, e.g., 180V260
5SM	3/4SM	Prevailing visibility: In U.S., Statute Miles and fractions; above 6 miles in TAF Plus6SM. (Or, 4-digit minimum visibility in meters and as required, lowest value with direction.)
	R28L/2600FT	Runway Visual Range: R; 2-digit runway designator Left, Center, or Right as needed; "/"; Minus or Plus in U.S., 4-digit value, FeeT in U.S. (usually meters elsewhere); 4-digit value Variability, 4-digit value (and tendency Down, Up, or No change)
HZ	TSRA	Significant present, forecast and recent weather: See table (Fig 7-1-22)
FEW020	OVC010CB	Cloud amount, height and type: SKy Clear 0/8, FEW >0/8-2/8, SCaTtered 3/8-4/8, BroKeN 5/8-7/8, OVerCast 8/8; 3-digit height in hundreds of feet; Towering CUmulus or CumulonimBus in METAR; in TAF, only CB. Vertical Visibility for obscured sky and height "VV004." More than 1 layer may be reported or forecast. In automated METAR reports only, CLeaR for "clear below 12,000 feet."
	18/16	Temperature: Degrees Celsius; first 2 digits, temperature "/" last 2 digits, dewpoint temperature; Minus for below zero, e.g., M06
	A2992	Altimeter setting: Indicator and 4 digits; in U.S., A: inches and hundredths; (Q: hectoPascals, e.g., Q1013)
WS010/31022KT		In U.S. TAF, nonconvective low-level ($\leq$2,000 feet) Wind Shear; 3-digit height (hundreds of feet); "/"; 3-digit wind direction and 2–3 digit wind speed above the indicated height, and unit, KT

Key to Aerodrome Forecast (TAF) and Aviation Routine Weather Report (METAR) *Back*

Forecast	Report	Explanation
	RMK SLP045 T01820159	In METAR, ReMarK indicator and remarks. For example: Sea-Level Pressure in hectoPascals and tenths, as shown: 1004.5 hPa; Temp/dewpoint in tenths °C, as shown: temp. 18.2°C, dewpoint 15.9°C
FM091930		FroM: Changes are expected at: 2-digit date, 2-digit hour, and 2-digit minute beginning time: indicates significant change. Each FM starts on a new line, indented 5 spaces
TEMPO 0920/0922		TEMPOrary: Changes expected for <1 hour and in total, < half of the period between the 2-digit date and 2-digit hour beginning, and 2-digit date and 2-digit hour ending time
PROB30 1004/1007		PROBability and 2-digit percent (30 or 40): Probable condition in the period between the 2-digit date and 2-digit hour beginning time, and the 2-digit date and 2-digit hour ending time
BECMG 1013/1015		BECoMinG: Change expected in the period between the 2-digit date and 2-digit hour beginning time, and the 2-digit date and 2-digit hour ending time

Table of Significant Present, Forecast and Recent Weather – Grouped in categories and used in the order listed below; or as needed in TAF, No Significant Weather

QUALIFIERS

Intensity or Proximity

"–" = Light   No sign = Moderate   "+" = Heavy

"VC" = Vicinity, but not at aerodrome. In the U.S. METAR, 5 to 10 SM from the point of observation. In the U.S. TAF, 5 to 10 SM from the center of the runway complex. Elsewhere, within 8000m.

Descriptor

| BC Patches | BL Blowing | DR Drifting | FZ Freezing |
| MI Shallow | PR Partial | SH Showers | TS Thunderstorm |

WEATHER PHENOMENA

Precipitation

DZ Drizzle	GR Hail	GS Small hail or snow pellets
IC Ice crystals	PL Ice pellets	RA Rain	SG Snow grains
SN Snow	UP Unknown precipitation in automated observations

Obscuration

| BR Mist (≥5/8SM) | DU Widespread dust | FG Fog (<5/8SM) | FU Smoke |
| HZ Haze | PY Spray | SA Sand | VA Volcanic ash |

Other

| DS Dust storm | FC Funnel cloud | +FC Tornado or waterspout |
| PO Well-developed dust or sand whirls | SQ Squall | SS Sandstorm |

- Explanations in parentheses "( )" indicate different worldwide practices.
- Ceiling is not specified; defined as the lowest broken or overcast layer, or the vertical visibility.
- NWS TAFs exclude BECMG groups and temperature forecasts, NWS TAFs do not use PROB in the first 9 hours of a TAF; NWS METARs exclude trend forecasts. U.S. Military TAFs include Turbulence and Icing groups.

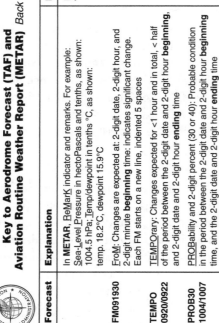

Figure 6-30. TAF/METAR key to codes in reports (from AIM)

The Altimeter group begins with A, of course, so the altimeter setting (what is set into aircraft altimeters) at KOKC is 2992. You might think "so what, we do not do that with our drone," which is true; however, knowing the current atmospheric pressure and its trend can tell you something about the weather. If the pressure is higher than 2992, then the weather will tend to be better (or getting better). If it is less than 2992, the opposite is true. If pressure is rising over time, this means better weather is likely to be heading your way. Watch out for rapidly falling pressure, as it indicates approaching poor weather.

All sorts of things show up in RMK (remarks). We learn that the METAR for KOKC came from an automated weather observing station (AUTO) with a precipitation discriminator that can tell the difference between liquid and freezing precipitation (AO2; AO1 would not have the discriminator), that the thunderstorms began at 25 minutes past the hour, are currently overhead, and are moving east. Sea Level Pressure (SLP) is 1032 millibars.

All of these abbreviations are great for passing knowledge tests; in real life, you would go to the ADDS METARs page, check Hover and Decoded, and the work would be done for you. Looking at past METARs for your local airports is an excellent way to tell if the weather at those stations is improving or getting worse. Is the temperature/dew point spread increasing or decreasing? Is the ceiling lowering? Is the wind increasing? If this is an out-and-back trip, which is likely the case with most sUAS operations, will the weather at the departure airport still be acceptable when you get back? (On the ADDS METAR page, there is a drop-down list under Data Options, Time.)

/ Textual FAs

You saw a textual Area Forecast (FA) on the Aviation Weather Center website under the Forecasts tab. The area forecast is your bridge to forecast weather between TAFs (remember that TAFs apply only to a five-mile circle around a primary airport and that only a few airports issue them). To interpret an area forecast, refer to the list of abbreviations in *Aviation Weather Services* (AC 00-45), which follows the key to reading METARs and TAFs fairly closely.

Area forecasts are issued three times daily and include four sections: a header giving the valid period for the synopsis and a second valid time for the clouds and weather section; a precautionary statement section; and two weather sections—synopsis and VFR CLOUDS/WX. The synopsis is a short description of the weather systems affecting a several-state area during the 18-hour valid period; it is the "big picture" that you should look to before getting down to specifics. A six-hour outlook categorical outlook (OTLK) follows the 12-hour specific clouds and weather forecast.

The VFR CLOUDS/WX section gives a general description of clouds and weather that cover more than 3,000 square miles and are significant to VFR flight operations. When reading an FA, all heights are above mean sea level unless prefaced by AGL or CIG (ceiling), and surface visibilities are given when forecast to be between 3 and 5 statute miles. When no visibility is given, the implication is that it is greater than 5 statute miles. Wind is mentioned in the forecast only when it is forecast to be sustained at 20 knots or greater.

Note: Area forecasts were discontinued in 2017. The NWS suggests that the same information (except for cloud tops) is available from Prog Charts, AIRMETs, and Significant Weather charts.

/ TAFs in Textual Form

Textual terminal area forecasts (Figure 6-31) are found by clicking the Forecasts tab on the AWC home page and selecting TAFs, just as you did when looking for graphic TAFs. Beneath the chart, there are two dialogue boxes: The first allows you to enter the identifier for the airport (or airports) you are interested in and returns a textual TAF; the second, "Show Impacts TAF board," lets you enter the identifiers for one or more airports and displays information in several forms. Play with it.

Looking at the TAF for MEM, note that the valid period is from 1800 on the 11th to 1800 on the 12th. Visibility is in statute miles and cloud heights are in hundreds of feet; the only cloud type included in a TAF is cumulonimbus—those that portend nasty weather. BECMG is a transitional phrase; at KOKC, "BECMG 2224… OVC020" means that the sky condition will become overcast at 2,000 feet between 2200 and 2400. If low-level wind shear (LLWS) was expected at MEM, that information would be appended at the end of the TAF.

TAF	
KMEM	121720Z 121818 20012KT 5SM HZ BKN030 PROB40 2022 1SM TSRA OVC008CB FM2200 33015G20KT P6SM BKN015 OVC025 PROB40 2202 3SM SHRA FM0200 35012KT OVC008 PROB40 0205 2SM-RASN BECMG 0608 02008KT BKN012 BECMG 1012 00000KT 3SM BR SKC TEMPO 1214 1/2SM FG FM1600 VRB06KT P6SM SKC=
KOKC	051130Z 051212 14008KT 5SM BR BKN030 TEMPO 1316 1 1/2SM BR FM1600 18010KT P6SM SKC BECMG 2224 20013G20KT 4SM SHRA OVC020 PROB40 0006 2SM TSRA OVC008CB BECMG 0608 21015KT P6SM SCT040=

Figure 6-31. Textual TAF (from computer testing supplement)

AUTOMATED WEATHER REPORTING STATIONS

Advances in sensor technology have made it possible for automated weather reporting stations to replace human observers in many locations. Some of these observations are incorporated in METARs, others are available by phone, and still others show up at the flight service station for use by the briefer. The Automated Weather Observing Station (AWOS), designed by the FAA, and the Automated Surface Observing Station (ASOS), designed by the NWS, are the most common. You'll find a blue circle with a reversed "A" in the frequency box when an automatic sensor is used.

A METAR from a sensor with no nearby human observer (unaugmented) will have "AUTO" following the date-time group. If the METAR from an automated site is fed to an observer for modification or augmentation, you will never know it because the METAR from that station won't give you a clue.

OTHER LESS FREQUENTLY USED RESOURCES

The following resources are available, but not as frequently used during preflight preparations or inflight operations.

/ Surface Analysis Chart

The NWS issues surface analysis charts eight times daily (every three hours). These charts reflect the observations of sky cover, visibility, surface wind direction and velocity, temperature, dew point, weather (obstructions to visibility), sea level pressure, and pressure trend. Using this information, meteorologists can locate high and low pressure systems, fronts, and pressure gradients, giving the user a big-picture view of the nation's weather at the time of the observations, as shown in the lower left corner of the chart (see Figure 6-32). Note how widely spaced the isobars (lines of constant barometric pressure) are over the southwestern states and consequently how light the surface winds are, compared to the more closely packed isobars between the low pressure area over Nebraska and the Great Lakes states.

By going to the ADDS page and typing "surface analysis + loop" into the search box, you will find a wide selection of surface charts that can be looped to show the movement of weather systems/fronts over a period of hours or days. You want to be alert to the movement of low-pressure areas, fronts, and anything else that would cause lifting.

/ Convective Forecast

You know that rising air means some degree of turbulence, increasing moisture content, and the possibility of thunderstorms. You can get a "big picture" of forecast convective activity by going to the ADDS page and clicking on Forecasts/Convection, Convective Outlook in the left column. Areas to the right of an arrow have convective potential (Figure 6-33). You can see that the Pacific Northwest and the states between the Great Lakes and the Gulf warrant further investigation.

PRACTICAL SOURCES FOR THE REMOTE PILOT

While the aviation weather products outlined above are informative and (mostly) accurate ways to learn about weather conditions, for practical purposes, you may want to use more intuitive and easy-to-access weather products. There is an almost endless list of weather applications for smartphones. There are hundreds if not thousands of weather websites. Moreover, just about every local community has weather reports and forecasts available from newspaper, television, and radio outlets. It is not hard to know what the weather is up to and how it is changing if you simply do a little snooping around. Everyone has their preferences, so pick a few "go-to" places to get your weather. Here are a few criteria to look for when selecting your handy weather sources:

- A reliable source—Places like the Weather Channel are obviously more trustworthy than "Uncle Bob's Best Guess about the Weather dot com."

- Up to date—Some websites update every minute (or even more often). Old weather = useless weather.

- Easy to use—The key is to find a source that allows you find what you need quickly and that is easy to understand. A good source will not bog you down with details you don't want or don't need.

- Mobile—You may very often be operating away from a computer and Internet access. You will want the capability to access weather, especially radar and maybe satellite data, in the field. If you are going somewhere with no cell service, be sure

to get all you need before getting out of range. (You could always use a pay phone or other "regular" phone—who knew those still existed?)

You should have access to local weather conditions, local weather forecasts, radar imagery, and an overview map of the weather (with fronts, lows, highs, etc.). Having satellite imagery and more sophisticated products would be helpful, but probably not essential. The nice thing about aviation-specific weather reports is that they mention wind, visibility, and cloud heights—all of which are helpful to sUAS operations. Non-aviation products tend to be more generic, which will work for you for the most part. Play around with a mix of reports, images, and other items to determine what is the best fit for you and your typical missions. Remember that you will want to monitor the weather while you are flying, because conditions can change fast.

Finally, remember that unless you are using a weather source that logs your access to it, like DUAT, the FAA will not have evidence of your weather-seeking activities. If something bad happens (i.e., an

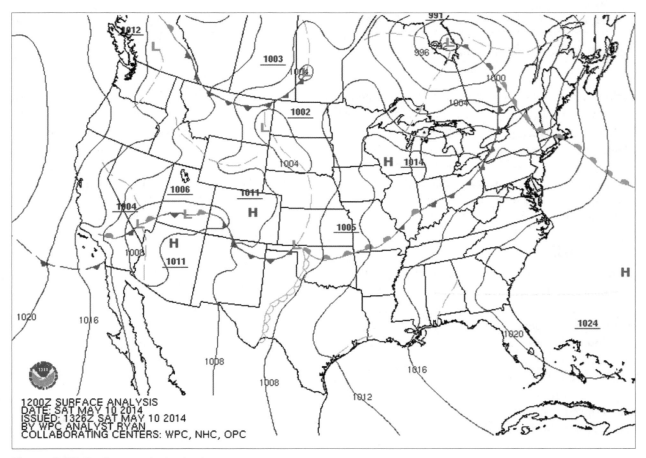

Figure 6-32. Surface analysis chart

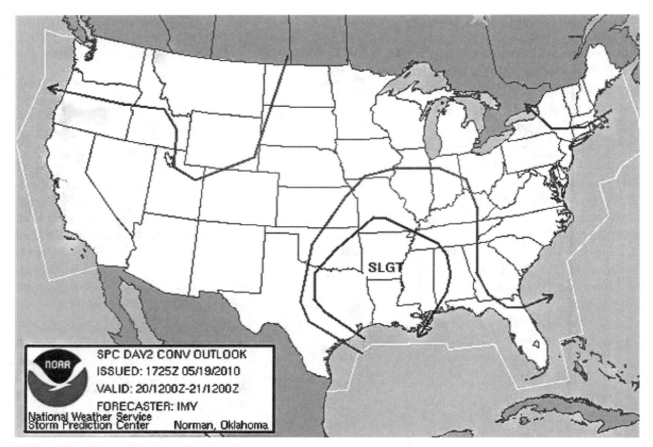

Figure 6-33. Convective outlook

accident), there may be some question into whether or not you checked the weather. You can always save or print some things out (or make sure your browser history is not erased), but all of this puts the burden on you and indirectly shows what you did. However, if you are doing your part and responsibly checking and monitoring the weather, you should have little to worry about.

SUMMARY

Mother Nature has many ways to make a pilot's life miserable. Remote pilots must be able to see, of course, so she comes up with obstructions to visibility in many forms. Understand that clouds and fog (which is a cloud, after all) will not form without moisture. Where does that moisture come from? Lakes, oceans, rain-soaked fields, snow-covered fields, plain old high humidity. Think about that. What makes that moisture into reduced visibility? Convection, being lifted by terrain, a frontal boundary? Reflect on that. Don't push

your luck, but fly safely. Thunderstorms are more of a threat to you than to your drone, so when storms approach, land and take cover. Pay attention to forecasts, observations, and your surroundings. Monitor radar and satellite images. If the sky looks like it is turning ugly or the winds start to increase, call it a day. By being a knowledgeable remote pilot and doing your homework, you can avoid unpleasant experiences at the hands of Mother Nature.

REVIEW QUESTIONS

Lesson 6 — Weather: General Weather Theory, Aviation Weather Sources, and Effects of Weather on sUAS Performance

1. Which of the following would not likely cause concerns about turbulence for remote pilots?

   A — Windy conditions near buildings

   B — A hot day in a parking lot area

   C — Overcast day with drizzle forecast later in the day

2. The primary hazard for a remote pilot when operating near thunderstorms is

   A — lightning.

   B — rain.

   C — wind shear.

3. Clouds, fog, or dew will always form when

   A — water vapor condenses.

   B — water vapor is present.

   C — relative humidity reaches 100 percent.

4. Steady precipitation preceding a front is an indication of

   A — stratiform clouds with moderate turbulence.

   B — cumuliform clouds with little or no turbulence.

   C — stratiform clouds with little or no turbulence.

5. How does frost affect the performance of sUAS lift-generating surfaces (wings and propellers)?

   A — Frost may disrupt airflow, thus preventing the aircraft from becoming airborne.

   B — Frost will change the camber of the wing, increasing lift during takeoff.

   C — Frost may cause the aircraft to be too heavy to lift off of the ground.

6. What types of fog depend upon wind in order to exist?

   A — Radiation fog and ice fog

   B — Steam fog and ground fog

   C — Advection fog and upslope fog

7. What conditions are necessary for the formation of thunderstorms?

   A — High humidity, lifting force, and unstable conditions

   B — High humidity, high temperature, and cumulus clouds

   C — Lifting force, moist air, and extensive cloud cover

8. What causes variations in weather between different geographical locations?

   A — Unequal heating of the Earth's surface

   B — Variation of terrain elevation

   C — Coriolis force

9. Refer to Figure 6-23. What type of front is shown extending from Michigan to Nebraska?

   A — Stationary

   B — Warm

   C — Cold

10. Every physical process of weather is accompanied by, or is the result of, a

   A — movement of air.

   B — pressure differential.

   C — heat exchange.

11. Ceiling is defined as the height above the Earth's surface of the

A — lowest reported obscuration and the highest layer of clouds reported as overcast.

B — lowest layer of clouds or obscuring phenomenon reported as broken or overcast.

C — lowest layer of clouds reported as scattered or broken.

12. From which primary source should information be obtained regarding expected weather at a specific airport at a particular time?

A — Low Level Prog Chart

B — Weather Depiction Chart

C — Terminal Aerodrome Forecast

13. In the standard atmosphere, the temperature at 5,000 feet above sea level should be

A — 15°C.

B — 10°C.

C — 5°C.

For review questions 14 through 18, refer to Figure Q6-1.

```
METAR KINK 121845Z 11012G18KT 15SM SKC 25/17 A3000
METAR KBOI 121854Z 13004KT 30SM SCT150 17/6 A3015
METAR KLAX 121852Z 25004KT 6SM BR SCT007 SCT250
16/15 A2991
SPECI KMDW 121856Z 32005KT 1 1/2SM RA OVC007 17/16
A2980 RMK RAB35
SPECI KJFK 121853Z 18004KT 1/2SM FG R04/2200
OVC005 20/18 A3006
```

Figure Q6-1. METAR

14. Which of the reporting stations have weather legal for sUAS operations under 14 CFR Part 107?

A — All

B — KINK, KBOI, and KJFK

C — KINK, KBOI, and KLAX

15. What is the maximum altitude can you operate your sUAS at KLAX while avoiding clouds?

A — 400 feet AGL

B — 300 feet AGL

C — 200 feet AGL

16. What are the wind conditions at Wink, Texas (KINK)?

A — 110° magnetic at 12 knots, gusts to 18 knots

B — 110° true at 12 knots, gusts to 18 knots

C — 111° true at 2 knots, gusts to 18 knots

17. The remarks section for KMDW has RAB35 listed. This entry means

A — blowing mist has reduced the visibility to 1½ SM.

B — rain began at 1835Z.

C — the barometer has risen .35" Hg.

18. What are the current conditions depicted for Chicago Midway Airport (KMDW)?

A — Sky 700 feet overcast, visibility 1½ SM, moderate rain

B — Sky 7,000 feet overcast, visibility 1½ SM, heavy rain

C — Sky 700 feet overcast, visibility 11, occasionally 2 SM, with rain

For review questions 19 through 25, refer to Figure Q6-2.

```
TAF KMEM 121720Z 121818 20012KT 5SM HZ BKN030 PROB40
2022 1SM TSRA OVC008CB
    FM2200 33015G20KT P6SM BKN015 OVC025 PROB40 2202
    3SM SHRA
    FM0200 35012KT OVC008 PROB40 0205 2SM -RASN
    BECMG 0608 02008KT NSW BKN012 BECMG 1012 00000KT
    3SM BR SKC TEMPO 1214 1/2SM FG
    FM1600 VRB04KT P6SM NSW SKC=

KOKC 051130Z 051212 14008KT 5SM BR BKN030 TEMPO 1316
1 1/2SM BR
    FM1600 16010KT P6SM NSW SKC BECMG 2224 20013G20KT
    4SM SHRA OVC020 PROB40 0006 2SM TSRA OVC008CB
    BECMG 0608 21015KT P6SM NSW SCT040=
```

Figure Q6-2. TAF

19. What is the valid time for the TAF for KMEM?

    A — 1200Z to 1200Z

    B — 1200Z to 1800Z

    C — 1800Z to 1800Z

20. In the TAF for KMEM, what does "SHRA" stand for?

    A — Rain showers.

    B — A shift in wind direction is expected.

    C — A significant change in precipitation is possible.

21. Between 1000Z and 1200Z, the visibility at KMEM is forecast to be

    A — ½ statute mile.

    B — 3 statute miles.

    C — 6 statute miles.

22. What is the forecast wind for KMEM from 1600Z until the end of the forecast?

    A — No significant wind

    B — 020° at 8 knots

    C — Variable in direction at 4 knots

23. In the TAF from KOKC, the "FM (FROM) Group" is

    A — forecast for the hours from 1600Z to 2200Z with the wind from 160° at 10 knots.

    B — forecast for the hours from 1600Z to 2200Z with the wind from 160° at 10 knots, becoming 220° at 13 knots with gusts to 20 knots.

    C — forecast for the hours from 1600Z to 2200Z with the wind from 160° at 10 knots, becoming 210° at 15 knots.

24. In the TAF from KOKC, the clear sky becomes

    A — overcast at 2,000 feet during the forecast period between 2200Z and 2400Z.

    B — overcast at 200 feet with a 40% probability of becoming overcast at 600 feet during the forecast period between 2200Z and 2400Z.

    C — overcast at 200 feet with the probability of becoming overcast at 400 feet during the forecast period between 2200Z and 2400Z.

25. During the time period from 0600Z to 0800Z, what significant weather is forecast for KOKC?

    A — Wind, 210° at 15 knots.

    B — Visibility, possibly 6 statute miles with scattered clouds at 4,000 feet.

    C — No significant weather is forecast for this time period.

26. Refer to Figure 6-28. Which state is not being subjected to widespread rainfall?

    A — Louisiana

    B — Kentucky

    C — Maine

27. Refer to Figure 6-29. Which is not true regarding the current weather conditions in eastern Texas?

    A — Overcast skies

    B — Extensive cloud cover

    C — Scattered cumulus clouds

28. What is the significance of closely spaced isobars on a surface analysis chart?

    A — Precipitation is likely.

    B — Likelihood of strong winds.

    C — A cold front is approaching.

Performance

A VERY BRIEF INTRODUCTION TO AERODYNAMICS

Although remote pilots by no means need to be able to cite the lift equation or know the finer details about aerodynamics, some basic knowledge is not only required for certification, but it can also make you a safer, better operator. While the following discussion is simplified, a few key concepts are important in understanding the basics about how wings and propellers generate lift and thrust, respectively. One of these concepts is something that Sir Isaac Newton discovered: for every action there is an equal and opposite reaction. Another was uncovered when a gentleman named Daniel Bernoulli applied Newtonian physics to liquids. Since air and liquids act in a similar manner (at least at slow speeds), Bernoulli's work is often cited in descriptions of lift. Bernoulli discovered that when liquid (or air) speeds up, the pressure in that area lowers (this is a function of the concept of conservation of energy). Lastly, liquids (and air) will follow the shape of a surface, a concept known as the Coanda Effect, and will potentially change direction depending upon the shape of the surface or deflection thereof. The combination of these elements can essentially explain how aircraft fly. In the following section, we'll look at an example while learning some key terms.

So how does a wing actually create lift? (Note that propellers also generate lift in the same manner, resulting in airflow displacement that we call thrust.) Wings are typically shaped with a curved surface on the top and flatter surface on the bottom. As airflow approaches the wing, it begins to follow the shape of the upper and lower surfaces. Since the top surface is more curved, thus "invading" more space within the atmosphere, the airflow must accelerate due to the reduced capacity for volume flow. The classic flight instructor explanation is that two friends start out at the front of the wing and agree to meet at the aft end of the wing at the same time. They both start working their way backward when the friend traveling over the top of the wing realizes that he must go further because a curved surface is longer than a straight one. So he must walk faster to meet up with his buddy down the road. Now instead of friends, imagine them as air molecules. Get it? (Although this is not factually accurate, as the air molecules traveling over the top surface actually go faster than the bottom molecules, thus there is no heartwarming reunion at the trailing edge of the wing). As we know, Bernoulli found that if liquid (or air) flows faster, pressure is reduced. Thus the wing is drawn upwards—creating lift—as the pressure on the top of the wing is lower than on the bottom. During the acceleration process, the airflow continues to follow the wing surface. The curvature of the wing (called camber) alters the airflow downward from the wing. This causes Newton's equal and opposite reaction. In reality, all of this is happening simultaneously. While this is all interesting, it gets even better, because pilots can control lift a variety of different ways.

The angle between the airflow (referred to as relative wind) and a wing reference called the chord line (which stretches from the wing's leading edge to trailing edge) is referred to as the angle of attack (AOA), since the airflow is "attacking" the leading edge of the wing (see Figure 7-1). A change in the AOA directly modifies lift. As the AOA increases, lift increases through the acceleration of airflow, further accelerating molecules and directing them downwards with more force. One way to think of this in a simpler way is to imagine a rudder on a ship. Move it a little and not much water is deflected, thus the bow does not move much; but deflect it a lot and hang on—the bow will move in reaction to the changing water flow. Downwash is most noticeable as the thrust produced by propellers when standing underneath a multicopter or behind a fixed-wing sUAS. However, you can only push things so far; if you keep increasing the AOA, there is a point at which the airflow will no longer smoothly adhere to the upper surface of the wing. When this occurs, you have reached what is called the critical AOA, and the wing is "stalled." It's also possible to stall by not having enough airflow over the wing, or simply by not flying fast enough. While wings are designed to stall in a way to help maintain controllability of the aircraft, exceeding the critical AOA will lead to rapid performance degradation and make continued flight difficult or impossible. The only way to recover from this condition is to realign the chord line with the airflow—i.e., reduce the angle of attack.

Lift can also be augmented by increasing airflow or changing the shape of the wing. You can increase airflow by going faster, and the shape or size of the wing can be changed by moving hinged surfaces, typically on the wing's trailing edge. The most common type of movable surface for increasing lift are trailing edge flaps, which are used for landing and sometimes takeoff. Other types of movable surfaces, referred to as flight controls, strategically manipulate lift—in some cases increasing it, in others decreasing it, or even causing lift laterally (i.e., on a horizontal plane). Flight controls include rudders (for shifting the nose left and right, i.e., yaw), elevators (for moving the nose up and down, i.e., pitch), and ailerons (which cause one wing to go up and the other down, i.e., bank) (Figure 7-2).

Let's take a look at how all of this works for fixed-wing sUAS in application. You first must generate enough lift to get airborne. This requires acceleration on the ground (takeoff) or via some other means, such as being thrown or via a catapult. The more the sUAS weighs, the faster it needs to go in order to get flying (or you can change the size/shape of the wing). Also, the thinner the air (higher density altitude), the faster you will need to go in order for the same weight (number of molecules) to pass over the wing each second. Of course, to keep flying, you will need something to push/pull the sUAS along, most likely a propeller. More weight = more power required. Higher altitude = faster speed required. Coming into land, you will need to slow down to minimize the distance required to stop. As previously explained, the sUAS cannot go too slow or it will not be able to continue to fly (it will stall). This is why flaps can be useful, by changing the shape/size of the wing in order to slow down enough to land in smaller areas.

Rotor-wing sUAS work a bit differently in regards to how they are controlled, but lift is a central part of it all, as is equal and opposite reaction. Of course, the upward and downward motion of copter-type sUAS is a function of thrust changes, which you now know is a result of lift generation. Pitch is controlled by varying the thrust of the motors at the front and back of the vehicle while bank is controlled by manipulating the thrust of the motors on either side of the vehicle. Yaw is changed by influencing the propeller speeds so as to cause the requested rotation in the vehicle orientation.

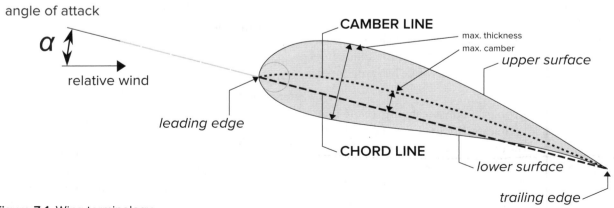

Figure 7-1. Wing terminology

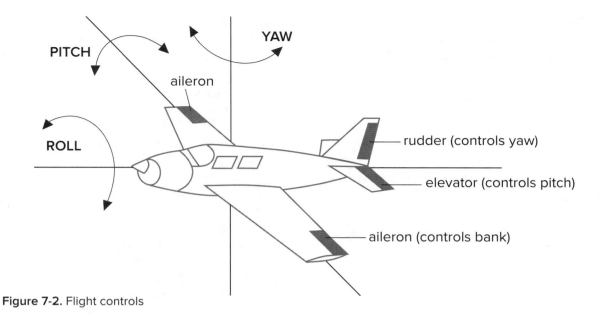

Figure 7-2. Flight controls

WEIGHT AND BALANCE

It would be nice to have an sUAS that could carry everything you need, such as batteries large enough to stay aloft for hours at a time, but that is seldom (if ever) possible. The manufacturer dictates a maximum gross weight figure based on several factors, including structural strength, power loading (weight per engine output), wing loading (weight per square foot of wing area), the strength of the wing/propeller structure, etc. *Overloading an sUAS can have serious consequences!*

If you overload an sUAS, the wing will have to be flown at a greater-than-normal angle of attack to develop enough lift to support the extra weight—and this increases the minimum speed at which the sUAS must fly to maintain enough airflow over the wing to remain aloft (i.e., stall speed). It also decreases the cruise speed and limits the angle you can bank before reaching the critical angle of attack (at which the plane loses airflow over the wing, i.e., reaches stall speed). For multicopters, the propellers and engines will have to work harder to keep the aircraft aloft, and the maximum capabilities of each or both may be exceeded. Moreover, wear and tear on both components will be greater, potentially reducing their longevity. Carrying more than the maximum design weight may seriously degrade the performance of the sUAS. It may not be able to climb as fast as is typical at normal weights, it will not be able to fly as high, and it will consume more power to stay aloft and maneuver, thus shortening its endurance. It may become slower to maneuver or even unstable.

Loads applied to the wing or propellers (multicopters) during maneuvering can overstress the structures. Figure 7-3 shows the relationship between bank angle and load factor while maintaining altitude. In a 60° bank, you will be doubling the load on the wing/propellers. So even though your sUAS may weigh 25 pounds, in this steep bank, the wing (or propellers) will have to generate enough lift to support 50 pounds of weight.

A one-time overload may not cause problems, but repeatedly overstressing components may cause them to fail many flight hours later while performing normal maneuvers.

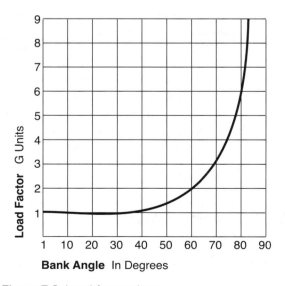

Figure 7-3. Load factor chart

An sUAS is maneuvered around three axes (pitch, bank, and yaw) that pass through the center of gravity (CG), which is the average location of the weight of the vehicle. All lift forces are concentrated at the center of pressure on the wing or propellers. The designer knows how the center of pressure will move as the angle of attack changes, and limits the allowable movement of the center of gravity so that a properly loaded airplane will always be controllable. CG location relates directly to longitudinal (pitch) and lateral (bank) stability.

If the CG is too far forward (too much weight in the front of the sUAS), it may be difficult to control the sUAS. In fixed-wing aircraft, this may result in the inability to pull out of a dive or to pitch-up during landing. In a multicopter, this may cause the sUAS to drift forward, requiring added control input and trim (and it may also exceed performance capabilities). If the CG is too far aft (too much weight in the rear of the sUAS), the opposite would be true: a fixed-wing may not be able to pitch down as easily or at all, while a multicopter may drift rearward or be unable to stop much motion. The extra control inputs and power required will reduce endurance.

Improper (or unbalanced) distribution of weight outside of the fuselage can also have undesirable effects. If weight is shifted away from the center of the sUAS body to the left or right, you will need extra control inputs to hold the wings level. Multicopters will drift left or right, depending on the location of the weight, which will require control and trim inputs (or may exceed the capability of the system). The extra control inputs and power required will reduce endurance.

Excessive weight, and weight far from the center of the aircraft, can have more than inconvenient effects. These conditions may cause loss of control or structural failures. An example of how this may occur unexpectedly is on some sUAS that do not have a fixed housing for the battery, but perhaps simply have it strapped to the bottom of the fuselage with Velcro. If installed improperly, the battery may slip or move in flight. This can lead to instability or loss of control.

WEIGHT AND BALANCE CALCULATIONS

In manned aircraft, weight and balance is serious business. Pilots calculate the center of gravity before each flight so that they can then reference performance charts to figure out how the aircraft will be able to achieve flight. Unfortunately, sUAS manufacturers provide little information about CG or weight and balance. While some sUAS have a marking to indicate the location of the CG, many leave the remote pilots-in-command (PICs) to rely on the fact that if the system is flown "out of the box" without modification, it is within weight and balance limits. For example, most multicopters have a CG at or near the middle of the vehicle, at the intersection of the "X" if lines were to be drawn from the motors to the center of the vehicle. However, users may want to modify their systems or even build the systems themselves. You can experiment to determine the CG. Hang the vehicle by a string (with tape, perhaps) in the location you estimate to be the CG. If it balances, you have found it; if not, move it to create a poised vehicle (i.e., it is not dipping from level). You also need to consider where the CG is in terms of height above or below the center of the fuselage. The higher the CG is on the fuselage, the less stable the vehicle (because the high CG location helps increase bank and pitch). The lower the CG is on the aircraft, the more stable it is (by helping to reduce bank and pitch). If the distance is excessive in either direction, it may cause instability or loss of control.

If your sUAS has items that are not in fixed locations, you should note their position and the CG when they are in such a position. For example, if the system has a battery that can be shifted forward or backward at the discretion of the remote PIC, you may want to mark the "ideal CG" position for the battery. Also, you will need to recalculate (i.e., re-experiment) anytime you change equipment, loading, or other aspects that may affect CG.

To get an idea how weight affects aircraft, consider the following equations:

$$weight \times arm = moment$$
and
$$CG = total\ moment \div total\ weight$$

Arm is the distance from the weight to the CG. Moment is the force that is applied to the vehicle as a result of the weight and its distance from the CG. So if your 2-pound battery moves 4 inches aft along the body of the sUAS, it will result in a moment of 8 pounds. Thus, a 2-pound battery affects the vehicle as though 8 pounds were at the rearward location, which would in turn need to be countered by control inputs. If the pitch capabilities are exceeded by this shift, the sUAS will become uncontrollable. By adding all of the weights and moments of the pieces of the sUAS, you could divide total moment by total weight to get the CG of the sUAS in that configuration. (The beginning CG would need to be provided by the manufacturer or determined via your experimentation.)

PERFORMANCE

sUAS are manufactured to fly all over the world, and remote pilots everywhere rely on consistent performance in accordance with the manufacturer's provided specifications. Would you expect a manufacturer to provide a different handbook to a Peruvian mountain remote pilot than is provided to a mining output surveyor in Death Valley?

Obviously, the operating conditions at different locations vary widely in altitude and temperature. It is not necessary (although it would be helpful) to have different data for each specific location, and the reason relates to the term International Standard Atmosphere (ISA). At manufacturing sites, engineering test flights launch in a variety of conditions, on calm and windy days, in summer and winter. All of the airspeeds, rates of climb, endurance, and takeoff and landing distances (if applicable) are determined by manufacturer testing and are most likely based on ideal conditions—i.e., a standard day at sea level.

By internationally accepted standards, a standard day has a barometric pressure of 29.92" Hg (inches of mercury) and a temperature of 15°C (59°F), and the standard atmospheric temperature lapse rate (decrease in temperature with increasing altitude) is assumed to be 2°C per 1,000 feet of altitude above sea level—the International Standard Atmosphere.

For manned aircraft, engineers take the information from the test flights, reduce it to its equivalent under standard conditions, and furnish the pilot with charts and graphs to predict airplane performance under widely varying pressure and temperature conditions. Without any details on performance provided by most sUAS manufacturers, remote PICs have to cautiously gain a working knowledge about how their system reacts, flies, and handles in a variety of conditions. Thankfully, we can learn a bit of what to expect based upon how manned aircraft performance is influenced by different conditions.

With the lack of information provided by sUAS manufacturers, it is often up to the remote PIC to figure out what performance metrics can be expected. Even if you are not interested in building or custom-izing your vehicles, if you ever need to replace parts, it is good to have an understanding of how much power and, in turn, thrust, is required to make things work. Unless you are a mathematician or an engineer, you probably don't want to do the calculations needed to determine these important factors. Thankfully, someone has done all of this work for us at this helpful website: www.ecalc.ch. With this tool, you can input the attributes of your sUAS and determine a wide range of performance measures such as thrust, thrust-to-weight ratio, endurance, operating temperatures, and more. You probably will want a minimum of a 2:1 thrust-to-weight ratio so as to provide enough performance under normal conditions with some extra for safety.

Let's look at an example situation. A typical sUAS quadcopter weighs somewhere around 3.5 pounds. With a minimum 2:1 thrust-to-weight ratio, this would mean you would want at least 7 pounds of thrust. That means each of the four motors has to support at least 1.75 pounds of thrust. If you are into tinkering, the different variables that can be tweaked on systems are numerous: different size motors, propellers, frames, etc. However, there are limitations, and some combinations of motors and frames work better than others. These subjects go beyond the scope of this book, but a good place to start is experimenting with various combinations in the aforementioned online calculator website.

DENSITY ALTITUDE

An important part of understanding performance is knowing how aircraft are influenced by changes in atmospheric conditions (i.e., weather). In particular, aircraft engines (especially gas ones), propellers, and wings are dependent on air molecules—the more, the better—to do their job. Engines use air to combine with fuel, which is then burned to provide the power needed for flight. (Obviously, this does not apply to electric motors, but they can be affected by reduced cooling efficiency due to "less" air). Propellers and wings rely on the forces generated through the interaction with the air molecules; therefore, if there are fewer molecules, less lift (from wings) and thrust (from propellers) is generated.

Several things can affect the number of molecules in a given volume of air, which essentially can reduce the capabilities of an sUAS as if it was operating at a higher altitude. This altitude at which the sUAS

humid air = less dense = worse performance

"thinks" or "feels" as though it is flying is referred to as density altitude. One such influence is altitude. There is a reason people wear oxygen masks when climbing Mount Everest. Air gets thinner with altitude—i.e., there are fewer air molecules. Another influence on density altitude is temperature: as the thermometer inches higher, density altitude increases. Other impacts on performance are atmospheric pressure and humidity. The simplest way to think about pressure is that just as it decreases as altitude increases, any lowering of the ambient pressure will negatively affect performance. Thus, as a low-pressure system moves into your area, the lower pressure will impact the performance of your sUAS. Humid air is less dense (a fact that relates to the weight of the air, since H_2O is lighter than other gases such as N_2 and O_2); thus, the more humid the day, the lower the performance of your sUAS. Humidity has a negligible impact, though, except in extreme conditions, so its effects may go unnoticed.

So let's look at the influence all of these factors have on an sUAS flight. The easiest way to calculate the current density altitude at your location is to use an app or website that provides a nifty calculator to handle all of the math for you. Alternatively, you can do it the old-fashioned way with formulas. With the math-by-hand method, start with your current elevation and make corrections based on the weather conditions. In a simple example, imagine you are getting ready to fly at sea level, elevation zero, to film some beautiful lighthouses in Maine. A nasty weather system is moving your way, so the local altimeter setting (i.e., sea level pressure) is 29.50" Hg, not to mention it is rather warm at 86°F/30°C. You can retrieve these values from nearby aviation weather reports (METARs) or your local weather report from the source of your choice. Recall that standard pressure is 29.92" Hg. So with lower-than-standard pressure, your sUAS would perform as though it was higher than sea level. But just how high? Consider the following equation for pressure altitude:

pressure altitude = (standard pressure – your current pressure setting) × 1,000 + field elevation

To help figure this out, we need to apply the rule of thumb that every inch of pressure is the equivalent of 1,000 feet in altitude. Pressure altitude is performance altitude being corrected for pressure. So using the values in our example:

pressure altitude = (29.92 – 29.50) × 1,000 + 0

Thus, pressure altitude works out to 420 feet.

Now we must correct for temperature, remembering that ISA for sea level is 15°C. To do this, we can use the following formula:

density altitude = pressure altitude + [120 × (current temperature – ISA temperature for your elevation)]

Temperatures must be in Celsius. (To adjust standard temperature [ISA] for your elevation, subtract 2°C from 15°C for each 1,000 increase in altitude from sea level). In this case:

density altitude = 420 + [120 × (30 – 15)]

density altitude = 2,220 feet

Adjusting for humidity is a bit more complex, but for simplicity, figuring the worst-case scenario (100% humidity), add the following to your density altitude calculation: at sea level, add 30%; at 3,000 feet, add 15%; at 5,000 feet, add 10%. Since we are right on the ocean, we could assume the 30% penalty, so 2,220 × 0.30 = 666, which we add back to our density altitude: 2,220 + 666 = 2,886 feet.

Thus, your sUAS would fly as if it were perched up at 2,886 feet above sea level. This would likely be noticed, as the system may be more sluggish, and may not react as fast or be able to climb or maneuver with as much agility. Some sUAS have such good performance that you may not notice a difference, but even the best of systems will suffer at high elevations, which is important to keep in mind if doing photo runs in the scenic mountains.

Go find a density altitude calculator online or an app for your smart device and play around with some scenarios. Watch out for high elevation, high temperature, low pressure, and high humidity situations. For example, tread carefully if up in the Rockies on a hot, muggy day with a low-pressure system sitting overhead.

TAKEOFF AND CLIMB PERFORMANCE

Takeoff performance is directly related to density altitude: the higher the altitude, the lower the performance. While takeoff capabilities will become quickly apparent in multicopters, in fixed-wing types, you may not find out how much takeoff performance has been degraded until it is too late. In high density altitude situations, the takeoff distance for fixed-wing sUAS will be increased, perhaps significantly. Moreover, as density altitude increases, recall that air becomes less dense; thus in order for the wing to create the same amount of lift, the aircraft must move faster so that the same number of air molecules pass over the wing as at sea-level conditions (it's all about the volume and density of air flowing over the wing). Therefore, at high density altitude, the system will be moving faster than you may be used to, especially if you typically operate near sea level.

You can determine the effects of density altitude on takeoff distance (fixed-wing) and climb performance (any type) using the Koch Chart (Figure 7-4). Simply connect the current temperature (°F) to the ambient pressure altitude. Where the line crosses the takeoff and climb scales is the value of penalty on normal performance in these phases of flight. In the example demonstrated in Figure 7-4, the temperature is 100°F, and the pressure altitude is 6,000 feet. This would add about 230% to your take-off distance and would reduce climb performance 75%. Those are big hits! If you are flying a fixed-wing sUAS, does it have enough room to take off and safely climb above local terrain and other obstacles? Extreme caution is required when operating in conditions different than the status quo. Even multicopter remote PICs need to use care in such situations. For example, a DJI Phantom advertises a 900 feet per minute maximum climb rate, but at high density altitude, this performance would be reduced to around 225 feet per minute. Maneuverability would also be reduced, potentially making you a test pilot of an sUAS that flies much differently than you are used to under ideal conditions.

Another consideration when planning takeoffs and climbs from the launch location is wind. If you are flying a fixed-wing sUAS, ideally you will want to take off and climb into the wind. This improves performance and keeps the ground speed of the vehicle to a minimum. For multicopters, the direction and speed of the wind should be considered to ensure that operations are conducted in the most favorable direction and positioning. Local terrain and obstacles should be deliberated, as they can affect the wind in ways that create unexpected challenges. Turbulent air can make controllability difficult and reduce performance. Destabilizing airflow can emanate adjacent to obstacles such as hills, buildings, or trees as well as over surfaces that may heat or cool more than the surrounding area. For example, unstable, rising air is common on sunny days above dark surfaces such as asphalt parking lots.

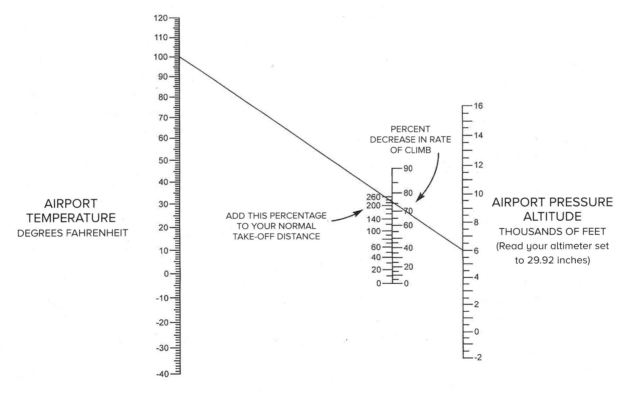

Figure 7-4. Koch Chart. (from *Density Altitude*, FAA–P–8740–2)

In short, setting up and getting ready to fly without careful thought into the influences of weather, locale, performance, and any miscellaneous factors is a mistake. Take the time to think things through. It will save having to learn the hard (and potentially expensive) way.

ENDURANCE

There is a whole slew of variables that are factors in the actual endurance of an sUAS, but we can make an estimate of endurance based on the battery capacity, accessories, and motor type(s) onboard. Probably the best place to run the numbers is at the "ecalc" website mentioned previously (www.ecalc.ch), though you can get a rough estimate by manual calculations. The formula is:

$$\left(\frac{battery\ capacity\ mAh \div 1000\ mA/Amp}{Current\ Draw\ A\ (Amps)} \right) \times 60\ min/hour$$

(mAh = milliampere hours)

Assuming a constant current draw of 20 A from a 3200 mAh LiPo battery, you will get:

$$\left(\frac{3200\ mAh \div 1000\ mA/Amp}{20\ A} \right) \times 60\ min/hour$$

$0.16 \times 60 = 9.6$ minutes flying time

Keep in mind, though, that you never want to run your batteries down to zero (minimum charge). Ideally you will want to leave about 20% capacity, otherwise you will greatly degrade the longevity of the battery and may increase the likelihood of damage and thus fires. Usually, "low battery" warnings provided by the sUAS manufacturer will provide enough capacity to return to base and still have enough juice to avoid messing up the battery, but it's recommended that you review the manufacturer's instructions for your specific sUAS.

Factors that will affect performance are weather conditions, weight, and balance. Anything that requires more maneuvering or control inputs will reduce performance. Thus, windy conditions will reduce endurance in general. Also, if an sUAS is slowed down by the wind, it will not travel as far in a given period, and thus will use up more fuel/battery to complete a mis-

sion. Greater weight will require more power to remain aloft and will also slow down the vehicle. If balance is off, it will require more control inputs, which will eat into the endurance. By planning ahead for such factors, you can avoid surprises such as running out of juice before completing your flight, or worse, not getting the vehicle back from a precarious position (such as over a canyon or out over the ocean). Some systems do much of this calculating for you. Fancy displays showing how many minutes you have left to fly (even factoring in how much flying is required to get back to your location) are becoming increasingly common. Regardless of the available technology, use common sense and do some mental math to ensure that what is being displayed makes sense.

LANDING DISTANCE

For fixed-wing sUAS, you will need a clear and open spot in which to recover the aircraft. Obviously, this should have been identified before the flight. You will most likely not need much real estate, but it is best to have more than you need. Be sure to pick a location clear of obstacles and with predictable wind conditions, if possible. You will also want to land into the wind to ensure your ground speed is as slow as possible and so you will not need to make any corrections for potential crosswinds. Just as atmospheric differences can affect takeoff and other in-flight performance parameters, these factors also play a role in impacting landing distance. Higher density altitudes will lead to less ideal performance with higher speeds, which in turn increases the roll-out/sliding distance of the landing aircraft. Multicopters will have reduced performance, which may require, for example, more power input to arrest the descent of the vehicle, as well as less agile movements.

AERODYNAMIC EFFECTS

Remote pilots need to be aware of the various aerodynamic effects that influence flight. Some are unique to rotor-type sUAS, while others may affect all types of UAS aircraft. While remote PICs do not need to be aeronautical engineers or rocket scientists, the more you know about how your aircraft fly and the various aerodynamic factors that impact their operation, the more competent and safe you will be as an operator. Be sure to take the time to read all available literature on your sUAS, including the experiences of other users, as many manufacturers provide minimal documentation and guidance for their devices.

VORTEX RING STATE

Vortex ring state (VRS) (also known as settling with power) is the descriptor of an unwanted aerodynamic effect that impacts rotorcraft (helicopters and multicopters). During normal flight, the primary airflow around the rotor blades/propellers is downward from above the aircraft through the blades and continuing downward below the aircraft. If you enter a vertical (or near vertical) moderate descent with power applied, you are at risk of VRS. The descent angles that are problematic are 45–90 degrees, while the rate of descent necessary to cause trouble varies, but is at least 300 feet per minute in manned rotorcraft. Note that vertical descent speeds lower than and much greater than this would result in a minimal risk for VRS.

When in VRS, the airflow around the rotors/propellers is no longer uniformly downward, but instead it forms rings of flow that includes some reverse (upward) airflow (Figure 7-5). This can lead to controllability issues, rapid descent, instability, or various combinations of these problems. Unfortunately, the profile for VRS is very similar to what is commonly encountered in everyday flight. As you conduct a near-vertical, slow descent down to land, you may inadvertently enter VRS. If you add power in an attempt to arrest the VRS-induced rapid descent, you can strengthen the vortices, increasing the descent rate further. If VRS occurs at a low enough altitude, the sUAS can literally fall out of the sky, potentially resulting in damage to the aircraft or property or injury to people around the landing zone.

To avoid VRS, use a combination of forward speed and descent when approaching to land. If you enter VRS, your two recovery options are initiating a faster forward speed or increasing the rate of descent (reducing power). Clearly, the choice in recovery should be influenced by the altitude of the aircraft and the people, property, obstacles, and hazards in the area.

GROUND EFFECT

When the wing or multicopter gets close to the ground (less than one-half the wingspan above the ground), drag is reduced by the interaction between the ground, the vortices, and downwash. This reduction in drag is called ground effect (Figure 7-6). When fixed-wing aircraft enter ground effect upon landing, they tend to be cushioned or to float. Rotorcraft may also appear to be cushioned or buoyed as they approach the ground

Figure 7-5. Vortex ring state

during landing. Ground effect can allow aircraft of any kind to lift off the ground prior to the speed/power necessary to sustain flight outside of ground effect (i.e., ground effect allows the aircraft to take off prematurely). If this occurs, once the aircraft exits ground effect, it may encounter controllability issues or stall, which can end up being detrimental since the aircraft is in such close proximity to the ground.

TRIM

To make flying easier, ground control stations commonly have trim capabilities, which are fine controls for pitch and bank (and sometimes yaw or throttle). These can be helpful to maintain desired flight conditions, especially when flying aircraft without GPS or sophisticated stabilization. It can also assist in cases of crosswinds or CG/balance issues. For example, what if you have installed a new camera on your multicopter, but while flying, the neutral position of the pitch (forward/backward) stick does not result in steady-state hovering? Instead, the sUAS inches forward. By adjusting the trim aft (backward), you can compensate for this unwanted forward drift. Simply click the pitch trim tab backward one input at a time until the aircraft returns to a steady hover. Or in another example, you may notice when flying your fixed-wing sUAS that the aircraft keeps wanting to bank to the right. To fix this, hit the bank trim tab to the left until the banking stops. Trim is a great tool allowing you to be more hands-off the controls without the aircraft immediately heading in an unwanted direction with a moment of inattention.

Airplane Out of Ground Effect

Upwash

Downwash

Tip Vortex

Airplane In Ground Effect

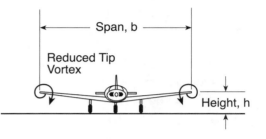

Reduced
Upwash

Reduced
Downwash

Span, b

Reduced Tip
Vortex

Height, h

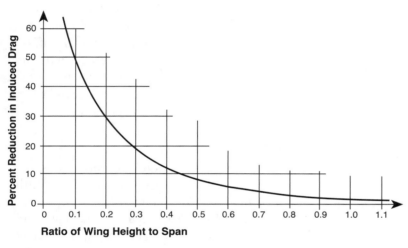

Figure 7-6. Ground effect

REVIEW QUESTIONS

Lesson 7 — Performance

1. Which is the best means of recovering from an aerodynamic stall?

   A — Reduce the aircraft pitch.

   B — Increase aircraft speed.

   C — Reduce the angle of attack.

2. Which combination of atmospheric conditions will reduce aircraft takeoff and climb performance?

   A — Low temperature, low relative humidity, and low density altitude

   B — High temperature, low relative humidity, and low density altitude

   C — High temperature, high relative humidity, and high density altitude

3. Your sUAS weighed 20 pounds prior to launch. While flying, you put your aircraft into a 30-degree bank. How much lift must be generated to support the vehicle while turning?

   A — 20 pounds

   B — 28 pounds

   C — 35 pounds

4. What effect does higher density altitude have on propeller efficiency?

   A — Increased efficiency due to less friction on the propeller blades.

   B — Reduced efficiency because the propeller exerts less force than at lower density altitudes.

   C — Increased efficiency because the propeller exerts less force on the thinner air.

5. Which is not a byproduct of entering ground effect?

   A — Reduced drag

   B — Reduced lift

   C — Increased performance

6. Which of the following is true about the weight and loading of an sUAS?

   A — Weight limits are more important than balance limits.

   B — Balance limits are more important than weight limits.

   C — Both weight and balance limits are equally critical to safety of flight.

7. You are planning to operate at a site where the elevation is 7,500 feet. The speed at which your sUAS will travel along the ground will be _____ when compared to when flying at sea level.

   A — the same as

   B — lower than

   C — higher than

8. As altitude increases, the angle of attack at which a given sUAS stalls will

   A — decrease as the true airspeed decreases.

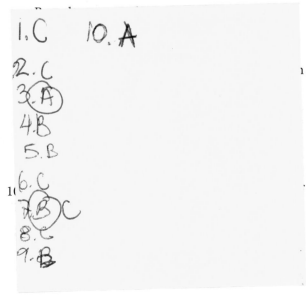

Emergency Procedures

CONTINGENCY PLANNING

The best way to deal with emergencies is to head them off before they even occur. A key component to avoiding the unexpected during a flight is proper mission planning. While what is deemed necessary to consider in such planning will vary greatly based upon the type of mission, following are examples of important things to contemplate:

- Flight path
- Emergency and contingency plans (e.g., potential landing areas)
- Software and hardware settings and setups
- Local terrain
- Nearby obstacles
- Visual line-of-sight requirements
- Micro-weather issues (such as wind speed increases between building in urban environments)
- Bystanders or other non-participants
- Animals
- Surrounding property
- Airspace
- Communication requirements and procedures
- Privacy concerns
- Property rights/trespass concerns
- Crew/operator experience
- Anything and everything else you can think of that is applicable to your operation

For each of these items, think about how you will conduct your mission so as to mitigate any impacts they may have on the safety or complexity of the mission. If other people in addition to yourself are participating, all of these items should be thoroughly discussed in your crew briefing. Make sure each person's duties are clearly delineated and procedures are known. For example, what does the visual observer do if he loses VLOS? What should the person operating the controls do if she spots a manned aircraft in the area? How does the remote PIC positively take control of the sUAS from the operator of the controls (in a way that avoids any possible confusion about "who's flying")? With these kinds of contingency plans, if anything goes wrong, it's likely there is a plan in place to deal with it and, if not, there is a chain of communications that is expected to occur that will ensure the situation is handled as it unfolds.

GROUND EMERGENCIES

If you're going to have an emergency, it's best to have it while your aircraft is still on the ground. Emergencies are no fun even on the ground, but generally they are easier to deal with there than in the air.

A serious concern when using high-capacity (i.e., LiPo) batteries is that they may catch on fire. As long as you take care of them properly and inspect them thoroughly prior to each use or charge, the fire risk should be very small. To prevent a fire, only discharge batteries to 20% of maximum charge during each cycle. However, if a fire happens, you should be prepared. Never leave a charging battery unattended. Avoid charging on or near flammable materials, in enclosed areas (such as cars), or in critical locations. Use a battery charging bag and ensure you're using it properly. All of these actions will minimize the danger if a battery ignites. Warning signs of an impending problem are bulges in the wrapping material surrounding the battery, smoke, or hissing sounds. Remove the battery from any power sources at the first indication of glitches. If it actually catches fire, the best thing is to try to prevent the thermal runaway from getting worse and spreading to other parts of the battery (all it takes is for one cell to ignite, which then heats the next one, and the next, and so on). Use whatever extinguishing capacity you have on hand, though it is likely the battery will have to burn itself out of "fuel" prior to being safely out. Even if the battery appears to be extinguished, use extreme caution, as it could reignite at any moment. Search the Internet for videos on LiPo battery fires and attempts to extinguish them—these events can be pretty scary. Always know who to call, such as the local fire department, if the situation gets out of hand.

What if the sUAS won't turn off? Spinning blades and body parts don't mix well. Usually, this situation occurs because of confusion by the onboard computer. Most sUAS have an emergency shutoff command or button on the ground controller. Alternatively, cycling through the start/stop sequence may help, or inputting some control commands may get the system to react properly. This is where system knowledge is paramount; a lot of headaches can be avoided if you actually know how to work all the features of the sUAS and are familiar with any and all of its quirks. Internet chat rooms and blogs are great sources to learn about some of the more common problems as well as solutions to issues you may encounter. In the worst case, try to access the "off" switch of the aircraft without hurting yourself, and shut the unit off manually. (With dangerous systems like those with large propeller blades, for example, it may be safer to allow the battery to drain to the point of system shutdown—it's better to lose a battery than a finger.)

Another ground emergency situation is if non-participants come into the launch or recovery area. It is shocking what some people have done when they feel as though they have been "harassed" by a drone. Again, search the Internet for a series of entertaining videos on the topic. With that said, you don't want anyone to get hurt, and sUAS can potentially be dangerous. If an unexpected guest (two- or four-legged) enters the scene, be sure to shut down the system immediately.

INFLIGHT EMERGENCIES

Prior to flying any sUAS, you should become intimately familiar with all of the aircraft's documentation. While some manufacturers provide ample details about their products, others do not. In such cases, it is wise to see what information is available online. A wide range of sources of helpful materials exist on sUAS discussion boards, including checklists and common problems or questions associated with specific sUAS models. Additionally, some preflight study is required to ensure you are well-versed on emergency procedures, because during an actual emergency is not the time to be wondering what to do next. While each sUAS is unique in terms of the potential emergencies that may be encountered, this section will discuss emergencies that are common in a variety of sUAS types as well as those that may have severe impact on the aircraft or persons and property. It is wise to develop emergency procedures or checklists for each sUAS you fly, if these resources are not available from the manufacturer (or other sources).

In manned aircraft, there's a saying used to describe what the priorities are when dealing with an emergency: aviate, navigate, communicate. The point is to keep flying the aircraft. The same can be applied to sUAS: Don't let a distraction lead you to letting the sUAS crash into something (especially a person!). The next priority is to maneuver the sUAS as needed to deal with the urgency or emergency. Lastly, you communicate—normally this means to ATC. For example, if you can't do what ATC has asked you to in Class D airspace because of a malfunction, communicate with them about it. To summarize: fly first, talk later.

One of the most concerning emergencies for remote pilots is the fly-away. A fly-away can be best described as an instance when the operator loses positive control of an sUAS. If you suspect that you have lost control, provide a control input; if the aircraft does not react, you're likely to have a serious problem. In extreme cases, fly-aways can involve an aircraft literally zooming off in an uncommanded direction with rather unfavorable results (for both the sUAS and anyone or anything in it way) (Figure 8-1). If you need examples of fly-aways, simply search for videos online using the key words "drone" and "fly away." There is little to nothing you can do in the event of a fly-away except perhaps to duck. Seriously, though, you will want to alert anyone in the immediate area that you have lost con-

Figure 8-1. This UAS crashed into the ground upside down following a fly-away. *(Bill Morrow; https://www.flickr.com/photos/billmorrow/14765710213; CC BY 2.0.)*

trol (yell "fly-away!"). It's recommended to include this procedure in your preflight crew briefing. Of course, attempts should be made to regain control, such as moving control sticks, and pressing emergency, land, or return to home buttons.

Another type of unpleasant emergency is engine failure. Until sUAS have been flown for a while, it is unclear as to exactly how long certain components are expected to last—but nothing lasts forever. Still, engine failures due to mechanical causes are rare; engine stoppages are often the result of running out of battery power (or fuel), which is an unforgivable and preventable sin. The individual at the controls of the sUAS and all crew should constantly be thinking of where to put down in case of an engine failure (or any other problem). Emergency landing spots should be away from people and property, preferably in an open area. When choosing possible landing sites, remember that the airplane itself is expendable, but people are not. If you can reduce momentum by shedding wings or other components against trees, bushes, or rocks, you will reduce the impact on bystanders.

Many emergency landings could have been avoided if the pilots had made precautionary landings when things started to unravel. There is nothing wrong with landing before the mission is complete or at a location other than the launch site. Never push your luck with battery (or fuel) levels; it's best to land with plenty of extra rather than find out you're a bit short. Don't let your ego write checks that your batteries can't cash.

For quadcopters, the loss of a single engine will most likely lead to loss of control. Multicopters with more than four engines will fare better (essentially the more engines, the better it will handle a single engine loss). Some larger multicopters are designed to be able to fly following an engine failure. Since most fixed-wing sUAS only have one engine, if it stops working, the aircraft becomes a glider. In this case, considering that you are not in the aircraft, figuring out how to maneuver the aircraft into a position to make a safe landing may be challenging. Thus, preflight planning is needed so that you will have a plan if this happens at various points during the mission, especially in critical areas (such as near people or property).

You can avoid user-induced engine failure most easily by always ensuring you have ample battery power (or fuel) to make it back to the recovery location or at least to a safe landing zone. With most new sUAS, there really is no excuse for running out of juice, as control stations provide a constant readout of battery. If yours doesn't, you need to pay close attention to warnings provided by the manufacturer (such as flashing lights on the fuselage). For sUAS using fuel, you will want to always know the amount of time the engine(s) have been running compared to how much time you can run the engines, based upon starting fuel quantity.

Structural failures can also turn a nice day of flying into a stressful event. Propellers can come apart if they are damaged or have some inherent weakness (such as damage encountered on a previous flight). Propeller blades can injure people proximate to the site of failure. Moreover, if a propeller fails, it is considered equivalent to an engine failure and must be handled accordingly.

If you properly inspect your battery prior to use and have cared for it properly (charging and discharging it within the manufacturer's guidelines), you should rarely if ever have to worry about a battery fire. If you notice hissing noises, smoke, or flames coming from any portion of the sUAS, land it immediately and shut down all engines. Unfortunately, there is not much you can do in the case of modern (LiPo) batteries, as the contents of the battery are the fuel and provide the heat source for continued ignition, which can quickly spread to other cells within the battery, igniting them as well. The best means of dealing with battery fires is to use whatever means you have to lower the temperature of the battery—e.g., water, a "typical" fire extinguisher, sand, etc. This may prevent the fire from spreading to other cells. Most likely, however, the fire will burn until the expendable contents of the battery are exhausted (Figure 8-2). Move all persons, property, and flammable items away from the area. If there is a risk that the fire will spread beyond the battery, call the local fire department for assistance.

Loss of datalink (lost link) can also be a major problem for some sUAS, although many systems have failsafes that engage automatic features—such as return to home following loss of link for more than a few seconds. This is why setting up the return home function is so important prior to launch. If you don't have the

Figure 8-2. LiPo battery fire

right parameters set, your sUAS may return home into trees or not have a lock on the "home" position. Efforts should be made to reestablish link, such as by moving ground station antennae, relocating into a clear signal line-of-sight (ensuring no buildings or other objects are close by or in between you and the aircraft), or moving closer to the sUAS. If you encounter two datalink losses on a flight, it is important to terminate the mission to investigate potential equipment problems.

Similar to loss of datalink, the failure of the ground control station (GCS) is another possible inflight emergency. The easiest way to avoid this is to ensure that the GCS is properly charged prior to operation. (I know this sounds obvious, but it has been overlooked by many unsuspecting pilots). If an actual hardware or software failure occurs, there is not much you can do unless you have a spare controller (and it is paired or pair-able to the sUAS). Otherwise, you will have to treat the event as a lost link scenario. Hopefully you have a system that will automatically return home or perform some other failsafe function. See Figure 8-3.

Not all sUAS use GPS, but more than likely you will be flying one that does at some point soon. Many sUAS use GPS for automatic flight capabilities and/or added stability. Losing GPS generally means that you will have to revert to "manual" flight, and typically this will result in a degraded mode that is a little more squirrely. Other than that, things should be all right for the majority of sUAS missions. However, as previously mentioned, if loss of GPS is then followed by loss of datalink, you may be in for some trouble. Any safety features, such as return to home, will not work (unless you're flying something pretty impressive with dead reckoning navigation onboard, which is unlikely).

Figure 8-3. Any lapse of attention or system failure could quickly turn into an emergency when flying sUAS, especially in confined spaces and around people or property.
(Lars Plougmann; www.flickr.com/photos/criminalintent/13931871659; CC BY-SA 2.0.)

If anything else unexpected happens—such as if you're on an automated flight plan and the autopilot software crashes or has a hiccup—it makes the most sense to manually take over and have the aircraft return to base so you can determine what went wrong. You really don't want to be experimenting with potentially problematic equipment; this is best done by conducting a test flight under controlled conditions where the effects of any failures can be managed. Perhaps your sUAS is not abiding by a geofence you set (this is a maximum altitude or distance that the onboard computer will let the aircraft fly from the ground controller). In this case, it is most likely because you set the geofence incorrectly—but it could be something else. Therefore, it is best to figure things out on the ground before troubleshooting more.

What if you are simply disoriented? If your sUAS gets a bit far out, it can be hard to tell which way it is flying or how it is oriented. This type of situation can get hairy quickly if you let it. If this occurs, the best

thing to do would be to make a small control input, such as left or right. You will then see if it is facing away from you (if you push left, it goes left) or facing towards you (if you push left, it moves right). You can then use the front/back control to bring it closer to reestablish orientation (or turn it towards you for a fixed-wing). You can also switch to "headless mode" if it is installed, which will always keep the vehicle moving per your control inputs regardless of which direction the sUAS is facing. This eliminates "having to think backwards" in terms of the flight controls when the aircraft to heading towards you. The key is not to panic. In most cases, if you simply let go for a little bit, things will calm down.

If you do have an emergency in Class B, C, D or special use airspace that requires authorization to enter, you will want to notify ATC as soon as practical. Remember that only FCC-licensed users can transmit on aviation frequencies. Regardless of the means of communication, don't expect a controller to understand your problem if you use highly technical terms such as "I lost my GCS." Most controllers are not likely to be remote pilots, so using language that would be crystal-clear only to another remote pilot may be useless. Instead, just say something like, "I am unable to control my drone."

Remember that the regulations allow the remote PIC to essentially do whatever is necessary in response to an emergency—even if it means disregarding other portions of the regulations. Of course, this does not provide an excuse to do whatever you want simply because you had a bad day flying, but if you need to do something outside of the rules to prevent harming people or property, you should not hesitate to do so. If you do bend any rules during an emergency situation, be prepared to write up a report for the FAA, if asked to do so.

There is an old wives' tale that a pilot who declares an emergency is inundated with a flood of paperwork when the emergency is over. This is not true. The controllers who handle the situation might ask for a phone call to get the details, but the purpose of the call will not be to issue a violation.

EMERGENCY COMMUNICATIONS

The international distress frequency for VHF is 121.5 MHz. It is highly recommended that you monitor (listen to) this frequency whenever possible. (Note: if you hear a weird siren sound on 121.5, this is likely an aircraft Emergency Locator Transmitter [ELT] emission. Unless it is within the first five minutes of the hour, when ELTs are allowed to be tested, this means a plane may have crashed nearby. Contact the closest FAA facility to report the situation.) In the case of a serious emergency for which you are not already in contact with ATC, you may want to arrange for assistance from other agencies, such as the local fire department. If you are already in contact with ATC, such as a control tower, simply communicate your emergency to them. The key word to use in emergencies is "mayday."

An "urgency" situation is supposed to be communicated by repeating the word PAN three times—but to my knowledge, nobody does this. You are in an urgency situation when you are concerned about the safety of your flight and need timely but not immediate assistance. Examples of an urgency situation include disorientation, low battery, deteriorating weather, etc.

OTHER "SURPRISES"

Each sUAS has its own unique personality in terms of odd manufacturer programming, required techniques, finesse necessary to maneuver, and so forth. Always be alert to the unexpected. Following are a few examples of things that may go awry.

You are all ready to go, but alas—your sUAS doesn't want to start. Before sticking your hands in harm's way of propellers, make sure you've done the required sequences to get the unit up and running. If necessary, go through your checklists again. Look for obvious issues first, then go on to the less common possible causes. I recall watching one remote pilot prepping to fly a demonstration flight, but he just couldn't seem to get the darned thing to start and fly. After about 30 minutes of embarrassing dilly-dallying, he determined that the sUAS would not allow the unit to fly because it was within the geofence parameters set up by the manufacturer due to the proximity to an airport. As previously mentioned, the more familiar you are with all aspects of your systems, the better off (and safer) you will be, avoiding heartache and unwanted surprises.

An sUAS may perform some unanticipated actions or movements without resulting in an actual fly-away or causing a major issue. If the unit appears to be doing something funky, it is best to troubleshoot on the ground. Consider tethering the system if you deem there is risk of a fly-away or other issue. Or alternatively, find a safe enclosure in which to do your testing. In short, you don't want to take an oddly acting sUAS on a mission without first diagnosing and solving the ailment.

Some of the unexpected situations associated with flying sUAS have nothing to do with you or the aircraft. People, wildlife, and property may all introduce themselves without warning. According to regulations, you must avoid overflying non-participants (unless you have a waiver). People are curious (or sometimes malicious) and may insert themselves below your aircraft or attempt to do things to it (e.g., grab it, break it). Calmly move the vehicle away from the person and out of harm's way, trying to secure a landing spot away from the disorder. Even if you have every right to fly your system in a location, respect people's concerns about privacy. You do not want to get into an argument with someone about the legality of your operation while the unit is flying. If there is a problem with persons in the area, it is best to abort the mission and seek help from local law enforcement, as necessary. If someone damages or destroys your sUAS in the process of their agitation, don't get sucked into doing something in retaliation. That's where you could end up in legal trouble yourself. Simply gather as much evidence as you can (you will likely have video; check to see if anyone in the area can be a witness) and call law enforcement to file a complaint.

Speaking of law enforcement, they themselves may be the cause of unsuspected strife. Again, it is best not to argue with officers of the law, particularly while your sUAS is still flying. Tell the officers you need to land the aircraft and then you can discuss the situation. Many police do not know or understand the laws controlling sUAS, but they also don't like to hear law lectures from citizens. It is all right to ask what law or other issue you are supposedly in noncompliance with. With that said, it is best to pick your fight another day by visiting their supervisor at a later point at the local headquarters or station.

REVIEW QUESTIONS

Lesson 8 — Emergency Procedures

1. The remote pilot-in-command is authorized to take any action necessary to deal with an emergency situation, including

   A — violating any regulation in 14 CFR Part 107.

   B — disregarding the safety of persons in the area.

   C — disregarding regulations that impede the response to the emergency.

2. When experiencing an emergency during a flight in Class D airspace, the remote pilot-in-command should immediately contact

   A — any station listening on 121.50.

   B — the control tower on the current frequency being used.

   C — the airport manager via the telephone.

3. Which action is recommended during a lithium polymer (LiPo) battery fire?

   A — Try to heat the battery to expedite the use of remaining fuel.

   B — Try to cool the battery to prevent further damage to cells.

   C — Place the battery into a battery charging bag.

4. Which is not something that can be done to prevent a lithium polymer (LiPo) battery fire?

   A — Charge the battery only when at room temperature.

   B — Place the battery into a battery charging bag.

   C — Be sure to drain the battery completely before recharging.

5. Which is something that can be done to prevent a lithium polymer (LiPo) battery fire?

   A — Charge the battery only when the outer coating is bloated.

   B — Only discharge batteries to 20% of maximum charge during each cycle.

   C — Be sure to top off the battery charge prior to flight even if it is assumed to be fully charged.

6. The best procedures to use during an emergency are

   A — those provided by the manufacturer.

   B — those provided by pilots who fly the same sUAS model.

   C — those outlined within the *Aeronautical Information Manual*.

1.C
2.B A B
3.B
4.B C
5.B
6.C

Answers:
1-C, 2-B, 3-B, 4-C, 5-B, 6-A.

8–8   The Complete Remote Pilot

Human Factors

HEALTH AND ENVIRONMENTAL FACTORS

/ Medical Factors for Pilots

Remote pilots are responsible for determining their fitness to fly sUAS. Additionally, anyone acting as a "crewmember," such as a visual observer, shares the same responsibility. Thus, careful attention to how you and other participants feel and act is necessary to ensure safe sUAS operations. Seemingly small things can create significant hazards when mixed with a fast-moving object with rapidly rotating propeller blades! For example, taking some medicine for your allergies could make you drowsy or dizzy, which may be enough of a distraction to cause you to accidently do something detrimental. If you have a question in your mind as to how a prescription or over-the-counter

drug, or even illness symptoms, may affect your fitness to fly, check with an Aviation Medical Examiner, not your family doctor, to be sure. Prescription analgesics and antihistamines, the very things that we reach for when we have problems, are the most likely to cause problems.

/ Drugs and Alcohol

The effects of drugs and alcohol on performance cannot be understated. Pilots are prohibited from flying within 8 hours of ingesting *any* alcoholic beverage and from flying while under the influence of any drug or medication. Even over-the-counter medications as seemingly innocuous as cough suppressants can affect judgment, memory, and alertness. Remote pilots should check with an Aviation Medical Examiner for advice if in doubt about any medication. Remember, you are required to ground yourself (and other crew should as well) if you have any medical condition which affects your abilities as a crewmember (Figure 9-1). Just as a reminder, remote pilots and crew must comply with the same regulations as manned pilots, per 14 CFR Part 107; this includes a minimum of 8 hours between drinking and flying as well as a maximum of 0.04 blood alcohol level. Also, if you get busted or refuse to submit to testing, your future application for certificates can be denied, or your current certificate revoked or suspended.

Figure 9-1. Self-grounding is required when a pilot is feeling ill.

/ Toxic Fumes

Don't fly immediately after using adhesives, solvents, or cleaners that leave fumes in or around the sUAS. Use caution when fueling the sUAS (for those that use fuel) to avoid unnecessary exposure to harmful fumes. This should be common sense, but it is sometimes overlooked in the rush to get the mission started.

/ Visual Illusions

As a remote pilot, you will rely on your eyes to keep you out of trouble—but under certain conditions, your eyes can lie. Here are a few subtle traps to watch out for:

Autokinesis: In low-light conditions, if you stare at a fixed light, it will appear to move. It might even lead you to believe it is a star (or a UFO). Solution? Don't stare at a fixed light. Instead look off-center of the light.

Featureless terrain illusion: This one gets you when flying over water or desert, with no structures or vegetation to help with depth perception. The terrain background, such as trees of different sizes, colors, and shapes, may also make it difficult to see an sUAS or be able to determine its orientation/direction.

Atmospheric illusions: Fog and haze will make you think that your sUAS is farther away than it really is. It will also make potentially conflicting aircraft seem farther away than they actually are.

Ground lighting illusions: Pilots have mistaken lights on roads and trains for runway lights. Check the CS to see what kind of approach lighting is installed, and check the sectional to see what nearby non-aviation activity might be confusing.

Disorientation: The farther away an sUAS gets from those operating it, the harder it can be to determine the features of the aircraft that provide clues about its orientation, heading, altitude, and speed. Before assuming a specific sUAS attitude or positioning, verify these by making small control inputs to confirm that the actual aircraft alignment is as anticipated. Rapid degradation of control can occur if care is not taken in times of disorientation.

Spatial disorientation: Spatial disorientation specifically refers to the lack of orientation with regard to the position, attitude, or movement of the airplane in space. It is a state of temporary confusion resulting from misleading information being sent to the brain by various sensory organs. The best way to overcome spatial disorientation is with training and by trusting the instruments and controls and disregarding the sensory perceptions.

/ Concerns While Out in the Elements

Unlike manned aircraft pilots, remote pilots work outside in Mother Nature and must directly deal with the elements. Thus, pre-planning should be undertaken to guarantee safe and comfortable operations. When preparing, think of what you would need if you were spending the day at a location similar to where you plan to operate. For example, if you are going to be up in the mountains, plan as though you were going for a hike in similar conditions and terrain. You will want proper protection from the environment in case the weather becomes unfavorable as well as any special equipment required to make getting in and out of the area easier (and innocuous). If you are flying at the beach, you will need sunscreen, sunglasses, and comfortable clothes. Also make sure your crew is well informed of what is required so they do not show up in mountain gear for the day at the beach, or vice versa. If going into remote areas, particularly if you are by yourself, be sure to leave information such as your location, plans, and anticipated length of the trip with a friend. Some common sense goes a long way.

In these days when virtually everyone seems to be carrying a bottle of water, it hardly seems necessary to warn anyone about the hazards of dehydration. The old advice about drinking six, eight-ounce glasses of water a day has been discredited, but no one denies that dehydration can cause disorientation and problems with speech. Make sure that you have plenty of liquids available, both for yourself and for other crewmembers. This is particularly important due to the sometimes harsh environments in which sUAS operations can occur (such as deserts) as well as the potentially long durations out in the sun. It is a good idea to pack some snacks, as well. You'd be surprised how much better your brain (and those of your crew) work when well fed and hydrated.

/ Looking Out for Other Aircraft

Scanning the sky for aircraft is just as important as maintaining control of your sUAS, and deserves equal attention. Do not limit your scan to those areas ahead of and at the same level as your sUAS, but instead scan systematically across the entire horizon, looking both below and above the altitude at which your system is flying. A constant sweep of the eyes will not be effective, because your eyes need time to focus on objects, so momentarily stopping for at least a second will enhance your ability to detect airplanes. A commonly used method is to pick a 10-degree section of the sky (visualizing the entire sky as 360 degrees), and then scan that section up and down before moving on to the next 10-degree section. It can be difficult to do a good job scanning while simultaneously flying an sUAS. Ideally, you will have a visual observer to look out for aircraft, but if not, you will have to divide your attention accordingly to ensure you're keeping watch for air traffic. If you receive a waiver to fly at night, because of the way your eyes work, you will see only those objects that are slightly out of your direct line of sight, and your scan will have to be slower and more deliberate.

If an airplane remains on the same relative bearing (it is not moving in your field of view, but is getting bigger), this means the aircraft is on a direct intercept course and may be a conflict to your operation. Keeping the right-of-way rules in mind, maneuver your sUAS well clear of the aircraft, or even better, land.

Hazy conditions are particularly challenging for pilots. With nothing specific to focus on, your eyes relax and "coast," seeking a comfortable focusing distance 10 to 30 feet in the direction of view. You are looking but not seeing. Because of the lack of contrast, terrain and obstacles appear to be farther away than their actual distance. Choose any distant object that presents itself, even the top of a distant object, to keep your eyes working.

/ Sun-Blindness

Flying directly toward a rising or setting sun can effectively blind you, making it impossible for you to track your sUAS or see obstacles or aircraft. Even a moment spent looking toward the sun can shrink your pupils to the size of BBs, and it will take a while for them to recover. It is best to be prepared with sunglasses, a hat/visor, or both. If possible, try to set up the mission to avoid having to look into the sun, keeping it behind the ground control station. Similar degradation to vision can occur when the sun reflects off of objects such as mirrored glass windows or snow-covered terrain. Whenever possible, the impact of these challenges should be minimized with adequate forethought.

DECISION-MAKING AND JUDGMENT

Approximately 80 percent of aviation accidents can be attributed to some form of human error; it might be because of an unwise decision under stress, or it might be the exercise of bad judgment. FAA psychologists have identified five subject areas for decision making, five risk elements, and five hazardous attitudes. By being familiar with these key concepts, remote PICs can be methodical about the decision-making process and the operational risks associated with each mission, which can be shared with all other operational participants. As part of good crew resource management (CRM), crewmembers can keep a lookout for "bad" attitudes among themselves and work them out before they interfere with safety.

The *five decision-making subject areas* are:

Pilot—Your state of health, level of fatigue, competency.

Aircraft—Any question about its airworthiness.

Environment—Weather, traffic, runway length and condition, etc.

Operation—The go/no-go decision.

Situation—Know what is going on around you.

The *five risk elements* follow the same pattern:

Pilot—Physical stress (too hot, too cold, too noisy, lack of oxygen); physiological stress (lack of sleep, missed meals); psychological stress (sick child, marital problems, work problems)

Aircraft—Radios OK? Fuel quantity sufficient?

Environment—Density altitude, day/night, deteriorating weather.

Operation—Pressure to keep a schedule.

Situation—"Get-home-itis" (see later section)

The *five hazardous attitudes* should be easy to identify:

Anti-authority—"Nobody is going to tell me what to do!" *Antidote:* Follow the rules.

Impulsivity—"Don't just sit there, do something even if it is wrong!" *Antidote:* Not so fast, think first.

Invulnerability—"Accidents happen to the other guy; I am too good a pilot to make a dumb mistake." *Antidote:* It could happen to me.

Macho—"I can do it despite _____" *Antidote:* Taking chances is foolish.

Resignation—"What's the use of trying, there's nothing I can do." *Antidote:* I am not helpless.

FAA Advisory Circular 60-22, *Aeronautical Decision Making*, contains example situations and grading sheets so that you can test yourself on decision-making, risk elements, and hazardous attitudes.

/ The DECIDE Model

Aeronautical decision making lays the groundwork for rational actions in flight. Even if you display none of the dangerous attitudes listed above, there are many points in every flight where a decision is called for, and you should have a mental template to use—this is the DECIDE model:

Detect the fact that a change has occurred (or is needed).

Estimate the need to react to the change (hardly anything in aviation requires immediate action).

Choose a desirable outcome for your decision.

Identify actions to take to achieve the desirable outcome.

Do. Take the necessary action.

Evaluate the effect of your action on the needed change.

Most preventable aviation accidents are caused by human error. Mechanical malfunctions are rare, and structural failure is many times a result of—you guessed it—human error. Accident investigators look for and identify an "error chain," in which one wrong decision leads to another—break just one link in the chain and the accident would not have happened.

Peer pressure ("Hey, we need those pictures of the listed houses by the end of the day") or self-induced pressure ("I do not want to disappoint my client") can lead to unpleasant outcomes. Just say no. Attempting to show colleagues that you have "the right stuff" instead of admitting that you have personal limitations or that the capabilities of the sUAS may be compromised can lead to disaster.

/ Get-Home-Itis and Completion Bias

The concept of "get-home-itis" leads to many aviation accidents each day. Symptoms include a tendency to overestimate one's abilities and to underestimate the problems and hazards that may present themselves. Pilots in this mindset are blinded by the desire to "finish the job." There is no cure for get-home-itis; however, there is nothing so important that it's worth the risk of damaging property, hurting people, or losing your sUAS for. Keeping this in mind will prevent you from being led down the path to succumb to get-home-itis.

A contributing factor is "completion bias." This sets in when you have begun a flight and have completed some or most of a particular mission. You simply want to go ahead and finish rather than scrubbing for the day or taking a delay.

You can save yourself from this kind of stress by establishing an unbreakable Code of Conduct for missions, such as setting weather restrictions or other parameters that restrict operations under certain conditions. For example, you may choose to set a maximum wind condition for certain types (or all kinds) of flights. This can certainly be less than the maximum recommended by the manufacturer. Remember, you're the remote PIC, and thus you're the one in charge. It is better to err on the side of safety.

REFRESHER TRAINING

Man was not meant to fly. Even stranger is flying from a third-person view—such as when you're looking up at an sUAS as it maneuvers around an object of interest. In short, the human organism was designed to operate in two dimensions on the surface of the earth. Operating outside such an environment requires training and mechanical devices to overcome the shortcomings of the human body. Even when the adaptive devices are present, if the training has been forgotten, things can go downhill fast.

Training is a process of substituting a new reaction for normal or typical responses. For example, for a novice multicopter operator whose aircraft encounters vortex ring state and begins to sink rapidly, the normal reaction is to gun the throttle to maximum and hold it there until the airplane hits the ground. The trained reaction, as you know (or will learn), is to alter the airflow around the propellers by increasing forward speed, reducing throttle, turning, or a combination of these reactions. All pilots know that it is counter-intuitive to reduce throttle if your aircraft is quickly sinking toward the ground, but if that is what it takes to recover, then it must be done. Another flight regime that can be problematic for remote pilots, especially when first learning to fly or after not flying for a while, is the reverse control inputs that are required for many systems when they are flown toward (inbound to) the user/ground control station.

It is wise to repeatedly go through such maneuvers from different starting scenarios, preferably under the watchful eye of a more experienced operator (at least at the beginning) and in a safe environment. According to physiologists, this repetition creates pathways in the brain that shortcut normal reactions, direct the muscles to react properly, and deliver what are called psychomotor responses. Unless they are refreshed with practice, these pathways lose their effectiveness, and when that happens normal reactions take their place. In that case, you will regress to the same state you were in before you took part in training.

In addition to keeping your flying skills sharp, the FAA wants you to stay on top of the knowledge required to continue to be a competent remote pilot. Thus, a regulatory requirement in 14 CFR Part 107 for aeronautical knowledge recency must be revisited every 24 calendar months. Completion of the necessary recurrent training can be fulfilled by taking a knowledge test or by completing a recurrent training course.

POSITIVE CONTROL

Whenever the remote PIC and the person manipulating the controls of an sUAS are not the same individual, it is critical always to ensure everyone knows who is responsible for flying and—if need be—how control is transferred from one individual to another. Accidents have occurred when someone tries to take over control unexpectedly or when a crewmember thought that someone else was in control. Eliminate all doubt and use a proven three-step procedure—

Person transferring control: "You have the flight controls."

Person taking over control: "I have the flight controls."

Person transferring control: "You have the flight controls."

RISK MANAGEMENT AND AERONAUTICAL DECISION MAKING

Additional subject areas that are key components of flight safety are risk management and aeronautical decision making. As is often the case, FAA provides acronyms and memory aids for you to use (the FAA just loves mnemonics!). You will notice much overlap between areas, but thinking about something twice is better than not thinking of it at all.

For those unfamiliar to the topics above (or as a refresher), take a look at the FAA's *Risk Management Handbook*. You will find that it is broken down by chapters, is well illustrated, and contains many cautionary tales culled from accident statistics. Following are the acronyms/memory aids that are covered on the FAA Knowledge Test and that should become part of every flight after you earn your certificate.

/ I'M SAFE

Illness: Any health related issue that might affect your ability to conduct a flight and respond to any emergency.

Medication: Over-the-counter and prescription medications have been involved in far too many accidents. "Do not operate heavy machinery" is a warning that is frequently shrugged off. "May cause drowsiness" is another. Remember, you're flying your sUAS in the same sky as airliners. Don't take unnecessary risks with other peoples' lives.

Stress: Job worries? Marital problems? Are bills getting you down? Flying deserves 100% of your attention. If in doubt, leave the sUAS on the ground.

Alcohol: Does this require explanation?

Fatigue: Professional pilots are limited in how many hours they can fly each day and how much rest time they must have between flights. The reason is obvious. If you're tired, call it a day. Do people on the ground, nearby, or in aircraft sharing the same airspace as your sUAS deserve any less?

Emotion: This goes hand-in-hand with stress. "Don't go to bed mad" applies equally to flying. Nothing is more important than the job at hand—the safe completion of the flight.

/ PAVE

The I'M SAFE memory aid applies before flight planning even begins. PAVE applies to the flight you are about to undertake:

P—Pilot. Physical and mental have been covered; this memory aid is about proper certification, flight experience, currency, etc.

A—Aircraft. Are all inspections current? Is this the right sUAS for the mission, or is it close to being overloaded? Does the sUAS have sufficient fuel/battery for the planned flight?

V—enVironment. First and foremost, this is about weather. Can you carry out your planned flight and stay in VLOS? Is weather forecast to deteriorate at any time during the intended operation? Any frontal weather to consider? Second consideration: Terrain. Check local aviation and/or topography maps to investigate natural terrain and obstacles. Also, do a visual inspection for potential hazards once on site.

E—External pressures. These are the most difficult decisions a pilot must make: Telling the customer that you cannot deliver what is being asked, at least not right now. Trying to do things for clients that you have never been trained for or practiced. Showing off: Low passes over someone's house or a group of people.

/ Three P's

Closely parallel to the DECIDE model are the Three P's: Perceive, Process, and Perform. When you *perceive* the need for a change (cloud cover increasing, visibility decreasing, etc.), you must *process* what that means to the successful completion of your flight; you then *perform* by taking the appropriate action.

The key here is your ability to recognize the need for change instead of just flying along without a care in the world. This brings up a few elements of risk management:

1. Situational awareness. If you do not know where you are, how can you avoid running into something vast and unyielding or violating an airspace restriction? Technology has provided the means for helping remote pilots complete missions with little or no input once programmed. Do not abdicate your pilot-in-command responsibilities to an electronic device. Always ensure that the device is doing what is intended, and if not, take over.

2. Controlled-flight-into-terrain. When loss of situational awareness is coupled with diminished visibility, or bad planning leads to loss of VLOS, it is all too easy to fly right into the side of a tree or a human-made obstacle.

3. Automation management. The more sophisticated the sUAS, flight planning software, and ground control station, the more interrelationships that exist between boxes. "Why is it doing that?" is a question asked by too many pilots. Know your systems and their capabilities, but do not rely on them to think for you.

4. Task management. Learn to prioritize your actions before, during, and after the flight. Think ahead: What are the next two things that must be accomplished? Is what you are planning the safest possible way to do things? The most logical?

Again, read the *Risk Management Handbook* to prepare yourself for the written exam and future planning decisions.

REVIEW QUESTIONS

Lesson 9 — Human Factors

1. A state of temporary confusion resulting from misleading information being sent to the brain by various sensory organs is defined as

   A — spatial disorientation.

   B — hyperventilation.

   C — hypoxia.

2. What is the most effective way to use the eyes during night flight?

   A — Look only at far away, dim lights.

   B — Scan slowly to permit off-center viewing.

   C — Concentrate directly on each object for a few seconds.

3. The danger of spatial disorientation during flight in poor visual conditions may be reduced by

   A — shifting the eyes quickly between the sUAS and the ground control station.

   B — having faith in the sUAS telemetry rather than relying on the sensory organs.

   C — leaning the body when turning the

4. What effect does haze have on the abilit traffic or terrain features during flight?

   A — Haze causes the eyes to focus at inf

   B — Contrasting colors become less dis making objects easier to see.

   C — All traffic or terrain features appear farther away than their actual dista

5. What is the most effective way to scan for during daytime flight?

   A — Focus on the distant horizon.

   B — Scan quickly, moving eyes back and using off-center viewing.

   C — Scan in deliberate, 10-degree increments of the sky.

6. What is the solution statement that should be used to deal with a crewmember suffering from resignation?

   A — You are not helpless; your actions are necessary.

   B — No matter what you do, it will not help; the situation is out of hand.

   C — It can happen to you; you are just like everyone else.

7. A crewmember who states that the mission can be completed no matter what hazards exist because the team is so experienced is exhibiting a ________ hazardous attitude.

   A — macho

   B — invulnerability

   C — impulsivity

8. The recommended mental model for remote pilots to use for the decision making required during flight is r e abbreviation

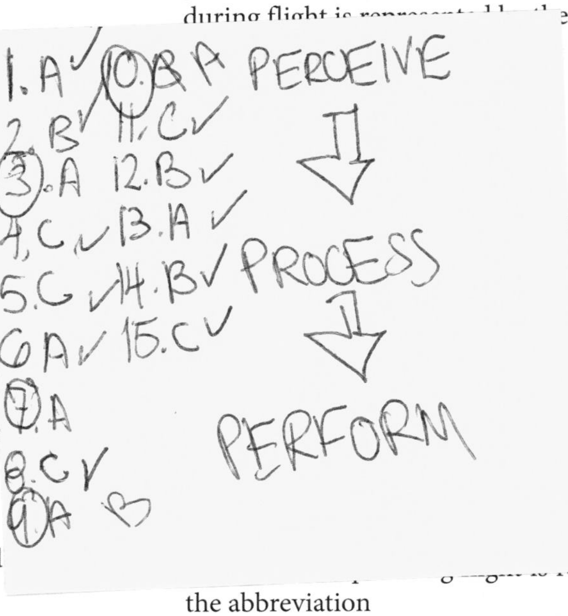

nended for use
s represented

model to use
emote pilots
presented by
the abbreviation

A — I'M SAFE

B — PAVE

C — DECIDE

11. The risk assessment process incorporates the "three P's." Which of the following is not one of the "p" words associated with this procedure?

   A — Perform

   B — Process

   C — Predict

12. What does the "V" in the PAVE model stand for?

   A — Visualize

   B — Environment

   C — Vigilance

13. Human error is a causal factor in _____ percent of all aviation accidents.

   A — 80

   B — 75

   C — 70

14. No one can act as remote pilot-in-command when their blood alcohol level exceeds _____.

   A — 0.40

   B — 0.04

   C — 0.004

15. Which situation would not exclude an individual from acting as remote pilot-in-command?

   A — Taking a medication prescribed by a physician that may cause drowsiness.

   B — Taking a non-prescription medication that may cause drowsiness.

   C — Taking a non-prescription medication that you have taken before, never experiencing any side effects.

Maintenance and Preflight Inspection Procedures

REGULATORY REQUIREMENTS

Since an sUAS potentially operates in proximity to and within the same airspace as manned aircraft, a high level of care is required to ensure that the aircraft is safe to operate and will not do anything to jeopardize the ability of the remote PIC to maintain positive control of the system while in use. The FAA explicitly spells this out in 14 CFR §107.15, stating that prior to each flight, "the remote pilot in command must check the small unmanned aircraft system to determine whether it is in a condition for safe operation." Further, if at any time it is determined that this condition is compromised, the operation must cease immediately. Unmanned aircraft pilots should mimic their manned counterparts who are very familiar with the preflight inspection process, which is (or should be) a very thorough evaluation of the aircraft before taking flight.

While manned aircraft manufacturers typically provide a comprehensive checklist to use for preflight inspections, not all sUAS manufacturers do so. It may be necessary to create your own checklist. However, you may not need to start from scratch—or worse, learn the "hard" way; instead, look online to find out what work has been done on your individual system. Some great resources are available on various websites, especially for systems with minimal documentation provided by the manufacturer. In short, if the aircraft comes with a checklist or procedure for ensuring safe operation, use it. Feel free to add to it if you find some additional things that you feel need to be checked prior to use. If no such guidance is provided, create your own. So what should you include? Let's take a look.

PREFLIGHT INSPECTION CONSIDERATIONS

While each sUAS will vary, here are some key areas to consider for careful inspection before flight or on a regular basis. Before every flight, it's important to do a thorough visual examination of the aircraft. Are there any loose parts? Is anything hanging off that should not be? Does anything look abnormal? Is there any damage to the structure? Next, you should take a look at the propellers. Before putting them on the aircraft, flex the blades slightly to confirm their integrity. While you are doing this, look over the blades and run your finger along their edges and surfaces. If there are nicks or cracks, you should replace the propeller. Once they are installed on the aircraft, propellers should be secure (and locked if applicable), but don't overtighten them, as that can damage the threads or connections.

While you are in the vicinity of the motors, check them for proper rotation and security. Do they spin freely? Is anything sticking? Are any motors too loose? The best way to know for sure is by comparing one motor to another (or if the sUAS only has one motor, comparing it to how it appeared the last time). If anything is abnormal, it is advisable to remove and replace the item in question. (More experienced users may want to do some bench tests prior to replacing or flying.)

Next, check all peripheral items, such as the camera gimbal or other payloads. Are they properly connected and secured? How about the camera or other sensors? These typically are expensive pieces of equipment; you do not want to accidentally damage or lose them because you were in a hurry to fly.

You will also want to inspect the battery prior to installation. Note: be sure you know the correct power-on procedures for your sUAS. Some will be powered once the battery is installed, so if that is the case, you will want to be ready for that change in status. Typically, the controller is turned on first and then the sUAS is turned on, to reduce the chances of something unexpected happening (and if it does, by following this procedure, you should have control).

Check the battery connection pins/slots to verify that they are not damaged or dirty. Check the body of the battery. Is there any "puffiness" or bulging of the outer coating or sides (*see* Figure 10-1)? If the answer is yes, your battery is failing. Never use a puffy or bulging battery. Is the battery warm or hot? If so, let it cool before using. Do you know the charging status? If not, it is best to know this before flight for quality assurance and performance tracking. Once you are happy with the battery's status, install it (or position it for installation).

The ground control station and any other equipment also should be inspected. Are the antennae properly installed and attached? Are there any missing or loose parts? What is the battery status of the components? Will the capacity be enough to complete the mission with an additional time cushion?

Is your crew briefed and ready to go? If yes, power on the sUAS (after completing necessary checklists) to check lights and other markings. Do a control check (if possible) and gimbal check. Does everything move freely without abnormal resistance or noises? Next, you will want to do an idle check with motors on (again,

only when ready and post-checklists). Check for any unusual noises or vibrations. If any are detected, shut down and investigate further before departing. The final check prior to initiating the mission is an airborne control check. For example, if you're using a quadcopter, lift the aircraft off to a hover just above the ground. Input left/right, forward/back, yaw, and power inputs to ensure the system reacts as expected. Additionally, confirm that there are no weird noises or "ticks" experienced during this operational check.

POSTFLIGHT INSPECTION CONSIDERATIONS

Upon completing a flight, the sUAS should be inspected again. Essentially you will want to check the same items as in the preflight inspection, noting any changes in aircraft status. Batteries will generally be warm because of discharging, but they should not be hot. Use caution if the battery condition changes between the pre- and post-flight inspections (e.g., it begins to bulge). Note any issues in your maintenance log (explained later) and replace any parts that are damaged or at the end of their service life.

INSPECTION INTERVALS

More heavy-duty inspections should occur at intervals determined by your experience or manufacturer guidance, but following are some ideas. Each week or every ten flights, conduct a more comprehensive visual inspection looking for cracks or other damage in the case, enclosures, on the landing gear, gimbals, sensor attachments, engine mounts, etc. Check retaining screws, such as those for the motors and shell. Clean battery and sensor attachments, as needed. Ensure that the batteries are being charged and discharged properly and that there are no major changes in either process. Recalibrate the navigation system (compass or inertial units) per manufacturer recommendations.

Every month or 30 flights, whichever is sooner, take a peek "under the hood" to verify that none of the wiring is coming loose or shows signs of wear (or even arcing—i.e., shorting of the electrical supply). Be sure all internal components are secure, and no unusual debris is present. Having a compressed air computer component cleaner handy will allow you to remove dust or debris without touching anything directly. Check the security of motors and gimbals, removing, replacing, and tightening them as needed.

Figure 10-1. Damaged LiPo battery with bulging exterior coating (*Mpt-matthew; https://en.wikipedia.org/wiki/ File:Expanded_lithium-ion-polymer_battery_from_an_ Apple_iPhone_3GS.jpg; CC BY-SA 3.0*)

(Some industry gurus suggest removing and inspecting the motors at this interval, but you should only do so if you are confident you will not damage the system.) This is a good time to check to see if any software updates are ready to be installed. For this, it is helpful to be on the email list of the manufacturer of your sUAS, or alternatively, you can regularly check their website for software updates.

BATTERY MAINTENANCE

The majority of sUAS these days use lithium polymer (LiPo) batteries, although you may occasionally come across a different type of battery. LiPo batteries are used because of their superior performance for high-demand situations in which light weight is desirable. In fact, these types of batteries are becoming common-place even in commercial aircraft such as the Boeing 787. Unlike batteries commonly used in other applications (such as in cars or flashlights), LiPo types require a bit more care and attention, mainly because if treated carelessly they may catch fire—or less dramatically, they will not last as long (which is an issue as they are not cheap). Improper use can reduce the number of cycles you get out of the battery by 50 to 75%.

It is recommended that batteries be broken in gently. They will come charged at around 40% capacity (around 3.8V per cell), which has been shown to be an ideal level for long-term storage (keep that in mind). You should fully charge the battery before use, and then only fly until it reaches around 50% capacity for the first few cycles. This has been shown to extend the life of LiPo batteries.

When charging LiPo batteries, be sure you are using a unit specifically designed to do so. If you are using a charger that allows you to select the type of battery you plan to charge, be absolutely certain it is set to LiPo. Proper cell balancing is a vital part of extending LiPo useful life, so use a charger that has this capability whenever possible (some batteries handle this themselves). Never overcharge your batteries (i.e., above 4.2V). This should not be a problem in most cases, as chargers have safety features and automatic shutoffs. In short, know not only your batteries but also the ins and outs of your chargers. Also, respect the maximum charge "speed" of your batteries. The general rule of thumb is to use 1C (multiply this by the battery rating—e.g., a 2200 mAh battery could safely be charged at 2.2A). Some batteries can be charged up to 3C, but more than this is not recommended. Considering that the majority of batteries are manufactured in China where quality assurance is not always high, the harder you charge your batteries, the higher the risk of bad things happening.

Do not charge cold (near or below freezing) or hot batteries; try to charge them only when they are at room temperature. Batteries that are being charged properly should not get hot. If they start to increase in temperature, stop charging. Do not try to charge damaged or bulging batteries. Also, do not "top off" batteries. If they are nearly fully charged, do not try to charge them to 100%. Never leave batteries to charge unattended, on or near flammable materials, or without special protective measures such as LiPo battery charging bags or fireproof containers.

To maximize the life of your batteries, do not over-discharge them. You should never allow battery capacity to get below 20% (3.6V per cell) unless you like buying new batteries. If you over drain your batteries, you may get as few as 50 cycles out of them compared to 150 to 300 cycles if treated properly. If you assume a 20-minute average mission, a 50 cycle limit on a $60 battery equates to 6 cents per cycle. Instead, if you get 300 cycles out of the battery, this results in a one penny cost per cycle. If you are flying a lot and abusing your batteries, these critical items can become a significant expense.

LiPo batteries have a range of temperatures at which they are most efficient. They do not like the cold—in fact, they can unexpectedly fail in temperatures near (or below) freezing. For multicopters, this means they will fall out of the sky, which is obviously not good for the aircraft or their payloads. Therefore, it is wise to keep batteries at room temperature prior to use. Alternatively, batteries that approach or exceed 60° Celsius (140° Fahrenheit) will result in battery damage and risk fire. In regards to storing batteries, a range of temperatures from 5 to 25°C (41 to 77°F) is best. Additionally, just as most new batteries are delivered, those you plan to store more than a few days should not be charged beyond approximately 3.8V per cell (around 40%). This will increase the longevity of your batteries and minimize the risks of damage or failure of internal components.

So when do you retire a battery? First, follow any manufacturer instructions. Second, batteries that consistently will not hold a minimum of 80% of full capacity should be removed from service. Third, once you get to 150–200 cycles, pay extra attention to battery performance, physical appearance, temperature, and charging times. Last, it is wise to track battery performance (i.e., how much flight time you get out of it) to gauge when it begins its final decline. When disposing of LiPo batteries, follow local regulations and policies as well as manufacturer instructions. The batteries should be fully discharged prior to getting rid of them. Do this outdoors and not on or near anything flammable. In order to avoid damaging sensitive components, do not use your sUAS to drain the power. Instead, connect a LiPo discharger or other slow discharging accessory. The discharging of damaged or puffy batteries is not recommended; take them to a battery recycling or disposal location.

FLIGHT AND MAINTENANCE LOGS

It is a good idea to maintain flight and maintenance logs (in fact, some operations require reporting to the FAA, so this is not optional in such cases). Keeping flight logs will ensure that you know exactly how much use your sUAS has seen. This will help you track the longevity of components—most importantly, the battery. If you notice that a fully charged battery does not last as long as it used to, it may be reaching the point at which it needs to be retired. Various vendors sell comprehensive sUAS logs (ASA offers a UAS operator logbook, and several applications for smartphones are available, as well).

Maintenance logs should also be kept to track any noted problems or component replacements. This will allow you to track how long a component has been in use, which helps determine the quality of components as well as if they are approaching their service limit (some manufacturers have recommended service limits to preclude unexpected failures). Both documents can be used to show that you are keeping track of operations and promoting safety of flight if any issues with the FAA or even legal issues occur. It can also serve as a means of tracking costs for business owners—which is never a bad idea, right?

MAINTENANCE, REPAIR, AND REPLACEMENT OF COMPONENTS

Regular inspection of your sUAS and its ground control station should preclude any major surprises regarding items in need of maintenance or repair. If it becomes time to replace an item that requires dismantling part of the sUAS, be sure to use manufacturer guidance and be careful! Also, you do not want to void your warranty, if one exists, so if in doubt, send the system back to the manufacturer for repair. Do not attempt to repair propellers. If they are damaged, they should be replaced. Other components should not be used beyond their service life, if one is specified. For some sUAS parts, only time will tell what their expected life is. How reliable are motors? Autopilots? Gimbals?

Ideally, your inspection, logging, and preventative maintenance plan will stay ahead of any major issues. If in doubt about a part or system, replace it; most things are modular and replaceable.

REVIEW QUESTIONS

Lesson 10 — Maintenance and Preflight Inspection Procedures

1. The _____ is responsible for ensuring that an sUAS is safe to operate.

   A — owner

   B — operator

   C — remote pilot-in-command

2. While you are flying a mission, it appears that one of the engines of your quadcopter is not responding to your inputs. You should

   A — keep flying as long as you are able to maintain altitude.

   B — land immediately.

   C — note the malfunction and complete the mission.

3. During your preflight inspection, you notice small nick in one of the propeller blades. T best course of action is

   A — to replace the propeller.

   B — dress the propeller blade by filing away the nick.

   C — use adhesives to strengthen the damage section of the blade.

4. During installation of the sUAS battery, you notice that one side of the outer coating is bulging. You should

   A — consult with the manufacturer to see if repair is possible.

   B — use the battery, as bulging is normal.

   C — discharge and recharge the battery.

5. After completing a flight, you notice that the sUAS battery is warm. What action should be taken prior to recharging the battery?

   A — Discharge the battery completely.

   B — No action is needed; begin recharging as soon as desired.

   C — Wait until the battery cools to room temperature.

6. When should you replace an sUAS battery?

   A — When it no longer will hold 40% charge.

   B — When it no longer will hold 80% charge.

   C — When it no longer will hold 100% charge.

7. What is the lowest percentage of battery capacity that you should allow to occur under normal circumstances?

   A — 0%

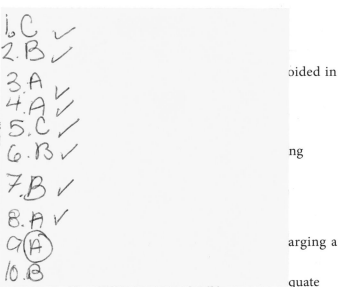

...ided in

...ng

...arging a

...quate power to the charger.

   B — Do not charge batteries on anything other than wood surfaces.

   C — Place the battery in a battery charging bag.

10. Which is true about maintenance logs?

   A — They are required by the FAA.

   B — They provide a means of tracking component life cycles.

   C — They are required by the manufacturer to maintain the warranty on the aircraft.

Answers:
1-C, 2-B, 3-A, 4-A, 5-C, 6-B, 7-B, 8-A, 9-C, 10-B

Glossary

above ground level (AGL). The height in feet of an object, such as a tower or UAS, above the local area terrain. For example, a cell phone tower that is 200 feet tall would be described as being 200 feet AGL.

Advisory Circular (AC). An advisory document released by the FAA to provide additional guidance on important subjects that goes beyond the explanations in the regulations and other documents. ACs are available free from the FAA's website. Be sure you are using the most recent version (expired versions are noted as such on the AC's first page or on the applicable download webpage).

aeronautical chart. A type of map used for aviation/aeronautical purposes. These charts come in various forms for both visual and non-visual (IFR) flying. The type of chart most commonly used by sUAS pilots is the sectional chart, which shows terrain, airports, airspace, landmarks, and other pertinent flight data.

aeronautical decision making (ADM). A systematic mental process for making decisions about tasks that must be undertaken in all phases of flight.

Aeronautical Information Manual (AIM). A reference publication applicable to all types of aviation/aerospace operations. Provides detailed information on topics such as air traffic control, weather, airports, and other subjects critical to remote pilots.

Air Defense Identification Zone (ADIZ). A designated piece of airspace around the border regions of a country to provide positive identification of aircraft for national security.

airport. A facility from which aircraft operate. Airports typically have runways, taxiways, and a variety of buildings (hangars, businesses, terminals, etc.).

Facilities exclusively reserved for helicopters are called heliports. Facilities specifically for seaplanes and amphibious aircraft are called seaplane bases. It is common for heliports and seaplane bases to be co-located with airports (though only the latter is typically indicated on aeronautical charts). *See also* heliport, seaplane base.

air traffic control (ATC). The entity in charge of separating aircraft in controlled airspace as well as in and around busy airports. ATC can also provide advisory and emergency assistance if requested. Remote pilots may have to contact ATC in specific situations.

air traffic control tower (ATCT). A facility responsible for handling departures, arrivals, and ground operations at an airport (or airports). These are almost always associated with Class B, C, and D airports.

airfoil. A structure specifically designed to produce lift. In sUAS, the typical airfoil is the wing or propeller/rotor blade(s).

Airman's Meteorological Information (AIRMET). A weather warning covering a specific area that is applicable to small aircraft and UAS (e.g., for windy conditions, turbulence, low visibilities).

airspace. The region of space above the ground in which aircraft operate. Airspace in the United States is generalized into two primary categories: controlled and uncontrolled. Airspace is further subdivided into classes: Classes A, B, C, D, and E are types of controlled airspace, while Class G is uncontrolled.

alert area. A designated area of airspace in which a large amount of flight training or other aviation activity takes place. Extreme caution should be used when operating in or near an alert area.

altimeter. An instrument that measures altitude (height) with respect to a reference plane. In manned aircraft, altitude is sensed via pressure changes in reference to sea level pressure (height above mean sea level [MSL]). For every 1,000 feet change in altitude, the barometric (atmospheric) pressure changes by 1 inch of mercury (" Hg) (e.g., a 1,000-foot increase in altitude results in a 1" Hg decrease). Altitude can also be measured in reference to height above the ground, or above ground level (AGL).

amp. The abbreviation for ampere, a measure of electric current. An amp is equivalent to the movement of one coulomb of charge per second. Using water as an example, this would be the water speed, such as in a river (current).

angle of attack (AOA). The angle between the middle of an airfoil (wing or rotor blade), referred to as the chord line, and the relative wind. Relative wind is equal to and opposite the direction the aircraft, wing, or rotor is moving.

Automatic Dependent Surveillance–Broadcast (ADS-B). A system that broadcasts aircraft position (and other information) to all users within range. This can be used by other aircraft to see the originator's position. It can also be used by ground users to determine the position of all aircraft that have ADS-B installed onboard.

Automatic Terminal Information Service (ATIS). A continuous broadcast of non-control aeronautical information. This service also provides weather information for the transmitting airport. Radio frequencies for ATIS can be found on aeronautical charts and in the *Chart Supplement*. Generally, only busy, controlled airports have ATIS.

Aviation Digital Data Service (ADDS). A government-operated website that "provides comprehensive, user-friendly aviation weather graphics, including icing, turbulence, and convection."[1]

Aviation Routine Weather Report (METAR). A weather report, usually distributed each hour, from airports with weather observation capabilities. METARs provide winds, visibility, weather phenomenon (e.g., rain, fog), temperature, dew point, atmospheric pressure (altimeter setting/sea level pressure), and any other pertinent weather data.

base. The leg of an airport traffic pattern at a 90-degree angle (perpendicular) to the approach end of the runway. This leg follows the downwind and precedes the final approach.

camber. The curvature of the surfaces of an airfoil. Camber improves the efficiency of an airfoil to generate pressure differences and downwash that results in lift.

ceiling. The lowest level of cloud cover that substantially covers the sky (i.e., referred to as broken or overcast and not designated thin or partial).

center of gravity (CG). The average location of the weight of an object in reference to a specific aircraft axis (usually the longitudinal axis, though there is also a lateral component to CG along the lateral axis).

Certificate of Waiver or Authorization (COA). A special waiver or authorization by the FAA to allow operations outside the parameters defined by Part 107. Operators with current COAs are allowed to continue to operate under them until they expire.

certificated flight instructor (CFI). An individual who is licensed by the FAA to provide flight and ground instruction.

Chart Supplement **(CS).** A government publication that provides "data on public and joint use airports, seaplane bases, heliports, VFR airport sketches, NAVAIDs, communications data, weather data, airspace, special notices, and operational procedures." The CS is available free from the FAA website.[2]

chord line. A reference line drawn from the leading edge to the trailing edge of an airfoil.

civil twilight. The time 30 minutes before official sunrise to 30 minutes after official sunset, local time. sUAS must have anti-collision lights to operate during civil twilight.

Code of Federal Regulations (CFR). The codification of the general and permanent rules and regulations published in the U.S. *Federal Register*. Title 14 of the CFR applies to areas of operation and certification of UAS and other aviation/aerospace vehicles.

cold front. A weather phenomenon indicated on weather maps with a blue line with triangles pointing in the direction in which the front is moving. A cold front is the division line between air masses in which

---

[1] www.aviationweather.gov/adds

[2] www.faa.gov/air_traffic/flight_info/aeronav/digital_products/dafd/

the approaching air mass is colder than the region adjacent to it. Cold fronts usually move quickly and have poor weather in a narrow band close to the frontal boundary.

Common Traffic Advisory Frequency (CTAF). The frequency used by aircraft in the vicinity of an airport to report their position and to communicate with other local aircraft. On aeronautical charts, it is designated with a "C" in a circle next to the applicable frequency. CTAF can also be found in the *Chart Supplement*.

control tower (CT). *See* air traffic control tower.

controlled airspace. Airspace in which aircraft may be subject to air traffic control. Controlled airspace includes Classes A, B, C, D, and E.

convective. The term that describes the vertical movement of air associated with cumulus clouds and thunderstorm activity. The term "convective activity" refers to the presence of thunderstorms or cumulus clouds with extensive vertical height (towering cumulus).

crewmember. An individual associated with the operation of the sUAS, such as the remote pilot-in-command, visual observer, or the operator of the sUAS itself. The remote PIC can be, but is not required to be, the operator.

crew resource management (CRM). A set of training procedures or curricula designed to avoid human errors, namely "group think" errors, in safety-critical environments. CRM is a process to ensure the use of all available resources, human or otherwise, to solve problems and work in a coordinated manner.

crosswind. The leg of an airport traffic pattern that occurs perpendicular to and beyond the departure end of the runway. It occurs after the upwind leg and precedes the downwind leg. It can also be used to describe aircraft operations in conditions when the wind is not aligned with the path of an aircraft.

cumulus cloud. A cloud that develops in unstable air due to rising air currents (convection). It has a puffy, cotton, or cauliflower-like appearance. It is generally associated with fair weather and often is indicative of turbulent conditions.

day. *See* daylight.

daylight. The period between sunrise and sunset in which sUAS operations are authorized to take place without a waiver or special equipment.

density altitude. The effective performance altitude for an aircraft. It is negatively impacted (increased) by higher elevation, temperatures, and humidity as well as lower atmospheric pressure. An example of how density altitude works: a sUAS is flying at sea level, yet if there are high temperatures and humidity in addition to low atmospheric pressure, the aircraft will perform as though it was flying in Denver, Colorado, at 5,000 feet in much thinner air. In short, the performance of the aircraft will be significantly degraded.

designated pilot examiner (DPE). A person designated by the FAA to represent the administration in the issuance of pilot certificates and to conduct practical exams.

dew point. The temperature at which air becomes completely saturated. Typically, fog or clouds will form when the temperature reaches the dew point.

drag. The aerodynamic force that resists forward movement of an aircraft or airfoil. It is the force opposite to thrust.

downwind. The leg of an airport traffic pattern that is parallel to the runway. It follows the crosswind leg and precedes the base. It is also a term used to describe when an aircraft is operating with a tailwind (i.e., the wind is from behind).

electronic speed controllers (ESC). A circuit designed to control the speed, braking, and direction of an electric motor.

endurance. The length of time that an aircraft can stay aloft. This is a function of the fuel/battery charge available as well as ambient conditions.

Federal Aviation Administration (FAA). The government entity charged with regulation, enforcement, and promotion of the aviation/aerospace industry in the United States. The FAA is tasked with ensuring safe operations in the National Airspace System (NAS), investigating accidents, and the certification of airmen, aircraft, airports, and other system components. sUAS involved in accidents that meet certain parameters are required to report such events to the FAA.

final. The leg of the traffic pattern that is aligned with and conducted toward the approach end of the runway. This leg comes after the base and usually ends in landing. Also referred to as "final approach."

first-person view (FPV). The ability of a remote pilot to utilize a camera onboard a UAS to see the perspective as if the user was in or on the UAS. This can be displayed on a screen that is part of the controller, on a tablet/smartphone, and/or in FPV goggles worn by the person manipulating the controls.

fixed wing. An aircraft that generates lift from a wing/airfoil that does not move. Instead, it produces lift by forward movement that forces air over the wing/airfoil. In other words, it does not produce the lift it needs to fly from a rotating airfoil such as a rotor blade or vertical propellers.

Flight Standards District Office (FSDO). A regional FAA office in charge of overseeing aviation/aerospace operations in a specific geographic area.

Flight Service Station (FSS). The provider of flight and weather services to pilots. FSS can be accessed via the Internet or phone.

flight visibility. *See* visibility.

fly-away. An unexpected loss of control over an sUAS. This may involve the rapid departure of the aircraft from the local environment.

fog. An atmospheric phenomenon that occurs when the air becomes saturated with moisture, resulting in reduced visibility. Fog is simply a cloud that occurs on or near the ground.

frequency. The numerical identification of a radio channel used for communication. For example, the aviation emergency frequency is 121.50. To use this frequency, you would tune your applicable air band radio to 121.50 MHz.

front. A division between air masses of different temperatures or humidities. Fronts often bring changing weather and, in some cases, poor weather.

frost. A deposit of frozen moisture that adheres to surfaces when both the air and surface temperatures are below freezing. Frost is not dew that freezes or rain that freezes to a surface. Frost creates a rough surface, which can disrupt airflow if it forms on an airfoil, significantly reducing performance (or even preventing flight).

Global Positioning System (GPS). A U.S.-based network of satellites that provide very accurate position information for navigation purposes. GPS is one of several Global Navigation Satellite Systems (GNSS); for example, Russia has its own system called GLONASS.

ground control station (GCS). The means of controlling a UAS. Also known as the controller.

ground effect. An aerodynamic effect when an airfoil comes near a surface (i.e., the ground) during which a portion of the airfoil drag is reduced. This increases performance slightly. Most notably, a fixed-wing aircraft may "float" when it gets close to the ground during landing.

ground speed (GS). The speed at which an aircraft travels in reference to objects on the ground. For example, an aircraft flying into a 20-knot headwind with an airspeed of 100 knots will only cross the ground at 80 knots. Thus we would say it has a ground speed of 80 knots.

ground visibility. *See* visibility.

heliport. An airport for rotorcraft such as helicopters. Instead of runways, heliports have one or more helipads, which are pieces of pavement to and from which helicopters/rotorcraft operate.

icing. The accumulation of frozen liquid on an aircraft or other object.

inertial measurement unit (IMU). A circuit that is capable of detecting movements and accelerations in different axes. IMUs are used by some sUAS for stability enhancement, navigation, and control.

instrument flight rules (IFR). A set of FAA rules that applies to aircraft that fly on IFR flight plans and to allow aircraft to fly in poor weather (less than 3 SM visibility and cloud ceiling heights below 1,000 AGL—referred to as Instrument Meteorological Conditions or IMC). IFR aircraft primarily navigate with sophisticated instruments and navigation systems, such as GPS.

Integrated Airman Certification and/or Rating Application (IACRA). The FAA's electronic application system, which should be used when applying for your remote pilot certificate.

knot. A unit of speed equivalent to one nautical mile per hour.

landing. The phase of flight when an aircraft is being recovered from flight. Landing also refers to the actual moment when an aircraft comes in contact with the appropriate surface to end a flight.

lapse rate. The rate at which temperature (or other measures) change with changes in altitude. In the International Standard Atmosphere (ISA), the temperature decreases at 2 degrees Celsius per 1,000 feet of altitude.

latitude. The navigation reference lines that are parallel to the equator. They are designated as north or south of the equator. Latitude is measured in degrees, minutes, and seconds. Each minute of latitude is approximately equal to 1 nautical mile (NM).

leading edge. The front surface of an airfoil. The surface of the airfoil that first contacts oncoming air.

left traffic. A traffic pattern in which all turns are to the left. Aircraft are to the left of the landing runway in this type of pattern. For example, if operating from runway 36 (to the north), left traffic would take the aircraft to the west while in the traffic pattern.

lift. The force of flight that supports the aircraft in the air. It acts vertically in opposition to weight.

lithium polymer (LiPo) battery. A rechargeable battery that uses lithium and a gelled polymer electrolyte in a pouch-like housing. The average consumer LiPo battery is essentially a Lithium-ion battery with minor modifications. LiPo batteries are preferred to NiCad batteries due to their lighter weight, higher capacities, and high potential discharge rates. Unfortunately, they are more susceptible to failure and fire. LiPo fires can quickly become uncontrollable.

load factor. The ratio of lift required to weight. Due to acceleration forces, when an aircraft enters a turn while holding altitude, the actual lift required to support it increases. Thus, a 100-pound sUAS in a steep turn (60 degrees) may, in fact, need to produce 200 pounds of lift.

longitude. The navigation reference lines that run from the north pole to the south pole. They are designated as east or west of the prime meridian, which passes through Greenwich, England. The other east/west border is the international date line in the Pacific Ocean.

magnetometer. An electronic, magnetic field detector. In short, it is a fancy term for an electric compass. Magnetometers are used by some sUAS for navigation and orientation purposes.

Military Operations Area (MOA). A type of special use airspace, designed to separate military aircraft training and activities occurring in the designated area from non-military air traffic. Remote pilots should avoid flight in these areas when they are active (referred to as "hot").

Military Training Route (MTR). Military flight routes indicated on aeronautical charts. The aircraft flying on MTRs tend to operate at high speeds and potentially at low altitudes. Remote pilots should use caution when operating near MTRs.

multicopter. A rotorcraft that utilizes more than one rotor/propeller system.

National Airspace System (NAS). The various types of airspace that exist in the United States as well as the systems that support this airspace (e.g., air traffic control).

National Transportation Safety Board (NTSB). The agency in charge of investigating transportation accidents in the United States. sUAS involved in accidents that meet certain parameters are required to report such events to the NTSB.

nautical mile (NM). A distance of 6,076 feet or approximately 1.15 statute miles. NM are used for most aviation navigation distance measurements.

nickel cadmium (NiCad) battery. A rechargeable battery that utilizes nickel (oxide hydroxide) and metallic cadmium as conductors.

Notice to Airmen (NOTAM). A notification of a change to expected or documented procedures or operations. For example, a NOTAM may be used to notify that a control tower frequency has been changed or that airspace is restricted due to the President being in the area. Be sure to check for NOTAMs before each flight to avoid unwanted attention from the FAA or law enforcement.

pilot-in-command (PIC). The person in charge of the operation of an aircraft. In the case of UAS, they are referred to as the remote PIC. Note: the remote PIC does not necessarily have to be at the controls of the UAS.

precipitation. Any liquid that falls from the sky. Examples include rain, drizzle, sleet, snow, and hail. Generally, precipitation and sUAS operations do not mix.

prohibited airspace. Designated areas of airspace in which all types of aircraft operations are prohibited. Although the regulations state that you can enter these areas with the permission of the controlling agency, this is not likely (unless you are the U.S. military or other government agency).

propeller. Essentially a set or array of rotating airfoils. Propellers produce thrust (lift) that can be used to push an aircraft forward or, in the case of multicopters, to take the aircraft aloft.

quadcopter. A rotorcraft with four motors and propellers.

relative wind. The airflow that moves parallel to and in the opposite direction of the movement of the aircraft (or airfoil). The angle between the relative wind and the chord line is referred to as the angle of attack (AOA).

remotely piloted aircraft system (RPAS). The term used by many countries outside the United States to describe UA or UAS. RPAS is synonymous with UAS.

remote pilot-in-command (remote PIC). The person in charge of the operation of a UAS. Note: the remote PIC does not necessarily have to be at the controls of the UAS.

restricted airspace. Designated areas of airspace in which certain types of aircraft operations are restricted. Although the regulations state that you can enter these areas with the permission of the controlling agency, this is not likely unless you are a participant or the restricted airspace is not currently effective (referred to as being "cold"). Restricted airspace can have dangerous and sometimes invisible hazards to aviation operations.

right traffic. A traffic pattern in which all turns are to the right. Aircraft are to the right of the landing runway in this type of pattern. For example, if operating from runway 36 (to the north), right traffic would take the aircraft to the east while in the traffic pattern.

ring vortex state (RVS). An aerodynamic condition that causes a disruption of airflow in the vicinity of rotor/propeller blades of rotorcraft. This occurs when the aircraft is descending at slow speed and in a steep, vertical manner. If left unchecked, it can lead to loss of control and/or a rapid increase in descent rate.

risk management. A procedure of predicting and assessing risks that may be encountered in flight so as to identify procedures to avoid or mitigate their impact.

revolutions per minute (RPM). Also referred to rotations per minute. The number of times a component, such as a motor or propeller, spins each minute.

rotor. The non-stationary part of a motor or engine. In the case of sUAS, it is the component of a motor/engine that drives propeller or rotor blades.

rotor blade. Essentially a large propeller blade, normally associated with helicopters and other rotorcraft, that produces the lift/thrust required to attain flight.

rotorcraft. An aircraft in which the primary lift-generation airfoil rotates, such as in the form of rotor blades or alternatively, vertically mounted propellers.

runway. Pavement used by aircraft for takeoff and landing. Although runways are typically reserved for manned aircraft, they may be needed by larger UAS.

seaplane base. An airport for seaplanes and amphibious aircraft. Waterways, lakes, and other bodies of water serve as the "runways" for these aircraft.

Significant Meteorological Information (SIGMET). A weather warning covering a specific area and that is applicable to all types of aircraft and UAS (e.g., for extreme and dangerous conditions).

small unmanned aircraft system (sUAS). UAS that are below 55 pounds (25 kg).

special use airspace (SUA). Airspace that is subject to special controls or restrictions. Examples include Military Operations Areas (MOAs) and Restricted Airspace.

stability (atmospheric). The general condition of the atmosphere in reference to how conducive such conditions are to the development of bad weather, namely convective activity. Unstable air has a higher tendency to produce turbulence, cumulus clouds, and thunderstorms than stable air. One can gauge the stability of the atmosphere by comparing ambient lapse rates with the standard lapse rate of 2 degrees Celsius per 1,000 feet. If the temperature decreases at a faster lapse rate (more than 2 degrees), the atmosphere is said to be unstable. The larger the deviation, the more unstable it is. The reverse is true: if temperature decreases at a rate less than 2 degrees (or even increases), we say that the atmosphere is stable.

stall. An aerodynamic condition in which the airflow over the top of the airfoil becomes detached, dramatically reducing the lift produced. This occurs when the angle of attack reaches or exceeds the critical angle of attack. This can occur if the aircraft flies too slow, pitches up too high, or conducts maneuvers that are too abrupt. The only way to recover from a stall is to reduce the angle of attack.

statute mile (SM). A distance of 5,280 feet. Commonly referred to as miles in non-aviation contexts. SM are sometimes used for distances in aviation, such as in aviation weather reports (METARs and TAFs).

stratus cloud. A type of cloud produced in stable air. Stratus clouds are sheet-like in appearance and are generally associated with smooth air.

take off. The maneuver in which an aircraft leaves the ground; the moment when the aircraft leaves the surface.

taxiway. Pavement used by aircraft to maneuver (taxi) to and from runways. Taxiways are typically reserved for manned aircraft; however, larger UAS may require the use of taxiways in some cases.

temperature. The amount of energy in the atmosphere measured in degrees Celsius (in aviation weather products).

temporary flight restriction (TFR). A restriction to flight operations issued via NOTAM. Flight into a TFR can have dramatic consequences usually involving law enforcement or government agencies. Be careful to avoid TFRs.

terminal area forecast (TAF). An aviation weather forecast for a specific airport. In general, the predicted weather is limited to within 5 miles of the airport, although this product can provide limited additional information to a 10-mile radius.

thermal. Upwards movement of air typically as a result of terrestrial heating. Thermals can be used for lift by aircraft, specifically gliders.

thrust. The aerodynamic force that opposes drag. The force produced by propeller or rotor blades.

thunderstorm. A cumulus cloud that becomes large enough to produce significant rainfall and lightning. Thunderstorms may also produce strong gusts, downdrafts, and hail.

traffic pattern. The rectangular pattern aircraft follow as they maneuver in the proximity of an airport. Aircraft enter, exit, or remain within the pattern depending upon their destination and intent.

trailing edge. The aft edge of an airfoil.

Transportation Security Administration (TSA). The government entity charged with the safety of transportation in the United States. The TSA vets potential remote pilots prior to the FAA issuing permanent certificates.

true airspeed (TAS). The speed at which an aircraft moves through the air. Simply, how fast air molecules pass by the aircraft. In still air, TAS will equal ground speed.

turbulence. Atmospheric condition that causes aircraft instability during flight. This can be caused by wind shear, thermals, or other disruptive conditions.

uncontrolled airspace. Airspace in which aircraft are not subject to air traffic control. Uncontrolled airspace is also referred to as Class G.

Universal Communications (UNICOM). A private, non-air traffic control radio facility that provides advisory communications capabilities for aircraft. It can be used to request services and assistance from onsite businesses or other providers. UNICOM is often available at both towered and non-towered airports.

Universal Time Coordinated (UTC). A standard time used in aviation operations based upon the time in Greenwich, England, uncorrected for daylight savings. Given in 24-hour time (military) format. Also referred to as ZULU time. UTC is used in communications, NOTAMs, and weather forecasts.

unmanned aircraft (UA). A term used to describe the actual aircraft that is part of a UAS (i.e., it excludes the ground station/controller).

unmanned aircraft system (UAS). The total system associated with an unmanned aircraft to include the ground station/controller, sensors, processors, and other components. Generically, it is used to describe what is also referred to as a drone or remote-controlled aircraft. Previously referred to as unmanned aerial vehicles (UAV).

unmanned aerial vehicles (UAV). *See* unmanned aircraft system (UAS).

upwind. The leg of an airport traffic pattern that occurs parallel to the departure runway immediately following take-off. The aircraft then turns 90-degrees to enter the crosswind leg. This can also be used to describe aircraft operations into the wind.

variation. The difference between references to magnetic and true north. For example, if you align your aircraft with a line of longitude facing the true north pole (360 or 000 degrees), and your magnetic compass (which points to the magnetic north pole) indicates a 010 heading, you have 10 degrees of variation.

virga. Precipitation that evaporates before it reaches the surface. Virga is usually associated with turbulent conditions.

visibility. The distance at which you can see prominent objects. Flight visibility refers to the ability to see prominent objects from the perspective of the cockpit (or ground control station), i.e., slant visibility. Ground visibility is that which is reported in weather reports and is controlling for manned aircraft in terms of adherence to the applicable flight rules (VFR or IFR).

visual flight rules (VFR). The set of FAA regulations that dictate operations by aircraft that are not flying under IFR. VFR flight requires good weather conditions (i.e., more than 3 SM visibility and cloud ceiling heights above 1,000). VFR aircraft navigate with the assistance of visual cues.

visual line-of-sight (VLOS). The remote pilot's ability to see the UAS without any aids to vision (such as using FPV or binoculars).

visual observer (VO). A crewmember who is responsible for maintaining visual contact with the sUAS and communicating this information to the remote pilot-in-command and person operating the controls.

very high frequency omnidirectional range (VOR). A navigational aid used by aircraft, often to define aircraft routes or position.

very high frequency omnidirectional range with tactical air navigation (VORTAC). A navigational aid used by aircraft, often to define aircraft routes or position coupled with a similar system used by military aircraft, Tactical Air Navigation (TACAN). This type of facility provides distance information from the facility with the appropriate onboard equipment.

volt. A measure of electromotive force or potential. It is the electrical "push" available. Using water as an example, it would be equivalent to the water pressure.

waiver. An authorization provided by the FAA for specific sUAS operations. Persons can apply for waivers directly with the FAA. Examples of potential waivable activities include operations in Class B airspace or at night.

wake turbulence. Turbulent air created behind, under, or near an aircraft as a result of the generation of lift (wing or rotor vortices) or from engine thrust.

warm front. The division line between air masses in which the approaching air mass is warmer than the region adjacent to it. This weather phenomenon is indicated on weather maps with a red line with half-circles pointing in the direction in which the front is moving. Warm fronts usually move slowly and have poor weather over a wide band ahead of the frontal boundary.

warning area. Designated areas of airspace in which there are certain dangerous and sometimes invisible hazards to aviation operations, much like restricted airspace. However, because warning areas are located far enough offshore to be outside of the authority of the United States, such airspace cannot technically be restricted.

weight. The force imparted on an aircraft due to the effect of gravity. This force is what must be countered by lift to support an aircraft in flight.

weight and balance. The procedure of properly loading an aircraft within its operational limits to ensure that it remains controllable and has the expected or printed performance capabilities specified by the manufacturer.

wildlife refuge area. An area in which manned aircraft are requested to avoid overflying at low altitude. These areas are designated to avoid disrupting local animal life. It is advisable that sUAS operations remain well clear of these areas. Violation of this airspace may open the operator to enforcement actions or liabilities to agencies other than the FAA.

wind shear. A rapid change in wind direction and/or speed. Wind shear can have a major impact on the controllability of an aircraft. It occurs when wind is affected by terrain or obstructions as well as poor weather conditions. Air traffic control will report wind shear on local frequencies, and if wind shear is present, sUAS operations should be terminated or conducted with extreme caution.

wing. The part of an aircraft that typically acts as the means to generate lift (i.e., an airfoil). Wings can also house electronic equipment, engines/motors, fuel, landing gear, and other components.

APPENDIX B

Chart Supplement Legend: Airport/Facility Directory

AIRPORT/FACILITY DIRECTORY LEGEND

SAMPLE

① CITY NAME

② AIRPORT NAME (ALTERNATE NAME) ③ (LTS)(KLTS) ④ CIV/MIL ⑤ 3 N ⑥ UTC–6(–5DT) ⑦ N34°41.93′ W99°20.20′ ⑧ JACKSONVILLE COPTER

⑪ 200 ⑫ B ⑬ TPA—1000(800) ⑭ AOE LRA ⑮ Class IV, ARFF Index A ⑯ NOTAM FILE ORL ⑰ Not insp. H–4G, L–19C IAP, DIAP, AD

⑨

⑱→ RWY 18–36: H12004X200 (ASPH–CONC–GRVD)
　　S–90, D–160, 2D–300 PCN 80 R/B/W/T HIRL CL
　　RWY 18: RLLS. MALSF. TDZL. REIL. PAPI(P2R)—GA 3.0° TCH 36′.
　　RVR–TMR. Thld dsplcd 300′. Trees. Rgt tfc. 0.3% up.
　　RWY 36: ALSF1. 0.4% down.
　　RWY 09–27: H6000X150 (ASPH) MIRL
　　RWY 173–353: H3515X150 (ASPH–PFC) AUW PCN 59 F/A/W/T

⑲→ LAND AND HOLD–SHORT OPERATIONS

LDG RWY	HOLD–SHORT POINT	AVBL LDG DIST
RWY 18	09–27	6500
RWY 36	09–27	5400

⑳→ RUNWAY DECLARED DISTANCE INFORMATION
　　RWY 18: TORA–12004 TODA–12004 ASDA–11704 LDA–11504
　　RWY 36: TORA–12004 TODA–12004 ASDA–12004 LDA–11704

㉑→ ARRESTING GEAR/SYSTEM
　　RWY 18 HOOK E5 (65′ OVRN) BAK–14 BAK–12B (1650′)
　　　　　　BAK–14 BAK–12B (1087′) HOOK E5 (74′ OVRN) RWY 36

㉒→ SERVICE: S4 FUEL 100LL, JET A OX 1, 3 LGT ACTIVATE MALSR Rwy
　　29, REIL Rwy 11, VASI Rwy 11, HIRL Rwy 11–29, PAPI Rwy 17
　　and Rwy 35, MIRL Rwy 17–35—CTAF. MILITARY—A–GEAR E–5
　　connected on dep end, disconnected on apch end.
　　JASU 3(AM32A–60) 2(A/M32A–86) FUEL J8(Mil)(NC–100, A)
　　FLUID W SP PRESAIR LOX OIL O–128 MAINT S1 Mon–Fri 1000–2200Z‡
　　TRAN ALERT Avbl 1300–0200Z‡ svc limited weekends.

㉓→ AIRPORT REMARKS: Special Air Traffic Rules—Part 93, see Regulatory Notices. Attended 1200–0300Z‡. Parachute Jumping. Deer invof arpt. Heavy jumbo jet training surface to 9000′. Twy A clsd indef. Flight Notification Service (ADCUS) avbl.

㉔→ MILITARY REMARKS: ANG PPR/Official Business Only. Base OPS DSN 638–4390, C503–335–4222. Ctc Base OPS 15 minutes prior to ldg and after dep. Limited tran parking.

㉕→ AIRPORT MANAGER: (580) 481–5739

㉖→ WEATHER DATA SOURCES: AWOS–1 120.3 (202) 426–8000. LAWRS.

㉗→ COMMUNICATIONS: SFA CTAF 122.8 UNICOM 122.95 ATIS 127.25 273.5 (202) 426–8003 PTD 372.2
　　NAME FSS (ORL) on arpt. 123.65 122.65 122.2
　　NAME RCO 112.2T 112.1R (NAME RADIO)
　　Ⓡ NAME APP/DEP CON 128.35 257.725 (1200–0400Z‡)
　　TOWER 119.65 255.6 (1200–0400Z‡) GND CON 121.7 GCO 135.075 (ORLANDO CLNC) CLNC DEL 125.55
　　CPDLC D–HZWXR, D–TAXI, DCL (LOGON KMEM)
　　NAME COMD POST (GERONIMO) 311.0 321.4 6761 PMSV METRO 239.8 NAME OPS 257.5

㉘→ AIRSPACE: CLASS B See VFR Terminal Area Chart.

㉙→ VOR TEST FACILITY (VOT): 116.7

㉚→ RADIO AIDS TO NAVIGATION: NOTAM FILE ORL. VHF/DF ctc FSS.
　　(H) VORTAC 112.2 MCO Chan 59 N28°32.55′ W81°20.12′ at fld. 1110/8E.
　　(H) TACAN Chan 29 CBU (109.2) N28°32.65′ W81°21.12′ at fld. 1115/8E.
　　HERNY NDB (LOM) 221 OR N28°37.40′ W81°21.05′ 177° 5.4 NM to fld.
　　ILS/DME 108.5 I–ORL Chan 22 Rwy 18. Class IIE. LOM HERNY NDB.
　　ASR/PAR (1200–0400Z‡)

㉛→ COMM/NAV/WEATHER REMARKS: Emerg frequency 121.5 not avbl at twr.

• • • • • • • • • • •

HELIPAD H1: H100X75 (ASPH)
HELIPAD H2: H60X60 (ASPH)
HELIPORT REMARKS: Helipad H1 lctd on general aviation side and H2 lctd on air carrier side of arpt. ①

• • • • • • • • • • •

187 TPA 1000(813)
WATERWAY 15–33: 5000X425 (WATER)
SEAPLANE REMARKS: Birds roosting and feeding areas along river banks. Seaplanes operating adjacent to SW side of arpt not visible from twr and are required to ctc twr.

Rwy 173–353: 3515 X 150 ⑩

All bearings and radials are magnetic unless otherwise specified. All mileages are nautical unless otherwise noted.
All times are Coordinated Universal Time (UTC) except as noted. All elevations are in feet above/below Mean Sea Level (MSL) unless otherwise noted.
The horizontal reference datum of this publication is North American Datum of 1983 (NAD83), which for charting purposes is considered equivalent to World Geodetic System 1984 (WGS 84).

AIRPORT/FACILITY DIRECTORY LEGEND

⑩ ## SKETCH LEGEND

RUNWAYS/LANDING AREAS

Hard Surfaced . . . .

Metal Surface . . . .

Sod, Gravel, etc. . . . .

Light Plane, ...
Ski Landing Area or Water

Under Construction . . . . .

Closed . . . .

Helicopter Landings Area . . . . Ⓗ

Displaced Threshold . . . .

Taxiway, Apron and Stopways . .

MISCELLANEOUS BASE AND CULTURAL FEATURES

Buildings . . . .

Power Lines . . . . —T—T—

Fence . . . .   ×××××××

Towers . . . .

Wind Turbine. . . . .

Tanks . . . .

Oil Well . . . .

Smoke Stack . . . .

Obstruction . . . .   5812 ∧

Controlling Obstruction . . . .   +5812

Trees . . . .

Populated Places . . . .

Cuts and Fills . . . . . .   Cut   Fill

Cliffs and Depressions . .

Ditch . . . .

Hill . . . .

RADIO AIDS TO NAVIGATION

VORTAC . . . ⬡   VOR . . . . ⬡

VOR/DME . . ⬡   NDB . . . . ◉

TACAN . . . .   NDB/DME . . . . ◙

DME . . . . ☐

MISCELLANEOUS AERONAUTICAL FEATURES

Airport Beacon . . . .   ☆ ✪

Wind Cone . . . .

Landing Tee . . . .

Tetrahedron . . . .

Control Tower . . . .   or TWR

When control tower and rotating beacon
are co-located beacon symbol will be
used and further identified as TWR.

APPROACH LIGHTING SYSTEMS

A dot "•" portrayed with approach lighting
letter identifier indicates sequenced flashing
lights (F) installed with the approach lighting
system e.g. Ⓐ) Negative symbology, e.g., Ⓐ)

Ⓥ indicates Pilot Controlled Lighting (PCL).

Runway Centerline Lighting . . . . .

Ⓐ Approach Lighting System ALSF-2 . .

Ⓐ₁ Approach Lighting System ALSF-1 . .

Ⓐ₂ Short Approach Lighting System
     SALS/SALSF . . . .

Ⓐ₃ Simplified Short Approach Lighting
     System (SSALR) with RAIL . . . . .

Ⓐ₄ Medium Intensity Approach Lighting System
     (MALS and MALSF)/(SSALS
     and SSALF) . . . .

Ⓐ₅ Medium Intensity Approach Lighting
     System (MALSR) and RAIL . . . . . .

⊕ Omnidirectional Approach
     Lighting System (ODALS) . . . .

Ⓓ Navy Parallel Row and Cross Bar . . .

⊕ Air Force Overrun . . . .

Ⓥ Visual Approach Slope Indicator with
     Standard Threshold Clearance provided

Ⓥ₂ Pulsating Visual Approach Slope Indicator
     (PVASI)

Ⓥ₃ Visual Approach Slope Indicator with a
     threshold crossing height to accomodate
     long bodied or jumbo aircraft

Ⓥ₄ Tri-color Visual Approach Slope Indicator
     (TRCV)

Ⓥ₅ Approach Path Alignment Panel (APAP)

Ⓟ Precision Approach Path Indicator (PAPI)

AIRPORT/FACILITY DIRECTORY LEGEND

LEGEND

This directory is a listing of data on record with the FAA on public–use airports, military airports and selected private–use airports specifically requested by the Department of Defense (DoD) for which a DoD Instrument Approach Procedure has been published in the U.S. Terminal Procedures Publication. Additionally this listing contains data for associated terminal control facilities, air route traffic control centers, and radio aids to navigation within the conterminous United States, Puerto Rico and the Virgin Islands. Civil airports and joint Civil/Military airports which are open to the public are listed alphabetically by state, associated city and airport name and cross–referenced by airport name. Military airports and private–use (limited civil access) joint Military/Civil airports are listed alphabetically by state and official airport name and cross–referenced by associated city name. Navaids, flight service stations and remote communication outlets that are associated with an airport, but with a different name, are listed alphabetically under their own name, as well as under the airport with which they are associated.

The listing of an airport as open to the public in this directory merely indicates the airport operator's willingness to accommodate transient aircraft, and does not represent that the airport conforms with any Federal or local standards, or that it has been approved for use on the part of the general public. Military airports, private–use airports, and private–use (limited civil access) joint Military/Civil airports are open to civil pilots only in an emergency or with prior permission. See Special Notice Section, Civil Use of Military Fields.

The information on obstructions is taken from reports submitted to the FAA. Obstruction data has not been verified in all cases. Pilots are cautioned that objects not indicated in this tabulation (or on the airports sketches and/or charts) may exist which can create a hazard to flight operation. Detailed specifics concerning services and facilities tabulated within this directory are contained in the Aeronautical Information Manual, Basic Flight Information and ATC Procedures.

The legend items that follow explain in detail the contents of this Directory and are keyed to the circled numbers on the sample on the preceding pages.

① CITY/AIRPORT NAME

Civil and joint Civil/Military airports which are open to the public are listed alphabetically by state and associated city. Where the city name is different from the airport name the city name will appear on the line above the airport name. Airports with the same associated city name will be listed alphabetically by airport name and will be separated by a dashed rule line. A solid rule line will separate all others. FAA approved helipads and seaplane landing areas associated with a land airport will be separated by a dotted line. Military airports and private–use (limited civil access) joint Military/Civil airports are listed alphabetically by state and official airport name.

② ALTERNATE NAME

Alternate names, if any, will be shown in parentheses.

③ LOCATION IDENTIFIER

The location identifier is a three or four character FAA code followed by a four–character ICAO code, when assigned, to airports. If two different military codes are assigned, both codes will be shown with the primary operating agency's code listed first. These identifiers are used by ATC in lieu of the airport name in flight plans, flight strips and other written records and computer operations. Zeros will appear with a slash to differentiate them from the letter "O".

④ OPERATING AGENCY

Airports within this directory are classified into two categories, Military/Federal Government and Civil airports open to the general public, plus selected private–use airports. The operating agency is shown for military, private–use and joint use airports. The operating agency is shown by an abbreviation as listed below. When an organization is a tenant, the abbreviation is enclosed in parenthesis. No classification indicates the airport is open to the general public with no military tenant.

A	US Army	MC	Marine Corps
AFRC	Air Force Reserve Command	MIL/CIV	Joint Use Military/Civil Limited Civil Access
AF	US Air Force	N	Navy
ANG	Air National Guard	NAF	Naval Air Facility
AR	US Army Reserve	NAS	Naval Air Station
ARNG	US Army National Guard	NASA	National Air and Space Administration
CG	US Coast Guard	P	US Civil Airport Wherein Permit Covers Use by
CIV/MIL	Joint Use Civil/Military Open to the Public		Transient Military Aircraft
DND	Department of National Defense Canada	PVT	Private Use Only (Closed to the Public)

⑤ AIRPORT LOCATION

Airport location is expressed as distance and direction from the center of the associated city in nautical miles and cardinal points, e.g., 4 NE.

⑥ TIME CONVERSION

Hours of operation of all facilities are expressed in Coordinated Universal Time (UTC) and shown as "Z" time. The directory indicates the number of hours to be subtracted from UTC to obtain local standard time and local daylight saving time UTC–5(–4DT). The symbol ‡ indicates that during periods of Daylight Saving Time (DST) effective hours will be one hour earlier than shown. In those areas where daylight saving time is not observed the (–4DT) and ‡ will not be shown. Daylight saving time is in effect from 0200 local time the second Sunday in March to 0200 local time the first Sunday in November. Canada and all U.S. Conterminous States observe daylight saving time except Arizona and Puerto Rico, and the Virgin Islands. If the state observes daylight saving time and the operating times are other than daylight saving times, the operating hours will include the dates, times and no ‡ symbol will be shown, i.e., April 15–Aug 31 0630–1700Z, Sep 1–Apr 14 0600–1700Z.

AIRPORT/FACILITY DIRECTORY LEGEND

⑦ **GEOGRAPHIC POSITION OF AIRPORT—AIRPORT REFERENCE POINT (ARP)**

Positions are shown as hemisphere, degrees, minutes and hundredths of a minute and represent the approximate geometric center of all usable runway surfaces.

⑧ **CHARTS**

Charts refer to the Sectional Chart and Low and High Altitude Enroute Chart and panel on which the airport or facility is located. Helicopter Chart locations will be indicated as COPTER. IFR Gulf of Mexico West and IFR Gulf of Mexico Central will be depicted as GOMW and GOMC.

⑨ **INSTRUMENT APPROACH PROCEDURES, AIRPORT DIAGRAMS**

IAP indicates an airport for which a prescribed (Public Use) FAA Instrument Approach Procedure has been published. DIAP indicates an airport for which a prescribed DoD Instrument Approach Procedure has been published in the U.S. Terminal Procedures. See the Special Notice Section of this directory, Civil Use of Military Fields and the Aeronautical Information Manual 5–4–5 Instrument Approach Procedure Charts for additional information. AD indicates an airport for which an airport diagram has been published. Airport diagrams are located in the back of each Chart Supplement volume alphabetically by associated city and airport name.

⑩ **AIRPORT SKETCH**

The airport sketch, when provided, depicts the airport and related topographical information as seen from the air and should be used in conjunction with the text. It is intended as a guide for pilots in VFR conditions. Symbology that is not self–explanatory will be reflected in the sketch legend. The airport sketch will be oriented with True North at the top. Airport sketches will be added incrementally.

⑪ **ELEVATION**

The highest point of an airport's usable runways measured in feet from mean sea level. When elevation is sea level it will be indicated as "00". When elevation is below sea level a minus "–" sign will precede the figure.

⑫ **ROTATING LIGHT BEACON**

B indicates rotating beacon is available. Rotating beacons operate sunset to sunrise unless otherwise indicated in the AIRPORT REMARKS or MILITARY REMARKS segment of the airport entry.

⑬ **TRAFFIC PATTERN ALTITUDE**

Traffic Pattern Altitude (TPA)—The first figure shown is TPA above mean sea level. The second figure in parentheses is TPA above airport elevation. Multiple TPA shall be shown as "TPA—See Remarks" and detailed information shall be shown in the Airport or Military Remarks Section. Traffic pattern data for USAF bases, USN facilities, and U.S. Army airports (including those on which ACC or U.S. Army is a tenant) that deviate from standard pattern altitudes shall be shown in Military Remarks.

⑭ **AIRPORT OF ENTRY, LANDING RIGHTS, AND CUSTOMS USER FEE AIRPORTS**

U.S. CUSTOMS USER FEE AIRPORT—Private Aircraft operators are frequently required to pay the costs associated with customs processing.

AOE—Airport of Entry. A customs Airport of Entry where permission from U.S. Customs is not required to land. However, at least one hour advance notice of arrival is required.

LRA—Landing Rights Airport. Application for permission to land must be submitted in advance to U.S. Customs. At least one hour advance notice of arrival is required.

NOTE: Advance notice of arrival at both an AOE and LRA airport may be included in the flight plan when filed in Canada or Mexico. Where Flight Notification Service (ADCUS) is available the airport remark will indicate this service. This notice will also be treated as an application for permission to land in the case of an LRA. Although advance notice of arrival may be relayed to Customs through Mexico, Canada, and U.S. Communications facilities by flight plan, the aircraft operator is solely responsible for ensuring that Customs receives the notification. (See Customs, Immigration and Naturalization, Public Health and Agriculture Department requirements in the International Flight Information Manual for further details.)

U.S. CUSTOMS AIR AND SEA PORTS, INSPECTORS AND AGENTS

Northeast Sector (New England and Atlantic States—ME to MD)	407–975–1740
Southeast Sector (Atlantic States—DC, WV, VA to FL)	407–975–1780
Central Sector (Interior of the US, including Gulf states—MS, AL, LA)	407–975–1760
Southwest East Sector (OK and eastern TX)	407–975–1840
Southwest West Sector (Western TX, NM and AZ)	407–975–1820
Pacific Sector (WA, OR, CA, HI and AK)	407–975–1800

⑮ **CERTIFICATED AIRPORT (14 CFR PART 139)**

Airports serving Department of Transportation certified carriers and certified under 14 CFR part 139 are indicated by the Class and the ARFF Index; e.g. Class I, ARFF Index A, which relates to the availability of crash, fire, rescue equipment. Class I airports can have an ARFF Index A through E, depending on the aircraft length and scheduled departures. Class II, III, and IV will always carry an Index A.

AIRPORT CLASSIFICATIONS

Type of Air Carrier Operation	Class I	Class II	Class III	Class IV
Scheduled Air Carrier Aircraft with 31 or more passenger seats	X			
Unscheduled Air Carrier Aircraft with 31 or more passengers seats	X	X		X
Scheduled Air Carrier Aircraft with 10 to 30 passenger seats	X	X	X	

AIRPORT/FACILITY DIRECTORY LEGEND

INDICES AND AIRCRAFT RESCUE AND FIRE FIGHTING EQUIPMENT REQUIREMENTS

Airport Index	Required No. Vehicles	Aircraft Length	Scheduled Departures	Agent + Water for Foam
A	1	<90′	≥1	500#DC or HALON 1211 or 450#DC + 100 gal H$_2$O
B	1 or 2	≥90′, <126′ ———— ≥126′, <159′	≥5 ———— <5	Index A + 1500 gal H$_2$O
C	2 or 3	≥126′, <159′ ———— ≥159′, <200′	≥5 ———— <5	Index A + 3000 gal H$_2$O
D	3	≥159′, <200′ ———— >200′	 ———— <5	Index A + 4000 gal H$_2$O
E	3	≥200′	≥5	Index A + 6000 gal H$_2$O

> Greater Than; < Less Than; ≥ Equal or Greater Than; ≤ Equal or Less Than;   H$_2$O–Water; DC–Dry Chemical.

NOTE: The listing of ARFF index does not necessarily assure coverage for non–air carrier operations or at other than prescribed times for air carrier. ARFF Index Ltd.—indicates ARFF coverage may or may not be available, for information contact airport manager prior to flight.

⑯ NOTAM SERVICE

All public use landing areas are provided NOTAM service. A NOTAM FILE identifier is shown for individual landing areas, e.g., "NOTAM FILE BNA". See the AIM, Basic Flight Information and ATC Procedures for a detailed description of NOTAMs. Current NOTAMs are available from flight service stations at 1–800–WX–BRIEF (992–7433) or online through the FAA PilotWeb at https://pilotweb.nas.faa.gov. Military NOTAMs are available using the Defense Internet NOTAM Service (DINS) at https://www.notams.faa.gov. Pilots flying to or from airports not available through the FAA PilotWeb or DINS can obtain assistance from Flight Service.

⑰ FAA INSPECTION

All airports not inspected by FAA will be identified by the note: Not insp. This indicates that the airport information has been provided by the owner or operator of the field.

⑱ RUNWAY DATA

Runway information is shown on two lines. That information common to the entire runway is shown on the first line while information concerning the runway ends is shown on the second or following line. Runway direction, surface, length, width, weight bearing capacity, lighting, and slope, when available are shown for each runway. Multiple runways are shown with the longest runway first. Direction, length, width, and lighting are shown for sea–lanes. The full dimensions of helipads are shown, e.g., 50X150. Runway data that requires clarification will be placed in the remarks section.

RUNWAY DESIGNATION

Runways are normally numbered in relation to their magnetic orientation rounded off to the nearest 10 degrees. Parallel runways can be designated L (left)/R (right)/C (center). Runways may be designated as Ultralight or assault strips. Assault strips are shown by magnetic bearing.

RUNWAY DIMENSIONS

Runway length and width are shown in feet. Length shown is runway end to end including displaced thresholds, but excluding those areas designed as overruns.

RUNWAY SURFACE AND SURFACE TREATMENT

Runway lengths prefixed by the letter "H" indicate that the runways are hard surfaced (concrete, asphalt, or part asphalt–concrete). If the runway length is not prefixed, the surface is sod, clay, etc. The runway surface composition is indicated in parentheses after runway length as follows:

(AFSC)—Aggregate friction seal coat	(GRVL)—Gravel, or cinders	(SAND)—Sand
(AM2)—Temporary metal planks coated with nonskid material	(MATS)—Pierced steel planking, landing mats, membranes	(TURF)—Turf
(ASPH)—Asphalt	(PEM)—Part concrete, part asphalt	(TRTD)—Treated
(CONC)—Concrete	(PFC)—Porous friction courses	(WC)—Wire combed
(DIRT)—Dirt	(PSP)—Pierced steel plank	
(GRVD)—Grooved	(RFSC)—Rubberized friction seal coat	

AIRPORT/FACILITY DIRECTORY LEGEND

RUNWAY WEIGHT BEARING CAPACITY

Runway strength data shown in this publication is derived from available information and is a realistic estimate of capability at an average level of activity. It is not intended as a maximum allowable weight or as an operating limitation. Many airport pavements are capable of supporting limited operations with gross weights in excess of the published figures. Permissible operating weights, insofar as runway strengths are concerned, are a matter of agreement between the owner and user. When desiring to operate into any airport at weights in excess of those published in the publication, users should contact the airport management for permission. Runway strength figures are shown in thousand of pounds, with the last three figures being omitted. Add 000 to figure following S, D, 2S, 2T, AUW, SWL, etc., for gross weight capacity. A blank space following the letter designator is used to indicate the runway can sustain aircraft with this type landing gear, although definite runway weight bearing capacity figures are not available, e.g., S, D. Applicable codes for typical gear configurations with S=Single, D=Dual, T=Triple and Q=Quadruple:

CURRENT	NEW	NEW DESCRIPTION
S	S	Single wheel type landing gear (DC3), (C47), (F15), etc.
D	D	Dual wheel type landing gear (BE1900), (B737), (A319), etc.
T	D	Dual wheel type landing gear (P3, C9).
ST	2S	Two single wheels in tandem type landing gear (C130).
TRT	2T	Two triple wheels in tandem type landing gear (C17), etc.
DT	2D	Two dual wheels in tandem type landing gear (B707), etc.
TT	2D	Two dual wheels in tandem type landing gear (B757, KC135).
SBTT	2D/D1	Two dual wheels in tandem/dual wheel body gear type landing gear (KC10).
None	2D/2D1	Two dual wheels in tandem/two dual wheels in tandem body gear type landing gear (A340–600).
DDT	2D/2D2	Two dual wheels in tandem/two dual wheels in double tandem body gear type landing gear (B747, E4).
TTT	3D	Three dual wheels in tandem type landing gear (B777), etc.
TT	D2	Dual wheel gear two struts per side main gear type landing gear (B52).
TDT	C5	Complex dual wheel and quadruple wheel combination landing gear (C5).

AUW—All up weight. Maximum weight bearing capacity for any aircraft irrespective of landing gear configuration.

SWL—Single Wheel Loading. (This includes information submitted in terms of Equivalent Single Wheel Loading (ESWL) and Single Isolated Wheel Loading).

PSI—Pounds per square inch. PSI is the actual figure expressing maximum pounds per square inch runway will support, e.g., (SWL 000/PSI 535).

Omission of weight bearing capacity indicates information unknown.

The ACN/PCN System is the ICAO standard method of reporting pavement strength for pavements with bearing strengths greater than 12,500 pounds. The Pavement Classification Number (PCN) is established by an engineering assessment of the runway. The PCN is for use in conjunction with an Aircraft Classification Number (ACN). Consult the Aircraft Flight Manual, Flight Information Handbook, or other appropriate source for ACN tables or charts. Currently, ACN data may not be available for all aircraft. If an ACN table or chart is available, the ACN can be calculated by taking into account the aircraft weight, the pavement type, and the subgrade category. For runways that have been evaluated under the ACN/PCN system, the PCN will be shown as a five–part code (e.g. PCN 80 R/B/W/T). Details of the coded format are as follows:

NOTE: Prior permission from the airport controlling authority is required when the ACN of the aircraft exceeds the published PCN or aircraft tire pressure exceeds the published limits.

(1) The PCN NUMBER—The reported PCN indicates that an aircraft with an ACN equal or less than the reported PCN can operate on the pavement subject to any limitation on the tire pressure.

(2) The type of pavement:
R — Rigid
F — Flexible

(3) The pavement subgrade category:
A — High
B — Medium
C — Low
D — Ultra–low

(4) The maximum tire pressure authorized for the pavement:
W — Unlimited, no pressure limit
X — High, limited to 254 psi (1.75 MPa)
Y — Medium, limited to 181 psi (1.25MPa)
Z — Low, limited to 73 psi (0.50 MPa)

(5) Pavement evaluation method:
T — Technical evaluation
U — By experience of aircraft using the pavement

RUNWAY LIGHTING

Lights are in operation sunset to sunrise. Lighting available by prior arrangement only or operating part of the night and/or pilot controlled lighting with specific operating hours are indicated under airport or military remarks. At USN/USMC facilities lights are available only during airport hours of operation. Since obstructions are usually lighted, obstruction lighting is not included in this code. Unlighted obstructions on or surrounding an airport will be noted in airport or military remarks. Runway lights nonstandard (NSTD) are systems for which the light fixtures are not FAA approved L–800 series: color, intensity, or spacing does not meet FAA standards. Nonstandard runway lights, VASI, or any other system not listed below will be shown in airport remarks or military

AIRPORT/FACILITY DIRECTORY LEGEND

service. Temporary, emergency or limited runway edge lighting such as flares, smudge pots, lanterns or portable runway lights will also be shown in airport remarks or military service. Types of lighting are shown with the runway or runway end they serve.

NSTD—Light system fails to meet FAA standards.
LIRL—Low Intensity Runway Lights.
MIRL—Medium Intensity Runway Lights.
HIRL—High Intensity Runway Lights.
RAIL—Runway Alignment Indicator Lights.
REIL—Runway End Identifier Lights.
CL—Centerline Lights.
TDZL—Touchdown Zone Lights.
ODALS—Omni Directional Approach Lighting System.
AF OVRN—Air Force Overrun 1000´ Standard Approach Lighting System.
MALS—Medium Intensity Approach Lighting System.
MALSF—Medium Intensity Approach Lighting System with Sequenced Flashing Lights.
MALSR—Medium Intensity Approach Lighting System with Runway Alignment Indicator Lights.
RLLS—Runway Lead–in Light System

SALS—Short Approach Lighting System.
SALSF—Short Approach Lighting System with Sequenced Flashing Lights.
SSALS—Simplified Short Approach Lighting System.
SSALF—Simplified Short Approach Lighting System with Sequenced Flashing Lights.
SSALR—Simplified Short Approach Lighting System with Runway Alignment Indicator Lights.
ALSAF—High Intensity Approach Lighting System with Sequenced Flashing Lights.
ALSF1—High Intensity Approach Lighting System with Sequenced Flashing Lights, Category I, Configuration.
ALSF2—High Intensity Approach Lighting System with Sequenced Flashing Lights, Category II, Configuration.
SF—Sequenced Flashing Lights.
OLS—Optical Landing System.
WAVE–OFF.

NOTE: Civil ALSF2 may be operated as SSALR during favorable weather conditions. When runway edge lights are positioned more than 10 feet from the edge of the usable runway surface a remark will be added in the "Remarks" portion of the airport entry. This is applicable to Air Force, Air National Guard and Air Force Reserve Bases, and those joint use airfields on which they are tenants.

VISUAL GLIDESLOPE INDICATORS

APAP—A system of panels, which may or may not be lighted, used for alignment of approach path.

PNIL	APAP on left side of runway	PNIR	APAP on right side of runway

PAPI—Precision Approach Path Indicator

P2L	2–identical light units placed on left side of runway	P4L	4–identical light units placed on left side of runway
P2R	2–identical light units placed on right side of runway	P4R	4–identical light units placed on right side of runway

PVASI—Pulsating/steady burning visual approach slope indicator, normally a single light unit projecting two colors.

PSIL	PVASI on left side of runway	PSIR	PVASI on right side of runway

SAVASI—Simplified Abbreviated Visual Approach Slope Indicator

S2L	2–box SAVASI on left side of runway	S2R	2–box SAVASI on right side of runway

TRCV—Tri–color visual approach slope indicator, normally a single light unit projecting three colors.

TRIL	TRCV on left side of runway	TRIR	TRCV on right side of runway

VASI—Visual Approach Slope Indicator

V2L	2–box VASI on left side of runway	V6L	6–box VASI on left side of runway
V2R	2–box VASI on right side of runway	V6R	6–box VASI on right side of runway
V4L	4–box VASI on left side of runway	V12	12–box VASI on both sides of runway
V4R	4–box VASI on right side of runway	V16	16–box VASI on both sides of runway

NOTE: Approach slope angle and threshold crossing height will be shown when available; i.e., –GA 3.5º TCH 37´.

PILOT CONTROL OF AIRPORT LIGHTING

Key Mike	Function
7 times within 5 seconds	Highest intensity available
5 times within 5 seconds	Medium or lower intensity (Lower REIL or REIL–Off)
3 times within 5 seconds	Lowest intensity available (Lower REIL or REIL–Off)

Available systems will be indicated in the Service section, e.g., **LGT** ACTIVATE HIRL Rwy 07–25, MALSR Rwy 07, and VASI Rwy 07—122.8.

Where the airport is not served by an instrument approach procedure and/or has an independent type system of different specification installed by the airport sponsor, descriptions of the type lights, method of control, and operating frequency will be explained in clear text. See AIM, "Basic Flight Information and ATC Procedures," for detailed description of pilot control of airport lighting.

RUNWAY SLOPE

When available, runway slope data will be provided. Runway slope will be shown only when it is 0.3 percent or greater. On runways less than 8000 feet, the direction of the slope up will be indicated, e.g., 0.3% up NW. On runways 8000 feet or greater, the slope will be shown (up or down) on the runway end line, e.g., RWY 13: 0.3% up., RWY 31: Pole. Rgt tfc. 0.4% down.

AIRPORT/FACILITY DIRECTORY LEGEND

RUNWAY END DATA

Information pertaining to the runway approach end such as approach lights, touchdown zone lights, runway end identification lights, visual glideslope indicators, displaced thresholds, controlling obstruction, and right hand traffic pattern, will be shown on the specific runway end. "Rgt tfc"—Right traffic indicates right turns should be made on landing and takeoff for specified runway end. Runway Visual Range shall be shown as "RVR" appended with "T" for touchdown, "M" for midpoint, and "R" for rollout; e.g., RVR-TMR.

⑲ **LAND AND HOLD–SHORT OPERATIONS (LAHSO)**

LAHSO is an acronym for "Land and Hold–Short Operations" These operations include landing and holding short of an intersection runway, an intersecting taxiway, or other predetermined points on the runway other than a runway or taxiway. Measured distance represents the available landing distance on the landing runway, in feet.

Specific questions regarding these distances should be referred to the air traffic manager of the facility concerned. The Aeronautical Information Manual contains specific details on hold–short operations and markings.

⑳ **RUNWAY DECLARED DISTANCE INFORMATION**

TORA—Take–off Run Available. The length of runway declared available and suitable for the ground run of an aeroplane take–off.
TODA—Take–off Distance Available. The length of the take–off run available plus the length of the clearway, if provided.
ASDA—Accelerate-Stop Distance Available. The length of the take–off run available plus the length of the stopway, if provided.
LDA—Landing Distance Available. The length of runway which is declared available and suitable for the ground run of an aeroplane landing.

㉑ **ARRESTING GEAR/SYSTEMS**

Arresting gear is shown as it is located on the runway. The a–gear distance from the end of the appropriate runway (or into the overrun) is indicated in parentheses. A–Gear which has a bi-direction capability and can be utilized for emergency approach end engagement is indicated by a (B). Up to 15 minutes advance notice may be required for rigging A–Gear for approach and engagement. Airport listing may show availability of other than US Systems. This information is provided for emergency requirements only. Refer to current aircraft operating manuals for specific engagement weight and speed criteria based on aircraft structural restrictions and arresting system limitations.

Following is a list of current systems referenced in this publication identified by both Air Force and Navy terminology:

BI–DIRECTIONAL CABLE (B)

TYPE	DESCRIPTION
BAK–9	Rotary friction brake.
BAK–12A	Standard BAK–12 with 950 foot run out, 1–inch cable and 40,000 pound weight setting. Rotary friction brake.
BAK–12B	Extended BAK–12 with 1200 foot run, 1¼ inch Cable and 50,000 pounds weight setting. Rotary friction brake.
E28	Rotary Hydraulic (Water Brake).
M21	Rotary Hydraulic (Water Brake) Mobile.

The following device is used in conjunction with some aircraft arresting systems:

BAK–14	A device that raises a hook cable out of a slot in the runway surface and is remotely positioned for engagement by the tower on request. (In addition to personnel reaction time, the system requires up to five seconds to fully raise the cable.)
H	A device that raises a hook cable out of a slot in the runway surface and is remotely positioned for engagement by the tower on request. (In addition to personnel reaction time, the system requires up to one and one–half seconds to fully raise the cable.)

UNI–DIRECTIONAL CABLE

TYPE	DESCRIPTION
MB60	Textile brake—an emergency one–time use, modular braking system employing the tearing of specially woven textile straps to absorb the kinetic energy.
E5/E5–1/E5–3	Chain Type. At USN/USMC stations E–5 A–GEAR systems are rated, e.g., E–5 RATING–13R–1100 HW (DRY), 31L/R–1200 STD (WET). This rating is a function of the A–GEAR chain weight and length and is used to determine the maximum aircraft engaging speed. A dry rating applies to a stabilized surface (dry or wet) while a wet rating takes into account the amount (if any) of wet overrun that is not capable of withstanding the aircraft weight. These ratings are published under Service/Military/A-Gear in the entry.

FOREIGN CABLE

TYPE	DESCRIPTION	US EQUIVALENT
44B–3H	Rotary Hydraulic (Water Brake)	
CHAG	Chain	E–5

UNI–DIRECTIONAL BARRIER

TYPE	DESCRIPTION
MA–1A	Web barrier between stanchions attached to a chain energy absorber.
BAK–15	Web barrier between stanchions attached to an energy absorber (water squeezer, rotary friction, chain). Designed for wing engagement.

NOTE: Landing short of the runway threshold on a runway with a BAK–15 in the underrun is a significant hazard. The barrier in the down position still protrudes several inches above the underrun. Aircraft contact with the barrier short of the runway threshold can cause damage to the barrier and substantial damage to the aircraft.

OTHER

TYPE	DESCRIPTION
EMAS	Engineered Material Arresting System, located beyond the departure end of the runway, consisting of high energy absorbing materials which will crush under the weight of an aircraft.

AIRPORT/FACILITY DIRECTORY LEGEND

22 SERVICE

SERVICING—CIVIL

S1: Minor airframe repairs.
S2: Minor airframe and minor powerplant repairs.
S3: Major airframe and minor powerplant repairs.
S4: Major airframe and major powerplant repairs.

S5: Major airframe repairs.
S6: Minor airframe and major powerplant repairs.
S7: Major powerplant repairs.
S8: Minor powerplant repairs.

FUEL—CIVIL

CODE	FUEL	CODE	FUEL
80	Grade 80 gasoline (Red)	A1+	Jet A–1, Kerosene with FS–II*, FP** minus 47° C.
100	Grade 100 gasoline (Green)	B	Jet B, Wide–cut, turbine fuel without
100LL	100LL gasoline (low lead) (Blue)		FS–II*, FP** minus 50° C.
115	Grade 115 gasoline (115/145 military specification) (Purple)	B+	Jet B, Wide–cut, turbine fuel with FS–II*, FP** minus 50° C
A	Jet A, Kerosene, without FS–II*, FP** minus 40° C.	J4 (JP4)	(JP–4 military specification) FP** minus 58° C.
A+	Jet A, Kerosene, with FS–II*, FP** minus 40ºC.	J5 (JP5)	(JP–5 military specification) Kerosene with FS–II, FP** minus 46ºC.
A++	Jet A, Kerosene, with FS–II*, CI/LI#, SDA##, FP** minus 40ºC.	J8 (JP8)	(JP–8 military specification) Jet A–1, Kerosene with FS–II*, CI/LI#, SDA##, FP** minus 47ºC.
A++100	Jet A, Kerosene, with FS–II*, CI/LI#, SDA##, FP** minus 40ºC, with +100 fuel additive that improves thermal stability characteristics of kerosene jet fuels.	J8+100	(JP–8 military specification) Jet A–1, Kerosene with FS–II*, CI/LI#, SDA##,FP** minus 47ºC, with +100 fuel additive that improves thermal stability characteristics of kerosene jet fuels.
A1	Jet A–1, Kerosene, without FS–II*, FP** minus 47ºC.	J	(Jet Fuel Type Unknown)
		MOGAS	Automobile gasoline which is to be used as aircraft fuel.

*(Fuel System Icing Inhibitor)   **(Freeze Point)   # (Corrosion Inhibitors/Lubricity Improvers)   ## (Static Dissipator Additive)

NOTE: Certain automobile gasoline may be used in specific aircraft engines if a FAA supplemental type certificate has been obtained. Automobile gasoline, which is to be used in aircraft engines, will be identified as "MOGAS", however, the grade/type and other octane rating will not be published.

Data shown on fuel availability represents the most recent information the publisher has been able to acquire. Because of a variety of factors, the fuel listed may not always be obtainable by transient civil pilots. Confirmation of availability of fuel should be made directly with fuel suppliers at locations where refueling is planned.

OXYGEN—CIVIL

OX 1   High Pressure
OX 2   Low Pressure

OX 3   High Pressure—Replacement Bottles
OX 4   Low Pressure—Replacement Bottles

SERVICE—MILITARY

Specific military services available at the airport are listed under this general heading. Remarks applicable to any military service are shown in the individual service listing.

JET AIRCRAFT STARTING UNITS (JASU)—MILITARY

The numeral preceding the type of unit indicates the number of units available. The absence of the numeral indicates ten or more units available. If the number of units is unknown, the number one will be shown. Absence of JASU designation indicates non–availability.

The following is a list of current JASU systems referenced in this publication:

USAF JASU (For variations in technical data, refer to T.O. 35–1–7.)
ELECTRICAL STARTING UNITS:

A/M32A–86	AC: 115/200v, 3 phase, 90 kva, 0.8 pf, 4 wire
	DC: 28v, 1500 amp, 72 kw (with TR pack)
MC–1A	AC: 115/208v, 400 cycle, 3 phase, 37.5 kva, 0.8 pf, 108 amp, 4 wire
	DC: 28v, 500 amp, 14 kw
MD–3	AC: 115/208v, 400 cycle, 3 phase, 60 kva, 0.75 pf, 4 wire
	DC: 28v, 1500 amp, 45 kw, split bus
MD–3A	AC: 115/208v, 400 cycle, 3 phase, 60 kva, 0.75 pf, 4 wire
	DC: 28v, 1500 amp, 45 kw, split bus
MD–3M	AC: 115/208v, 400 cycle, 3 phase, 60 kva, 0.75 pf, 4 wire
	DC: 28v, 500 amp, 15 kw
MD–4	AC: 120/208v, 400 cycle, 3 phase, 62.5 kva, 0.8 pf, 175 amp, "WYE" neutral ground, 4 wire, 120v, 400 cycle, 3 phase, 62.5 kva, 0.8 pf, 303 amp, "DELTA" 3 wire, 120v, 400 cycle, 1 phase, 62.5 kva, 0.8 pf, 520 amp, 2 wire

AIRPORT/FACILITY DIRECTORY LEGEND

AIR STARTING UNITS

AM32–95	150 +/– 5 lb/min (2055 +/– 68 cfm) at 51 +/– 2 psia
AM32A–95	150 +/– 5 lb/min @ 49 +/– 2 psia (35 +/– 2 psig)
LASS	150 +/– 5 lb/min @ 49 +/– 2 psia
MA–1A	82 lb/min (1123 cfm) at 130° air inlet temp, 45 psia (min) air outlet press
MC–1	15 cfm, 3500 psia
MC–1A	15 cfm, 3500 psia
MC–2A	15 cfm, 200 psia
MC–11	8,000 cu in cap, 4000 psig, 15 cfm

COMBINED AIR AND ELECTRICAL STARTING UNITS:

AGPU	AC: 115/200v, 400 cycle, 3 phase, 30 kw gen
	DC: 28v, 700 amp
	AIR: 60 lb/min @ 40 psig @ sea level
AM32A–60*	AIR: 120 +/– 4 lb/min (1644 +/– 55 cfm) at 49 +/– 2 psia
	AC: 120/208v, 400 cycle, 3 phase, 75 kva, 0.75 pf, 4 wire, 120v, 1 phase, 25 kva
	DC: 28v, 500 amp, 15 kw
AM32A–60A	AIR: 150 +/– 5 lb/min (2055 +/– 68 cfm at 51 +/– psia
	AC: 120/208v, 400 cycle, 3 phase, 75 kva, 0.75 pf, 4 wire
	DC: 28v, 200 amp, 5.6 kw
AM32A–60B*	AIR: 130 lb/min, 50 psia
	AC: 120/208v, 400 cycle, 3 phase, 75 kva, 0.75 pf, 4 wire
	DC: 28v, 200 amp, 5.6 kw

*NOTE: During combined air and electrical loads, the pneumatic circuitry takes preference and will limit the amount of electrical power available.

USN JASU

ELECTRICAL STARTING UNITS:

NC–8A/A1	DC: 500 amp constant, 750 amp intermittent, 28v;
	AC: 60 kva @ .8 pf, 115/200v, 3 phase, 400 Hz.
NC–10A/A1/B/C	DC: 750 amp constant, 1000 amp intermittent, 28v;
	AC: 90 kva, 115/200v, 3 phase, 400 Hz.

AIR STARTING UNITS:

GTC–85/GTE–85	120 lbs/min @ 45 psi.
MSU–200NAV/A/U47A–5	204 lbs/min @ 56 psia.
WELLS AIR START SYSTEM	180 lbs/min @ 75 psi or 120 lbs/min @ 45 psi. Simultaneous multiple start capability.

COMBINED AIR AND ELECTRICAL STARTING UNITS:

NCPP–105/RCPT	180 lbs/min @ 75 psi or 120 lbs/min @ 45 psi. 700 amp, 28v DC. 120/208v, 400 Hz AC, 30 kva.

ARMY JASU

59B2–1B	28v, 7.5 kw, 280 amp.

OTHER JASU

ELECTRICAL STARTING UNITS (DND):

CE12	AC 115/200v, 140 kva, 400 Hz, 3 phase
CE13	AC 115/200v, 60 kva, 400 Hz, 3 phase
CE14	AC/DC 115/200v, 140 kva, 400 Hz, 3 phase, 28vDC, 1500 amp
CE15	DC 22–35v, 500 amp continuous 1100 amp intermittent
CE16	DC 22–35v, 500 amp continuous 1100 amp intermittent soft start

AIR STARTING UNITS (DND):

CA2	ASA 45.5 psig, 116.4 lb/min

COMBINED AIR AND ELECTRICAL STARTING UNITS (DND)

CEA1	AC 120/208v, 60 kva, 400 Hz, 3 phase DC 28v, 75 amp
	AIR 112.5 lb/min, 47 psig

ELECTRICAL STARTING UNITS (OTHER)

C–26	28v 45kw 115–200v 15kw 380–800 Hz 1 phase 2 wire
C–26–B, C–26–C	28v 45kw: Split Bus: 115–200v 15kw 380–800 Hz 1 phase 2 wire
E3	DC 28v/10kw

AIR STARTING UNITS (OTHER):

A4	40 psi/2 lb/sec (LPAS Mk12, Mk12L, Mk12A, Mk1, Mk2B)
MA–1	150 Air HP, 115 lb/min 50 psia
MA–2	250 Air HP, 150 lb/min 75 psia

CARTRIDGE:

MXU–4A	USAF

AIRPORT/FACILITY DIRECTORY LEGEND

FUEL—MILITARY

Fuel available through US Military Base supply, DESC Into–Plane Contracts and/or reciprocal agreement is listed first and is followed by (Mil). At commercial airports where Into–Plane contracts are in place, the name of the refueling agent is shown. Military fuel should be used first if it is available. When military fuel cannot be obtained but Into–Plane contract fuel is available, Government aircraft must refuel with the contract fuel and applicable refueling agent to avoid any breach in contract terms and conditions. Fuel not available through the above is shown preceded by NC (no contract). When fuel is obtained from NC sources, local purchase procedures must be followed. The US Military Aircraft Identaplates DD Form 1896 (Jet Fuel), DD Form 1897 (Avgas) and AF Form 1245 (Avgas) are used at military installations only. The US Government Aviation Into–Plane Reimbursement (AIR) Card (currently issued by AVCARD) is the instrument to be used to obtain fuel under a DESC Into–Plane Contract and for NC purchases if the refueling agent at the commercial airport accepts the AVCARD. A current list of contract fuel locations is available online at https://cis.energy.dla.mil/ip_cis/. See legend item 14 for fuel code and description.

SUPPORTING FLUIDS AND SYSTEMS—MILITARY

CODE	
ADI	Anti–Detonation Injection Fluid—Reciprocating Engine Aircraft.
W	Water Thrust Augmentation—Jet Aircraft.
WAI	Water–Alcohol Injection Type, Thrust Augmentation—Jet Aircraft.
SP	Single Point Refueling.
PRESAIR	Air Compressors rated 3,000 PSI or more.
De–Ice	Anti–icing/De–icing/Defrosting Fluid (MIL–A–8243).

OXYGEN:

LPOX	Low pressure oxygen servicing.
HPOX	High pressure oxygen servicing.
LHOX	Low and high pressure oxygen servicing.
LOX	Liquid oxygen servicing.
OXRB	Oxygen replacement bottles. (Maintained primarily at Naval stations for use in acft where oxygen can be replenished only by replacement of cylinders.)
OX	Indicates oxygen servicing when type of servicing is unknown.

NOTE: Combinations of above items is used to indicate complete oxygen servicing available;

LHOXRB	Low and high pressure oxygen servicing and replacement bottles;
LPOXRB	Low pressure oxygen replacement bottles only, etc.

NOTE: Aircraft will be serviced with oxygen procured under military specifications only. Aircraft will not be serviced with medical oxygen.

NITROGEN:

LPNIT — Low pressure nitrogen servicing.

HPNIT — High pressure nitrogen servicing.

LHNIT — Low and high pressure nitrogen servicing.

OIL—MILITARY

US AVIATION OILS (MIL SPECS):

CODE	GRADE, TYPE
O–113	1065, Reciprocating Engine Oil (MIL–L–6082)
O–117	1100, Reciprocating Engine Oil (MIL–L–6082)
O–117+	1100, O–117 plus cyclohexanone (MIL–L–6082)
O–123	1065, (Dispersant), Reciprocating Engine Oil (MIL–L–22851 Type III)
O–128	1100, (Dispersant), Reciprocating Engine Oil (MIL–L–22851 Type II)
O–132	1005, Jet Engine Oil (MIL–L–6081)
O–133	1010, Jet Engine Oil (MIL–L–6081)
O–147	None, MIL–L–6085A Lubricating Oil, Instrument, Synthetic
O–148	None, MIL–L–7808 (Synthetic Base) Turbine Engine Oil
O–149	None, Aircraft Turbine Engine Synthetic, 7.5c St
O–155	None, MIL–L–6086C, Aircraft, Medium Grade
O–156	None, MIL–L–23699 (Synthetic Base), Turboprop and Turboshaft Engines
JOAP/SOAP	Joint Oil Analysis Program. JOAP support is furnished during normal duty hours, other times on request. (JOAP and SOAP programs provide essentially the same service, JOAP is now the standard joint service supported program.)

TRANSIENT ALERT (TRAN ALERT)—MILITARY

Tran Alert service is considered to include all services required for normal aircraft turn–around, e.g., servicing (fuel, oil, oxygen, etc.), debriefing to determine requirements for maintenance, minor maintenance, inspection and parking assistance of transient aircraft. Drag chute repack, specialized maintenance, or extensive repairs will be provided within the capabilities and priorities of the base. Delays can be anticipated after normal duty hours/holidays/weekends regardless of the hours of transient maintenance operation. Pilots should not expect aircraft to be serviced for TURN–AROUNDS during time periods when servicing or maintenance manpower is not available. In the case of airports not operated exclusively by US military, the servicing indicated by the remarks will not always be available for US military aircraft. When transient alert services are not shown, facilities are unknown. NO PRIORITY BASIS—means that transient alert services will be provided only after all the requirements for mission/tactical assigned aircraft have been accomplished.

AIRPORT/FACILITY DIRECTORY LEGEND

㉓ AIRPORT REMARKS

The Attendance Schedule is the months, days and hours the airport is actually attended. Airport attendance does not mean watchman duties or telephone accessibility, but rather an attendant or operator on duty to provide at least minimum services (e.g., repairs, fuel, transportation).

Airport Remarks have been grouped in order of applicability. Airport remarks are limited to those items of information that are determined essential for operational use, i.e., conditions of a permanent or indefinite nature and conditions that will remain in effect for more than 30 days concerning aeronautical facilities, services, maintenance available, procedures or hazards, knowledge of which is essential for safe and efficient operation of aircraft. Information concerning permanent closing of a runway or taxiway will not be shown. A note "See Special Notices" shall be applied within this remarks section when a special notice applicable to the entry is contained in the Special Notices section of this publication.

Parachute Jumping indicates parachute jumping areas associated with the airport. See Parachute Jumping Area section of this publication for additional Information.

Landing Fee indicates landing charges for private or non–revenue producing aircraft. In addition, fees may be charged for planes that remain over a couple of hours and buy no services, or at major airline terminals for all aircraft.

Note: Unless otherwise stated, remarks including runway ends refer to the runway's approach end.

㉔ MILITARY REMARKS

Joint Civil/Military airports contain both Airport Remarks and Military Remarks. Military Remarks published for these airports are applicable only to the military. Military and joint Military/Civil airports contain only Military Remarks. Remarks contained in this section may not be applicable to civil users. When both sets of remarks exist, the first set is applicable to the primary operator of the airport. Remarks applicable to a tenant on the airport are shown preceded by the tenant organization, i.e., (A) (AF) (N) (ANG), etc. Military airports operate 24 hours unless otherwise specified. Airport operating hours are listed first (airport operating hours will only be listed if they are different than the airport attended hours or if the attended hours are unavailable) followed by pertinent remarks in order of applicability. Remarks will include information on restrictions, hazards, traffic pattern, noise abatement, customs/agriculture/immigration, and miscellaneous information applicable to the Military.

Type of restrictions:

CLOSED: When designated closed, the airport is restricted from use by all aircraft unless stated otherwise. Any closure applying to specific type of aircraft or operation will be so stated. USN/USMC/USAF airports are considered closed during non–operating hours. Closed airports may be utilized during an emergency provided there is a safe landing area.

OFFICIAL BUSINESS ONLY: The airfield is closed to all transient military aircraft for obtaining routine services such as fueling, passenger drop off or pickup, practice approaches, parking, etc. The airfield may be used by aircrews and aircraft if official government business (including civilian) must be conducted on or near the airfield and prior permission is received from the airfield manager.

AF OFFICIAL BUSINESS ONLY OR NAVY OFFICIAL BUSINESS ONLY: Indicates that the restriction applies only to service indicated.

PRIOR PERMISSION REQUIRED (PPR): Airport is closed to transient aircraft unless approval for operation is obtained from the appropriate commander through Chief, Airfield Management or Airfield Operations Officer. Official Business or PPR does not preclude the use of US Military airports as an alternate for IFR flights. If a non–US military airport is used as a weather alternate and requires a PPR, the PPR must be requested and confirmed before the flight departs. The purpose of PPR is to control volume and flow of traffic rather than to prohibit it. Prior permission is required for all aircraft requiring transient alert service outside the published transient alert duty hours. All aircraft carrying hazardous materials must obtain prior permission as outlined in AFJI 11–204, AR 95–27, OPNAVINST 3710.7.

Note: OFFICIAL BUSINESS ONLY AND PPR restrictions are not applicable to Special Air Mission (SAM) or Special Air Resource (SPAR) aircraft providing person or persons on aboard are designated Code 6 or higher as explained in AFJMAN 11–213, AR 95–11, OPNAVINST 3722–8J. Official Business Only or PPR do not preclude the use of the airport as an alternate for IFR flights.

㉕ AIRPORT MANAGER

The phone number of the airport manager.

㉖ WEATHER DATA SOURCES

Weather data sources will be listed alphabetically followed by their assigned frequencies and/or telephone number and hours of operation.

ASOS—Automated Surface Observing System. Reports the same as an AWOS–3 plus precipitation identification and intensity, and freezing rain occurrence;

AWOS—Automated Weather Observing System

AWOS–A—reports altimeter setting (all other information is advisory only).

AWOS–AV—reports altimeter and visibility.

AWOS–1—reports altimeter setting, wind data and usually temperature, dew point and density altitude.

AWOS–2—reports the same as AWOS–1 plus visibility.

AWOS–3—reports the same as AWOS–1 plus visibility and cloud/ceiling data.

AWOS–3P reports the same as the AWOS–3 system, plus a precipitation identification sensor.

AWOS–3PT reports the same as the AWOS–3 system, plus precipitation identification sensor and a thunderstorm/lightning reporting capability.

AIRPORT/FACILITY DIRECTORY LEGEND

AWOS–3T reports the same as AWOS–3 system and includes a thunderstorm/lightning reporting capability.

See AIM, Basic Flight Information and ATC Procedures for detailed description of Weather Data Sources.

AWOS–4—reports same as AWOS–3 system, plus precipitation occurrence, type and accumulation, freezing rain, thunderstorm and runway surface sensors.

HIWAS—See RADIO AIDS TO NAVIGATION

LAWRS—Limited Aviation Weather Reporting Station where observers report cloud height, weather, obstructions to vision, temperature and dewpoint (in most cases), surface wind, altimeter and pertinent remarks.

LLWAS—indicates a Low Level Wind Shear Alert System consisting of a center field and several field perimeter anemometers.

SAWRS—identifies airports that have a Supplemental Aviation Weather Reporting Station available to pilots for current weather information.

SWSL—Supplemental Weather Service Location providing current local weather information via radio and telephone.

TDWR—indicates airports that have Terminal Doppler Weather Radar.

WSP—indicates airports that have Weather System Processor.

When the automated weather source is broadcast over an associated airport NAVAID frequency (see NAVAID line), it shall be indicated by a bold ASOS, AWOS, or HIWAS followed by the frequency, identifier and phone number, if available.

㉗ COMMUNICATIONS

Airport terminal control facilities and radio communications associated with the airport shall be shown. When the call sign is not the same as the airport name the call sign will be shown. Frequencies shall normally be shown in descending order with the primary frequency listed first. Frequencies will be listed, together with sectorization indicated by outbound radials, and hours of operation. Communications will be listed in sequence as follows:

Single Frequency Approach (SFA), Common Traffic Advisory Frequency (CTAF), Aeronautical Advisory Stations (UNICOM) or (AUNICOM), and Automatic Terminal Information Service (ATIS) along with their frequency is shown, where available, on the line following the heading "COMMUNICATIONS." When the CTAF and UNICOM frequencies are the same, the frequency will be shown as CTAF/UNICOM 122.8.

The FSS telephone nationwide is toll free 1–800–WX–BRIEF (1–800–992–7433). When the FSS is located on the field it will be indicated as "on arpt". Frequencies available at the FSS will follow in descending order. Remote Communications Outlet (RCO) providing service to the airport followed by the frequency and FSS RADIO name will be shown when available. FSS's provide information on airport conditions, radio aids and other facilities, and process flight plans. Airport Advisory Service (AAS) is provided on the CTAF by FSS's for select non–tower airports or airports where the tower is not in operation.

(See AIM, Para 4–1–9 Traffic Advisory Practices at Airports Without Operating Control Towers or AC 90–42C.)

Aviation weather briefing service is provided by FSS specialists. Flight and weather briefing services are also available by calling the telephone numbers listed.

Remote Communications Outlet (RCO)—An unmanned air/ground communications facility that is remotely controlled and provides UHF or VHF communications capability to extend the service range of an FSS.

Civil Communications Frequencies–Civil communications frequencies used in the FSS air/ground system are operated on 122.0, 122.2, 123.6; emergency 121.5; plus receive–only on 122.1.

    a. 122.0 is assigned as the Enroute Flight Advisory Service frequency at selected FSS RADIO outlets.

    b. 122.2 is assigned as a common enroute frequency.

    c. 123.6 is assigned as the airport advisory frequency at select non–tower locations. At airports with a tower, FSS may provide airport advisories on the tower frequency when tower is closed.

    d. 122.1 is the primary receive–only frequency at VOR's.

    e. Some FSS's are assigned 50 kHz frequencies in the 122–126 MHz band (eg. 122.45). Pilots using the FSS A/G system should refer to this directory or appropriate charts to determine frequencies available at the FSS or remoted facility through which they wish to communicate.

Emergency frequency 121.5 and 243.0 are available at all Flight Service Stations, most Towers, Approach Control and RADAR facilities.

Frequencies published followed by the letter "T" or "R", indicate that the facility will only transmit or receive respectively on that frequency. All radio aids to navigation (NAVAID) frequencies are transmit only.

TERMINAL SERVICES

SFA—Single Frequency Approach.

CTAF—A program designed to get all vehicles and aircraft at airports without an operating control tower on a common frequency.

ATIS—A continuous broadcast of recorded non–control information in selected terminal areas.

D–ATIS—Digital ATIS provides ATIS information in text form outside the standard reception range of conventional ATIS via landline & data link communications and voice message within range of existing transmitters.

AUNICOM—Automated UNICOM is a computerized, command response system that provides automated weather, radio check capability and airport advisory information selected from an automated menu by microphone clicks.

UNICOM—A non–government air/ground radio communications facility which may provide airport information.

PTD—Pilot to Dispatcher.

APP CON—Approach Control. The symbol ® indicates radar approach control.

TOWER—Control tower.

GCA—Ground Control Approach System.

GND CON—Ground Control.

AIRPORT/FACILITY DIRECTORY LEGEND

GCO—Ground Communication Outlet—An unstaffed, remotely controlled, ground/ground communications facility. Pilots at uncontrolled airports may contact ATC and FSS via VHF to a telephone connection to obtain an instrument clearance or close a VFR or IFR flight plan. They may also get an updated weather briefing prior to takeoff. Pilots will use four "key clicks" on the VHF radio to contact the appropriate ATC facility or six "key clicks" to contact the FSS. The GCO system is intended to be used only on the ground.

DEP CON—Departure Control. The symbol Ⓡ indicates radar departure control.

CLNC DEL—Clearance Delivery.

CPDLC—Controller Pilot Data Link Communication. FANS ATC data communication capability from the aircraft to the ATC Data Link system.

PRE TAXI CLNC—Pre taxi clearance.

VFR ADVSY SVC—VFR Advisory Service. Service provided by Non–Radar Approach Control.
  Advisory Service for VFR aircraft (upon a workload basis) ctc APP CON.

COMD POST—Command Post followed by the operator call sign in parenthesis.

PMSV—Pilot–to Metro Service call sign, frequency and hours of operation, when full service is other than continuous. PMSV installations at which weather observation service is available shall be indicated, following the frequency and/or hours of operation as "Wx obsn svc 1900–0000Z‡" or "other times" may be used when no specific time is given. PMSV facilities manned by forecasters are considered "Full Service". PMSV facilities manned by weather observers are listed as "Limited Service".

OPS—Operations followed by the operator call sign in parenthesis.

CON

RANGE

FLT FLW—Flight Following

MEDIVAC

NOTE: Communication frequencies followed by the letter "X" indicate frequency available on request.

㉘ AIRSPACE

Information concerning Class B, C, and part–time D and E surface area airspace shall be published with effective times, if available.

CLASS B—Radar Sequencing and Separation Service for all aircraft in CLASS B airspace.

CLASS C—Separation between IFR and VFR aircraft and sequencing of VFR arrivals to the primary airport.

TRSA—Radar Sequencing and Separation Service for participating VFR Aircraft within a Terminal Radar Service Area.

Class C, D, and E airspace described in this publication is that airspace usually consisting of a 5 NM radius core surface area that begins at the surface and extends upward to an altitude above the airport elevation (charted in MSL for Class C and Class D). Class E surface airspace normally extends from the surface up to but not including the overlying controlled airspace.

When part–time Class C or Class D airspace defaults to Class E, the core surface area becomes Class E. This will be formatted as:
AIRSPACE: **CLASS C** svc "times" ctc **APP CON** other times CLASS E:
or
AIRSPACE: **CLASS D** svc "times" other times CLASS E.

When a part–time Class C, Class D or Class E surface area defaults to Class G, the core surface area becomes Class G up to, but not including, the overlying controlled airspace. Normally, the overlying controlled airspace is Class E airspace beginning at either 700′ or 1200′ AGL and may be determined by consulting the relevant VFR Sectional or Terminal Area Charts. This will be formatted as:
AIRSPACE: **CLASS C** svc "times" ctc **APP CON** other times CLASS G, with CLASS E 700′ (or 1200′) AGL & abv:
or
AIRSPACE: **CLASS D** svc "times" other times CLASS G with CLASS E 700′ (or 1200′) AGL & abv:
or
AIRSPACE: **CLASS E** svc "times" other times CLASS G with CLASS E 700′ (or 1200′) AGL & abv.

NOTE: AIRSPACE SVC "TIMES" INCLUDE ALL ASSOCIATED ARRIVAL EXTENSIONS. Surface area arrival extensions for instrument approach procedures become part of the primary core surface area. These extensions may be either Class D or Class E airspace and are effective concurrent with the times of the primary core surface area. For example, when a part–time Class C, Class D or Class E surface area defaults to Class G, the associated arrival extensions will default to Class G at the same time. When a part–time Class C or Class D surface area defaults to Class E, the arrival extensions will remain in effect as Class E airspace.

NOTE: CLASS E AIRSPACE EXTENDING UPWARD FROM 700 FEET OR MORE ABOVE THE SURFACE, DESIGNATED IN CONJUNCTION WITH AN AIRPORT WITH AN APPROVED INSTRUMENT PROCEDURE.
Class E 700′ AGL (shown as magenta vignette on sectional charts) and 1200′ AGL (blue vignette) areas are designated when necessary to provide controlled airspace for transitioning to/from the terminal and enroute environments. Unless otherwise specified, these 700′/1200′ AGL Class E airspace areas remain in effect continuously, regardless of airport operating hours or surface area status. These transition areas should not be confused with surface areas or arrival extensions.

(See Chapter 3, AIRSPACE, in the Aeronautical Information Manual for further details)

AIRPORT/FACILITY DIRECTORY LEGEND

㉙ VOR TEST FACILITY (VOT)

The VOT transmits a signal which provided users a convenient means to determine the operational status and accuracy of an aircraft VOR receiver while on the ground. Ground based VOTs and the associated frequency shall be shown when available. VOTs are also shown with identifier, frequency and referenced remarks in the VOR Receiver Check section in the back of this publication.

㉚ RADIO AIDS TO NAVIGATION

The Airport/Facility Directory section of the Chart Supplement lists, by facility name, all Radio Aids to Navigation that appear on FAA, Aeronautical Information Services Visual or IFR Aeronautical Charts and those upon which the FAA has approved an Instrument Approach Procedure, with exception of selected TACANs. All VOR, VORTAC, TACAN and ILS equipment in the National Airspace System has an automatic monitoring and shutdown feature in the event of malfunction. Unmonitored, as used in this publication, for any navigational aid, means that monitoring personnel cannot observe the malfunction or shutdown signal. The NAVAID NOTAM file identifier will be shown as "NOTAM FILE IAD" and will be listed on the Radio Aids to Navigation line. When two or more NAVAIDS are listed and the NOTAM file identifier is different from that shown on the Radio Aids to Navigation line, it will be shown with the NAVAID listing. NOTAM file identifiers for ILSs and its components (e.g., NDB (LOM) are the same as the associated airports and are not repeated. Automated Surface Observing System (ASOS), Automated Weather Observing System (AWOS), and Hazardous Inflight Weather Advisory Service (HIWAS) will be shown when this service is broadcast over selected NAVAIDs.

NAVAID information is tabulated as indicated in the following sample:

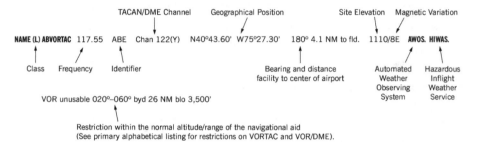

Note: Those DME channel numbers with a (Y) suffix require TACAN to be placed in the "Y" mode to receive distance information.

HIWAS—Hazardous Inflight Weather Advisory Service is a continuous broadcast of inflight weather advisories including summarized SIGMETs, convective SIGMETs, AIRMETs and urgent PIREPs. HIWAS is presently broadcast over selected VOR's throughout the U.S.

ASR/PAR—Indicates that Surveillance (ASR) or Precision (PAR) radar instrument approach minimums are published in the U.S. Terminal Procedures. Only part–time hours of operation will be shown.

AIRPORT/FACILITY DIRECTORY LEGEND

RADIO CLASS DESIGNATIONS

VOR/DME/TACAN Standard Service Volume (SSV) Classifications

SSV Class	Altitudes	Distance (NM)
(T) Terminal	1000′ to 12,000′	25
(L) Low Altitude	1000′ to 18,000′	40
(H) High Altitude	1000′ to 14,500′	40
	14,500′ to 18,000′	100
	18,000′ to 45,000′	130
	45,000′ to 60,000′	100

NOTE: Additionally, (H) facilities provide (L) and (T) service volume and (L) facilities provide (T) service. Altitudes are with respect to the station's site elevation. Coverage is not available in a cone of airspace directly above the facility.

The term VOR is, operationally, a general term covering the VHF omnidirectional bearing type of facility without regard to the fact that the power, the frequency protected service volume, the equipment configuration, and operational requirements may vary between facilities at different locations.

AB	Automatic Weather Broadcast.
DF	Direction Finding Service.
DME	UHF standard (TACAN compatible) distance measuring equipment.
DME(Y)	UHF standard (TACAN compatible) distance measuring equipment that require TACAN to be placed in the "Y" mode to receive DME.
GS	Glide slope.
H	Non–directional radio beacon (homing), power 50 watts to less than 2,000 watts (50 NM at all altitudes).
HH	Non–directional radio beacon (homing), power 2,000 watts or more (75 NM at all altitudes).
H–SAB	Non–directional radio beacons providing automatic transcribed weather service.
ILS	Instrument Landing System (voice, where available, on localizer channel).
IM	Inner marker.
LDA	Localizer Directional Aid.
LMM	Compass locator station when installed at middle marker site (15 NM at all altitudes).
LOM	Compass locator station when installed at outer marker site (15 NM at all altitudes).
MH	Non–directional radio beacon (homing) power less than 50 watts (25 NM at all altitudes).
MM	Middle marker.
OM	Outer marker.
S	Simultaneous range homing signal and/or voice.
SABH	Non–directional radio beacon not authorized for IFR or ATC. Provides automatic weather broadcasts.
SDF	Simplified Direction Facility.
TACAN	UHF navigational facility–omnidirectional course and distance information.
VOR	VHF navigational facility–omnidirectional course only.
VOR/DME	Collocated VOR navigational facility and UHF standard distance measuring equipment.
VORTAC	Collocated VOR and TACAN navigational facilities.
W	Without voice on radio facility frequency.
Z	VHF station location marker at a LF radio facility.

AIRPORT/FACILITY DIRECTORY LEGEND

ILS FACILITY PEFORMANCE CLASSIFICATION CODES

Codes define the ability of an ILS to support autoland operations. The two portions of the code represent Official Category and farthest point along a Category I, II, or III approach that the Localizer meets Category III structure tolerances.

Official Category: I, II, or III; the lowest minima on published or unpublished procedures supported by the ILS.

Farthest point of satisfactory Category III Localizer performance for Category I, II, or III approaches: A – 4 NM prior to runway threshold, B – 3500 ft prior to runway threshold, C – glide angle dependent but generally 750–1000 ft prior to threshold, T – runway threshold, D – 3000 ft after runway threshold, and E – 2000 ft prior to stop end of runway.

ILS information is tabulated as indicated in the following sample:

  ILS/DME   108.5   I-ORL   Chan 22   Rwy 18.   Class IIE.   LOM HERNY NDB.

ILS Facility Performance
Classification Code

FREQUENCY PAIRING TABLE

VHF FREQUENCY	TACAN CHANNEL	VHF FREQUENCY	TACAN CHANNEL	VHF FREQUENCY	TACAN CHANNEL	VHF FREQUENCY	TACAN CHANNEL
108.10	18X	108.55	22Y	111.05	47Y	114.85	95Y
108.30	20X	108.65	23Y	111.15	48Y	114.95	96Y
108.50	22X	108.75	24Y	111.25	49Y	115.05	97Y
108.70	24X	108.85	25Y	111.35	50Y	115.15	98Y
108.90	26X	108.95	26Y	111.45	51Y	115.25	99Y
109.10	28X	109.05	27Y	111.55	52Y	115.35	100Y
109.30	30X	109.15	28Y	111.65	53Y	115.45	101Y
109.50	32X	109.25	29Y	111.75	54Y	115.55	102Y
109.70	34X	109.35	30Y	111.85	55Y	115.65	103Y
109.90	36X	109.45	31Y	111.95	56Y	115.75	104Y
110.10	38X	109.55	32Y	113.35	80Y	115.85	105Y
110.30	40X	109.65	33Y	113.45	81Y	115.95	106Y
110.50	42X	109.75	34Y	113.55	82Y	116.05	107Y
110.70	44X	109.85	35Y	113.65	83Y	116.15	108Y
110.90	46X	109.95	36Y	113.75	84Y	116.25	109Y
111.10	48X	110.05	37Y	113.85	85Y	116.35	110Y
111.30	50X	110.15	38Y	113.95	86Y	116.45	111Y
111.50	52X	110.25	39Y	114.05	87Y	116.55	112Y
111.70	54X	110.35	40Y	114.15	88Y	116.65	113Y
111.90	56X	110.45	41Y	114.25	89Y	116.75	114Y
108.05	17Y	110.55	42Y	114.35	90Y	116.85	115Y
108.15	18Y	110.65	43Y	114.45	91Y	116.95	116Y
108.25	19Y	110.75	44Y	114.55	92Y	117.05	117Y
108.35	20Y	110.85	45Y	114.65	93Y	117.15	118Y
108.45	21Y	110.95	46Y	114.75	94Y	117.25	119Y

FREQUENCY PAIRING TABLE

The following is a list of paired VOR/ILS VHF frequencies with TACAN channels.

TACAN CHANNEL	VHF FREQUENCY	TACAN CHANNEL	VHF FREQUENCY	TACAN CHANNEL	VHF FREQUENCY	TACAN CHANNEL	VHF FREQUENCY
2X	134.5	25X	108.80	36X	109.90	47X	111.00
2Y	134.55	25Y	108.85	36Y	109.95	47Y	111.05
11X	135.4	26X	108.90	37X	110.00	48X	111.10
11Y	135.45	26Y	108.95	37Y	110.05	48Y	111.15
12X	135.5	27X	109.00	38X	110.10	49X	111.20
12Y	135.55	27Y	109.05	38Y	110.15	49Y	111.25
17X	108.00	28X	109.10	39X	110.20	50X	111.30
17Y	108.05	28Y	109.15	39Y	110.25	50Y	111.35
18X	108.10	29X	109.20	40X	110.30	51X	111.40
18Y	108.15	29Y	109.25	40Y	110.35	51Y	111.45
19X	108.20	30X	109.30	41X	110.40	52X	111.50
19Y	108.25	30Y	109.35	41Y	110.45	52Y	111.55
20X	108.30	31X	109.40	42X	110.50	53X	111.60
20Y	108.35	31Y	109.45	42Y	110.55	53Y	111.65
21X	108.40	32X	109.50	43X	110.60	54X	111.70
21Y	108.45	32Y	109.55	43Y	110.65	54Y	111.75
22X	108.50	33X	109.60	44X	110.70	55X	111.80
22Y	108.55	33Y	109.65	44Y	110.75	55Y	111.85
23X	108.60	34X	109.70	45X	110.80	56X	111.90
23Y	108.65	34Y	109.75	45Y	110.85	56Y	111.95
24X	108.70	35X	109.80	46X	110.90	57X	112.00
24Y	108.75	35Y	109.85	46Y	110.95	57Y	112.05

AIRPORT/FACILITY DIRECTORY LEGEND

TACAN CHANNEL	VHF FREQUENCY	TACAN CHANNEL	VHF FREQUENCY	TACAN CHANNEL	VHF FREQUENCY	TACAN CHANNEL	VHF FREQUENCY
58X	112.10	77X	113.00	96X	114.90	115X	116.80
58Y	112.15	77Y	113.05	96Y	114.95	115Y	116.85
59X	112.20	78X	113.10	97X	115.00	116X	116.90
59Y	112.25	78Y	113.15	97Y	115.05	116Y	116.95
60X	133.30	79X	113.20	98X	115.10	117X	117.00
60Y	133.35	79Y	113.25	98Y	115.15	117Y	117.05
61X	133.40	80X	113.30	99X	115.20	118X	117.10
61Y	133.45	80Y	113.35	99Y	115.25	118Y	117.15
62X	133.50	81X	113.40	100X	115.30	119X	117.20
62Y	133.55	81Y	113.45	100Y	115.35	119Y	117.25
63X	133.60	82X	113.50	101X	115.40	120X	117.30
63Y	133.65	82Y	113.55	101Y	115.45	120Y	117.35
64X	133.70	83X	113.60	102X	115.50	121X	117.40
64Y	133.75	83Y	113.65	102Y	115.55	121Y	117.45
65X	133.80	84X	113.70	103X	115.60	122X	117.50
65Y	133.85	84Y	113.75	103Y	115.65	122Y	117.55
66X	133.90	85X	113.80	104X	115.70	123X	117.60
66Y	133.95	85Y	113.85	104Y	115.75	123Y	117.65
67X	134.00	86X	113.90	105X	115.80	124X	117.70
67Y	134.05	86Y	113.95	105Y	115.85	124Y	117.75
68X	134.10	87X	114.00	106X	115.90	125X	117.80
68Y	134.15	87Y	114.05	106Y	115.95	125Y	117.85
69X	134.20	88X	114.10	107X	116.00	126X	117.90
69Y	134.25	88Y	114.15	107Y	116.05	126Y	117.95
70X	112.30	89X	114.20	108X	116.10		
70Y	112.35	89Y	114.25	108Y	116.15		
71X	112.40	90X	114.30	109X	116.20		
71Y	112.45	90Y	114.35	109Y	116.25		
72X	112.50	91X	114.40	110X	116.30		
72Y	112.55	91Y	114.45	110Y	116.35		
73X	112.60	92X	114.50	111X	116.40		
73Y	112.65	92Y	114.55	111Y	116.45		
74X	112.70	93X	114.60	112X	116.50		
74Y	112.75	93Y	114.65	112Y	116.55		
75X	112.80	94X	114.70	113X	116.60		
75Y	112.85	94Y	114.75	113Y	116.65		
76X	112.90	95X	114.80	114X	116.70		
76Y	112.95	95Y	114.85	114Y	116.75		

(31) **COMM/NAV/WEATHER REMARKS:** These remarks consist of pertinent information affecting the current status of communications, NAVAIDs and weather.

Chart Supplement Excerpts

ELLENSBURG

BOWERS FLD (ELN)(KELN)   2 N   UTC–8(–7DT)   N47°01.98′ W120°31.84′ SEATTLE
H–1C, L–13A
IAP

1764   B   S4   **FUEL** 100LL, JET A   TPA—2598(834)   NOTAM FILE ELN

RWY 07–25: H5590X150 (ASPH)   S–12.5   0.8% up E

   RWY 07: P–line.

   RWY 25: PAPI(P4R).

RWY 11–29: H4301X150 (CONC)   S–35, D–57, 2D–100   MIRL 0.4% up NW

   RWY 29: REIL. PAPI(P2R)—GA 3.0° TCH 40′.

AIRPORT REMARKS: Attended Mon–Sat 1500–0000Z‡. 100LL self service avbl, credit card. Rwy 07–25 CLOSED Dec 15–Feb 28, no maintenance avbl. Rwy 07–25 cracks in rwy sfc. Rwy 07–25 has weeds growing through cracks in pavement first 2000′. ACTIVATE MIRL Rwy 11–29—123.0.

AIRPORT MANAGER: 509-962-7523

WEATHER DATA SOURCES: ASOS 118.375 (509) 925–2040. **HIWAS** 117.9 ELN.

COMMUNICATIONS: CTAF/UNICOM 123.0

   ELLENSBURG RCO 122.2 (SEATTLE RADIO)

   SEATTLE CENTER APP/DEP CON 132.6

RADIO AIDS TO NAVIGATION: NOTAM FILE ELN.

   ELLENSBURG (H) VORTACW 117.9   ELN   Chan 126   N47°01.46′ W120°27.50′   259° 3.0 NM to fld. 1770/21E.   **HIWAS.**

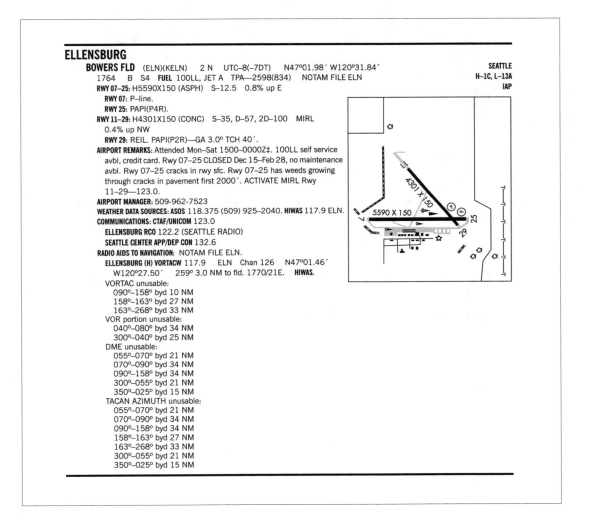

VORTAC unusable:
   090°–158° byd 10 NM
   158°–163° byd 27 NM
   163°–268° byd 33 NM
VOR portion unusable:
   040°–080° byd 34 NM
   300°–040° byd 25 NM
DME unusable:
   055°–070° byd 21 NM
   070°–090° byd 34 NM
   090°–158° byd 34 NM
   300°–055° byd 21 NM
   350°–025° byd 15 NM
TACAN AZIMUTH unusable:
   055°–070° byd 21 NM
   070°–090° byd 34 NM
   090°–158° byd 34 NM
   158°–163° byd 27 NM
   163°–268° byd 33 NM
   300°–055° byd 21 NM
   350°–025° byd 15 NM

OLYMPIA

[...]

- -

OLYMPIA RGNL (OLM)(KOLM) 4 S UTC–8(–7DT) N46°58.16′ W122°54.15′   **SEATTLE**
  208 B S4 **FUEL** 100LL, JET A OX 1, 3, 4 LRA NOTAM FILE OLM   **H–1B, L–1D**
  RWY 17–35: H5500X150 (ASPH–GRVD) S–75, D–94, 2S–87, 2D–142   **IAP, AD**
    HIRL
    RWY 17: MALSR. PAPI(P4L)—GA 3.0° TCH 54′.
    RWY 35: REIL. PAPI(P4L)—GA 3.0° TCH 50′. Rgt tfc.
  RWY 08–26: H4157X150 (ASPH) S–30
    RWY 08: Trees. Rgt tfc.
    RWY 26: Tree.
  AIRPORT REMARKS: Attended 1600–0200Z‡. Twy lgts on Twy A, Twy B, Twy
    L and Twy W. PAPI Rwy 17 and Rwy 35 opr continuously. When twr
    clsd ACTIVATE HIRL Rwy 17–35, MALSR Rwy 17, REIL Rwy 35, twy
    lgts and directional signage—CTAF.
  AIRPORT MANAGER: 360-528-8074
  WEATHER DATA SOURCES: ASOS 135.725 (360) 943–1278. **HIWAS** 113.4 OLM.
    SAWRS.
  COMMUNICATIONS: CTAF 124.4 **ATIS** 135.725 **UNICOM** 122.95
  ®**SEATTLE APP/DEP CON** 121.1
    TOWER 124.4 (1600–0400Z‡) **GND CON** 121.6
  AIRSPACE: CLASS D svc 1600–0400Z‡ other times CLASS E.
  RADIO AIDS TO NAVIGATION: NOTAM FILE OLM.
    (H) VORTACW 113.4 OLM Chan 81 N46°58.30′
    W122°54.11′ at fld. 200/19E. **HIWAS.**
    TACAN AZIMUTH & DME unusable:
      223°–258° byd 20 NM blo 4,100′
      258°–283° byd 30 NM blo 4,100′
      358°–043° byd 10 NM blo 6,000′
      358°–043° byd 20 NM blo 7,000′
    ILS 111.9 I–OLM Rwy 17. Unmonitored when ATCT closed. LOC unusable byd 25° rgt of course.
  COMM/NAV/WEATHER REMARKS: Emerg frequency 121.5 not avbl at twr.

®**SEATTLE CENTER** – 121.5 **121.5**   **H–1–3, L–1–2–11–13**
  Antelope Mountain – 124.85   **(KZSE)**
  Arcata – 124.85
  Badger Mountain – 134.95 **134.95** 127.05 **127.05**
  Beacon Hill – 127.05 **127.05** 120.3 **120.3**
  Cottonwood – 123.95 **118.55**
  Dallesport – 126.6 **126.6**
  Ferndale – **135.15** 124.85
  Fort Lawton – 127.05 **127.05**
  Hoquiam – 128.3
  Horton – **132.075** 125.8 121.4
  Kimberly – **135.45**
  Klamath Falls – **134.9** 127.6
  Lakeside – 123.95
  Lakeview – **135.35** 127.6
  Larch Mountain – 128.3 **128.3** 126.6 **126.6**
  Marlin – 126.1
  Medford – **135.15** 124.85 121.4
  Mohler – **128.45**
  Mullan Pass – **128.45**
  Nassel – 124.2
  Neah Bay – 125.1 **125.1**
  Redmond – **135.35 134.9** 128.15 **121.35**
  Rex-Parrett – **121.35**
  Scappoose – 128.15 124.2
  Spokane – 123.95 119.225
  Stampede Pass – 134.95 **134.95**
  The Dalles – **135.45** 119.65
  Wallula – 132.6
  Wenatchee – 126.1
  Whidbey Island – 134.95 **134.95** 128.5 125.1 **125.1**
  Yakima – 135.525 **135.525** 132.6 120.3 **120.3 118.55**

CONTROL TOWER FREQUENCIES ON SEATTLE SECTIONAL CHART

Airports with control towers are indicated on the face of the chart by the letters CT followed by the primary VHF local control frequency (ies). Information for each tower is listed in the table below. Operational hours are local time. The primary VHF and UHF local control frequencies are listed. An asterisk (*) indicates the part-time tower frequency is remoted to a collocated full-time FSS for use as Airport Advisory Service (AAS) during hours the tower is closed. The primary VHF and UHF ground control frequencies are listed.

Automatic Terminal Information Service (ATIS) frequencies shown on the face of the chart are primary arrival VHF/UHF frequencies. All ATIS frequencies are listed in the table below. ATIS operational hours may differ from tower operational hours.

ASR and/or PAR indicate Radar Instrument Approach available.

"MON-FRI" indicates Monday through Friday.

O/T indicates other times.

CONTROL TOWER	OPERATES	TWR FREQ	GND CON	ATIS	ASR/PAR
ABBOTSFORD	0700-2300	119.4 (INNER) 121.0 (OUTER) 295.0	121.8	119.8	
BELLINGHAM INTL	0700-2230	124.9 379.3	127.4 379.3	134.45	
BOEING/KING CO INTL	CONTINUOUS	118.3 (E) 257.8	121.9	127.75	
EASTERN OREGON RGNL	0600-2000	119.7 257.8	121.9 257.8		
FAIRCHILD AFB	CONTINUOUS	120.35 233.7	123.6 275.8	257.625	
FELTS	0600-2000	132.5 239.025	121.7	120.55	
GRANT CO INTL	0600-2200	118.25 (E) 128.0 (W) 257.8	121.9	119.05	
GRAY AAF (JB LEWIS–MCCHORD)	CONTINUOUS EXC HOL	119.325 256.8	121.9 290.2	124.65 306.2	PAR
LEWISTON–NEZ PERCE CO	0600-2200	119.4 318.8	121.9		
MCCHORD (JB LEWIS–MCCHORD)	CONTINUOUS	124.8 259.3	118.175 279.65	109.6 270.1	
MCNARY	0700-2100	119.1 257.2	121.9	124.55	
OLYMPIA RGNL	0800-2000	124.4 254.25	121.6	135.725	
PORTLAND–HILLSBORO	0600-2200	119.3 239.3	121.7	127.65	
PORTLAND INTL	CONTINUOUS	118.7 257.8 (RWY 10L/28R) 123.775 251.125 (RWYS 3/21 & 10R/28L)	121.9 348.6	128.35 269.9	
PORTLAND–TROUTDALE	0700-2200	120.9 254.3	121.8	135.625	
RENTON	0700-2000 OCT–APR 0700-2100 MAY–SEP	124.7 256.9	121.6 256.9	126.95	
SEATTLE–TACOMA INTL	CONTINUOUS	119.9 239.3 (RWYS 16L/34R, 16C/34C) 120.95 239.3 (RWY 16R/34L)	121.7	118.0	
SNOHOMISH CO (PAINE)	0700-2100	120.2 (ARR E OF CNTRLN OR DEP RWY 16L/34R) 132.95 (ARR W OF CNTRLN OR DEP RWY 16R/34L) 256.7	121.8 339.8	128.65	
SPOKANE INTL	CONTINUOUS	118.3 278.3	121.9 348.6	124.325 254.375	
TACOMA NARROWS	0800-2000	118.5 253.5	121.8	124.05	
TRI-CITIES	0600-2200	135.3 323.3	121.8	125.65	
VICTORIA INTL	0600-2400	119.1 (OUTER) 119.7 (INNER) 239.6	121.9 361.4	118.8	
WALLA WALLA RGNL	0600-1830	118.5 289.4	121.6 289.4		
WHIDBEY ISLAND NAS/AULT	CONTINUOUS	127.9 340.2	121.75 336.4	134.15 281.5	ASR/PAR
YAKIMA/MCALLISTER	0600-2200	133.25 257.8	121.9	125.25	

CLASS B, CLASS C, TRSA, AND SELECTED APPROACH CONTROL FREQUENCIES

FACILITY	FREQUENCIES	SERVICE AVAILABILITY
SEATTLE CLASS B	119.2 284.7 (341°-075°) 120.1 290.9 (199°-300°) 126.5 377.15 (161°-198°) 119.2 284.7 (RWYS 16 076°-160°) 125.9 290.9 (RWYS 16 301°-340°) 120.4 269.125 (RWYS 34 301°-340°) 125.9 290.9 (RWYS 34 076°-160°)	CONTINUOUS
FAIRCHILD AFB/SPOKANE CLASS C	123.75 282.25 (205°-025°) 133.35 263.0 (026°-204°)	CONTINUOUS
PORTLAND CLASS C	118.1 284.6 (100°-279°) 124.35 299.2 (280°-099°)	CONTINUOUS
WHIDBEY ISLAND CLASS C	118.2 285.65 (W) 120.7 270.8 (E)	CONTINUOUS

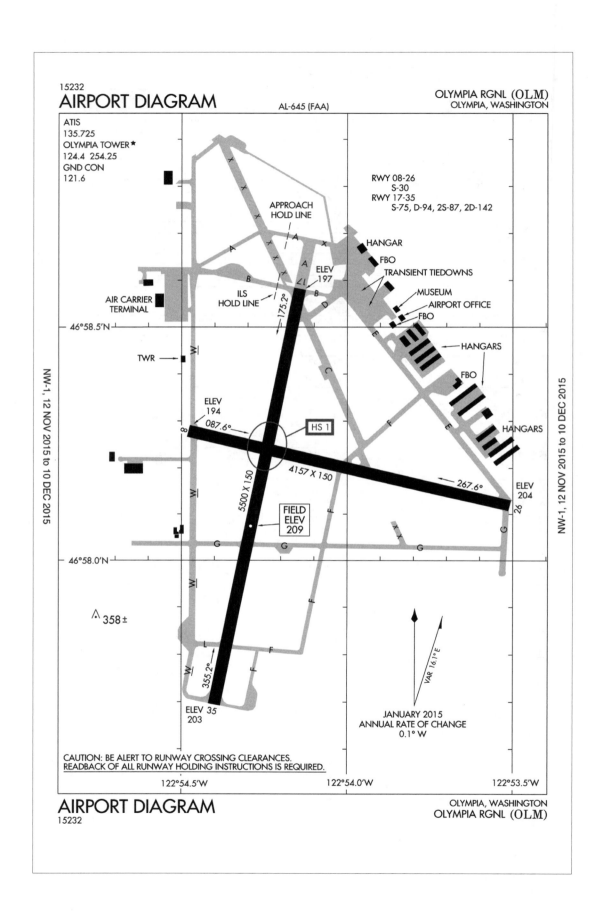

AIRPORT DIAGRAM

15232

AL-645 (FAA)

OLYMPIA RGNL (OLM)
OLYMPIA, WASHINGTON

ATIS
135.725
OLYMPIA TOWER ★
124.4 254.25
GND CON
121.6

RWY 08-26
S-30
RWY 17-35
S-75, D-94, 2S-87, 2D-142

APPROACH
HOLD LINE

HANGAR
FBO
TRANSIENT TIEDOWNS

ELEV
197

ILS
HOLD LINE

MUSEUM
AIRPORT OFFICE
FBO

AIR CARRIER
TERMINAL

46°58.5'N

TWR

HANGARS

FBO

ELEV
194

087.6°

HS 1

HANGARS

4157 X 150

267.6°

ELEV
204

5500 X 150

FIELD
ELEV
209

46°58.0'N

358±

VAR 16.1° E

JANUARY 2015
ANNUAL RATE OF CHANGE
0.1° W

355.2°

ELEV 35
203

CAUTION: BE ALERT TO RUNWAY CROSSING CLEARANCES.
READBACK OF ALL RUNWAY HOLDING INSTRUCTIONS IS REQUIRED.

122°54.5'W

122°54.0'W

122°53.5'W

AIRPORT DIAGRAM

15232

OLYMPIA, WASHINGTON
OLYMPIA RGNL (OLM)

NW-1, 12 NOV 2015 to 10 DEC 2015

NW-1, 12 NOV 2015 to 10 DEC 2015

Additional Full-Color Illustrations

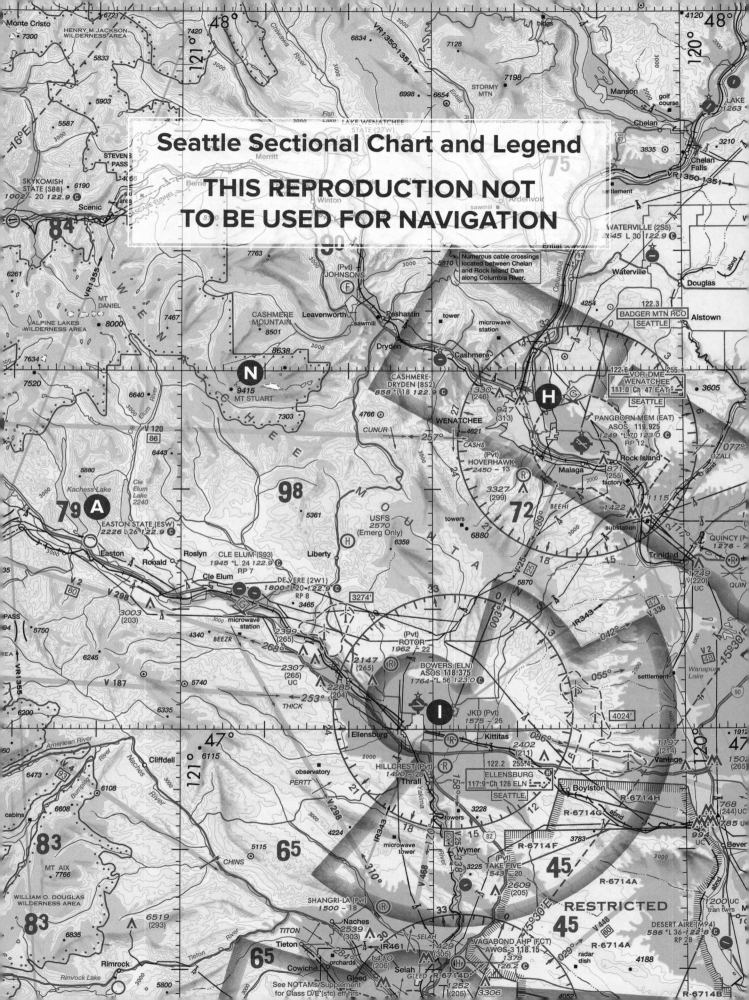

Seattle Sectional Chart and Legend

THIS REPRODUCTION NOT TO BE USED FOR NAVIGATION

SOUTH

SEATTLE
LEGEND

 NORTH

Airports having <u>Control Towers</u> are shown in <u>Blue</u>, all others in <u>Magenta</u>. Consult Chart Supplement for details involving airport lighting, navigation aids, and services. All times are local. For additional symbol information refer to the Chart User's Guide.

AIRPORTS

○ ○ — Other than hard-surfaced runways

⚓ Seaplane Base

◐ ⊗ — Hard-surfaced runways 1500 ft. to 8069 ft. in length

▮ ✖ — Hard-surfaced runways greater than 8069 ft. or some multiple runways less than 8069 ft.

◕ ✖ — Open dot within hard-surfaced runway configuration indicates approximate VOR, VOR-DME, DME or VORTAC location.

All recognizable hard-surfaced runways, including those closed, are shown for visual identification. Airports may be public or private.

ADDITIONAL AIRPORT INFORMATION

(R) — Private "(Pvt)" - Non-public use having emergency or landmark value

◎◎ — Military - Other than hard-surfaced; all military airports are identified by abbreviations AFB, NAS, AAF, etc.

(H) Heliport Selected   (U) Unverified   ⊗ Abandoned - paved having landmark value, 3000 ft. or greater   (F) Ultralight Flight Park Selected

✦ ✦ ✦ — Fuel - available Mon thru Fri 10:00 A.M. to 4:00 P.M. depicted by use of ticks around basic airport symbol. Consult Supplement for details and for availability at airports with hard-surfaced runways greater than 8069 ft.

☆ Rotating airport beacon in operation Sunset to Sunrise

OBJECTIONABLE - Airport may adversely affect airspace use.

AIRPORT DATA

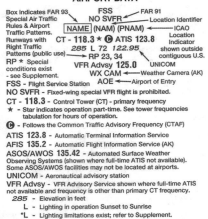

Box indicates FAR 93 Special Air Traffic Rules & Airport Traffic Patterns.
Runways with Right Traffic Patterns (public use)
RP ★ Special conditions exist - see Supplement.
FSS - Flight Service Station
NO SVFR - Fixed-wing special VFR flight is prohibited.
CT - 118.3 - Control Tower (CT) - primary frequency
★ - Star indicates operation part-time. See tower frequencies tabulation for hours of operation.
Ⓒ - Follows the Common Traffic Advisory Frequency (CTAF)
ATIS 123.8 - Automatic Terminal Information Service
AFIS 135.2 - Automatic Flight Information Service (AK)
ASOS/AWOS 135.42 - Automated Surface Weather Observing Systems (shown where full-time ATIS not available). Some ASOS/AWOS facilities may not be located at airports.
UNICOM - Aeronautical advisory station
VFR Advsy - VFR Advisory Service shown where full-time ATIS not available and frequency is other than primary CT frequency.
285 - Elevation in feet
L - Lighting in operation Sunset to Sunrise
*L - Lighting limitations exist; refer to Supplement.
72 - Length of longest runway in hundreds of feet; usable length may be less.
When information is lacking, the respective character is replaced by a dash. Lighting codes refer to runway edge lights and may not represent the longest runway or full length lighting.

Labels in box: FSS / NO SVFR / FAR 91 / Location Identifier / NAME (NAM) (PNAM) / ICAO Location Indicator shown outside contiguous U.S. / CT - 118.3 ★ Ⓒ ATIS 123.8 / 285 L 72 122.95 / UNICOM / RP 23, 34 / VFR Advsy 125.0 / WX CAM ← Weather Camera (AK) / AOE ← Airport of Entry

AIRPORT TRAFFIC SERVICE AND AIRSPACE INFORMATION

Only the controlled and reserved airspace effective below 18,000 ft. MSL are shown.

▬ Class B Airspace
▬ Class C Airspace (Mode C - see FAR 91.215/AIM.)
▬ ▬ Class D Airspace
[40] Ceiling of Class D Airspace in hundreds of feet (A minus ceiling value indicates surface up to but not including that value.)
▭ Class E (sfc) Airspace
▬ Class E Airspace with floor 700 ft. above surface that laterally abuts Class G Airspace.
CLASS G
▬ Class E Airspace with floor 700 ft. above surface that laterally abuts 1200 ft. or higher Class E Airspace
▬ Class E Airspace with floor 1200 ft. or greater above surface that laterally abuts Class G Airspace

2400 MSL / 4500 MSL — Differentiates floors of Class E Airspace greater than 700 ft. above surface.

Class E Airspace exists at 1200' AGL unless otherwise designated as shown above.
Class E Airspace low altitude Federal Airways are indicated by center line.
Intersection - Arrows are directed towards facilities which establish intersection.

132° → V 69 ↗↖
[169]

Total mileage between NAVAIDs on direct Airways
Class E Airspace low altitude RNAV 2 Routes are indicated by center line.

T 319   TK 313 ◆
(Helicopter Only)   RNAV Waypoint

▨▨▨ Prohibited, Restricted, and Warning Areas; Canadian Advisory, Danger, and Restricted Areas
▨▨▨ Alert Area and MOA - Military Operations Area
⟋⟋⟋ Special Airport Traffic Area (See FAR 93 for details.)
∴∴∴ ADIZ - Air Defense Identification Zone
▬ ▬ MODE C (See FAR 91.215/AIM.)
▬ National Security Area
▬ Terminal Radar Service Area (TRSA)
← IR211 MTR - Military Training Route

COMMUNICATION BOXES

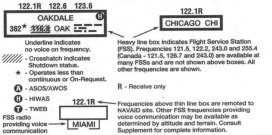

122.1R 122.6 123.6
OAKDALE Ⓗ
362 ★ ▨▨▨ OAK ▭▭▭

122.1R
CHICAGO CHI

Underline indicates no voice on frequency.
▨▨▨ - Crosshatch indicates Shutdown status.
★ - Operates less than continuous or On-Request.
Ⓐ - ASOS/AWOS
Ⓗ - HIWAS
Ⓣ - TWEB
FSS radio providing voice communication

122.1R
MIAMI

Heavy line box indicates Flight Service Station (FSS). Frequencies 121.5, 122.2, 243.0 and 255.4 (Canada - 121.5, 126.7 and 243.0) are available at many FSSs and are not shown above boxes. All other frequencies are shown.

R - Receive only

Frequencies above thin line box are remoted to NAVAID site. Other FSS frequencies providing voice communication may be available as determined by altitude and terrain. Consult Supplement for complete information.

RADIO AIDS TO NAVIGATION

⊡ VHF OMNI RANGE (VOR)
⊡ VOR-DME
▢ DME
⊚ VORTAC
⊙ Other facilities, i.e., FSS Outlet, RCO, WX CAM (AK) (see Supplement), etc.
◎ Non-Directional Radio Beacon (NDB)
◙ NDB - DME

OBSTRUCTIONS

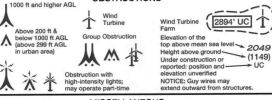

1000 ft and higher AGL
Above 200 ft & below 1000 ft AGL (above 299 ft AGL in urban area)
Wind Turbine
Group Obstruction
Wind Turbine Farm
(2894' UC)
Elevation of the top above mean sea level → 2049
Height above ground → (1149)
Under construction or reported: position and elevation unverified → UC
Obstruction with high-intensity lights; may operate part-time
NOTICE: Guy wires may extend outward from structures.

MISCELLANEOUS

⬙ STADIUM
◆ Intermittent TFR site (within 3 NM, up to & incl 3000' AGL)
🚀 Space Launch Activity Area (See Supplement.)
A - Aerobatic Practice Area (See Supplement.)
G - Glider Operations
H - Hang Glider Activity
U - Ultralight Activity
UA - Unmanned Aircraft Activity
⛱ Parachute Jumping Area (See Supplement.)
● Marine Light
—1°E— Isogonic Line (2015 VALUE)
◇ VPXYZ VFR Waypoints (See chart tabulation for latitude/longitude.)
△ NAME (VPXYZ)

TOPOGRAPHIC INFORMATION

⊥⊥⊥ Power Transmission Line
▬●▬ Aerial Cable
⊙ Lookout Tower 618 (Elevation Base of Tower)

) (Mountain Pass
11823 (Elevation of Pass)
Pass symbol does not indicate a recommended route or direction of flight and pass elevation does not indicate a recommended clearance altitude. Hazardous flight conditions may exist within and near mountain passes.

Sectional chart legend

SEATTLE SECTIONAL
SECTIONAL AERONAUTICAL CHART SCALE 1:500,000

NORTH ▶

Federal Aviation
Administration

TM

93RD **EDITION EFFECTIVE** 0901Z **25 MAY 2017**

TO 0901Z **7 DEC 2017**

Includes airspace amendments effective **27 APR 2017**
and all other aeronautical data received by **30 MAR 2017**

Information on this chart will change; consolidated major updates of chart changes are available every 56 days in the CHART SUPPLEMENT Aeronautical Chart Bulletin section (online at http://faa.gov/go/ais). Also consult appropriate NOTICES TO AIRMEN (NOTAMs) and other FLIGHT INFORMATION PUBLICATIONS (FLIPs) for the latest changes. Consult/Subscribe to FAA Safety Alerts and Charting Notices at:
http://www.faa.gov/air_traffic/flight_info/aeronav/safety_alerts/

Published from digital files compiled in accordance with Interagency Air Cartographic Committee specifications and agreements approved by Department of Defense - Federal Aviation Administration.

Warning: Refer to current foreign charts and flight information publications for information within foreign airspace.

Flight Following Services are available on request and highly recommended in and around Class B, C, and TRSA areas.

CAUTION: This chart is primarily designed for VFR navigational purposes and does not purport to indicate the presence of all power transmission and telecommunication lines, terrain or obstacles which may be encountered below reasonable and safe altitudes.

Lambert Conformal Conic Projection Standard Parallels 41° 20' and 46° 40'
Horizontal Datum: North American Datum of 1983 (World Geodetic System 1984)

CONVERSION OF ELEVATIONS

FEET (Thousands) 0 2 4 6 8 10 12 14 16 18 20 22 24 26 28 30
METERS (Thousands) 0 1 2 3 4 5 6 7 8 9

CONTOUR INTERVAL 500 *feet*
Intermediate contours 250 *feet*
━━ 500 ━━   ━━ 250 ━━
HIGHEST TERRAIN elevation is *14410 feet*
located at 46° 51' N - 121° 46'W
Spot elevation. *4254*
Approximate elevation. . . . . x *3200*

┌─14410─
GLACIER
12000
9000
7000
5000
3000
2000
1000
Sea Level─┘

Class G Airspace within the United States extends up to 14,500 feet MSL. At and above this altitude all airspace is within Class E Airspace, excluding the airspace less than 1500 feet above the terrain and certain special use airspace areas.

Features normally used as checkpoints for controlling VFR traffic are emphasized on this series of charts so they may be readily identified.

Example: ■ ⌐ **POWER PLANT**

The name shown is that used by the controlling personnel and is not necessarily the official name of the feature.

MILITARY TRAINING ROUTES (MTRs)

All IR and VR MTRs are shown, and may extend from the surface upwards. Only the route centerline, direction of flight along the route, and the route designator are depicted - route widths and altitudes are not shown.

Since these routes are subject to change every 56 days, you are cautioned and advised to contact Flight Service for route dimensions and current status for those routes affecting your flight.

Routes with a change in the alignment of the charted route centerline will be indicated in the Aeronautical Chart Bulletin of the Chart Supplement.

DoD users refer to Area Planning AP/1B Military Training Routes North and South America for current routes.

ATTENTION

THIS CHART CONTAINS MAXIMUM ELEVATION FIGURES (MEF). The Maximum Elevation Figures shown in quadrangles bounded by ticked lines of latitude and longitude are represented in THOUSANDS and HUNDREDS of feet above mean sea level. The MEF is based on information available concerning the highest known feature in each quadrangle, including terrain and obstructions (trees, towers, antennas, etc.).

Example: 12,500 feet **12**⁵

Sectional chart legend (continued)

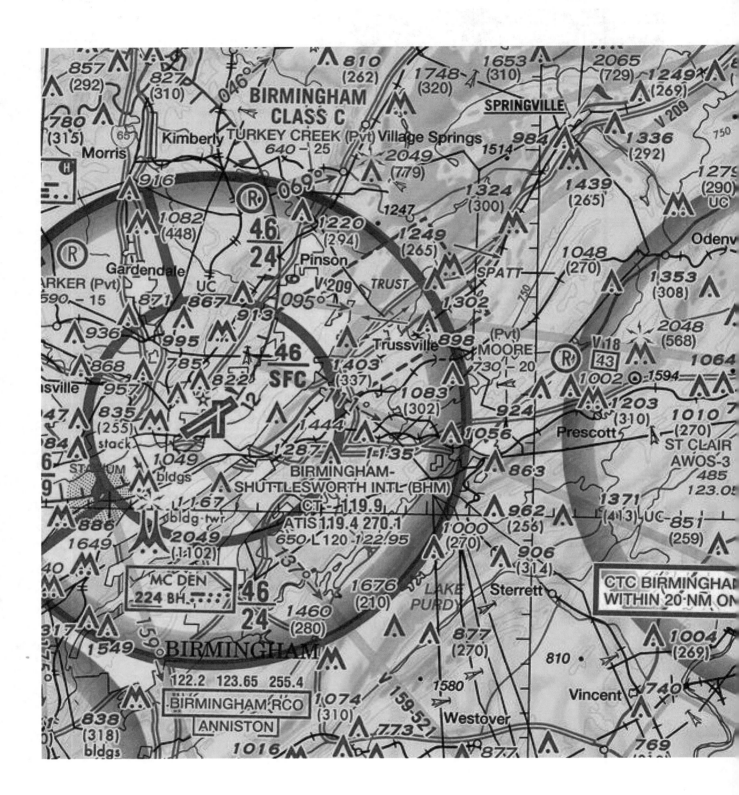

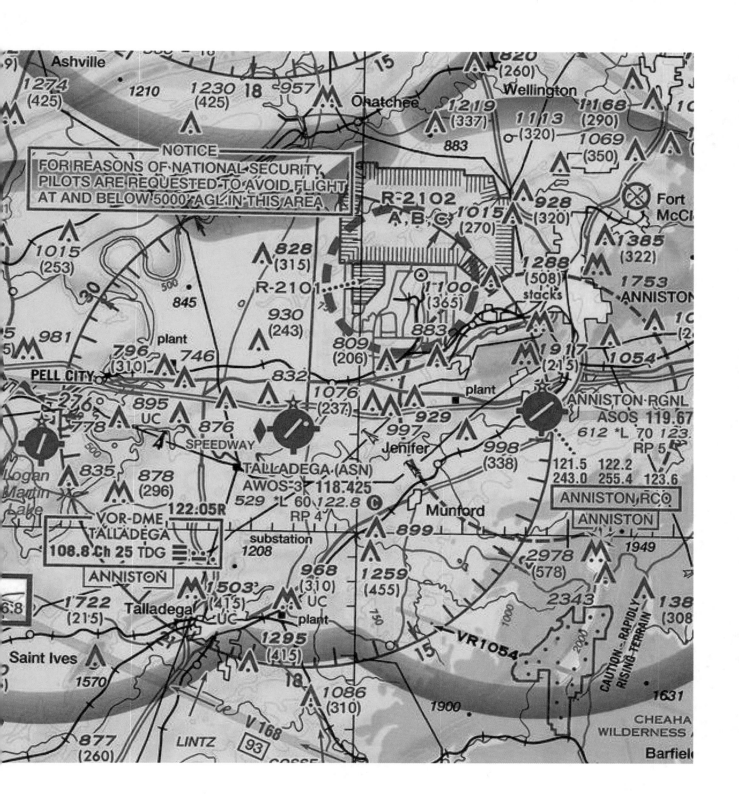

AIRPORT SIGNS

From Aeronautical Information Manual (AIM)

Figure A. Runway Holding Position Sign

Figure B. Holding Position Sign at beginning of takeoff runway

Figure C. Holding Position Sign for a Taxiway that intersects the intersection of two runways

Figure D. Holding Position Sign for ILS Critical Area

Figure E. Holding Position Sign for a runway approach area

Figure F. Sign Prohibiting Aircraft Entry into an area

Figure G. Runway Location Sign

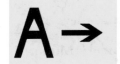

Figure H. Direction Sign for runway exit

Figure I. Destination Sign for common taxiing route to two runways

Figure J. Destination Sign for different taxiing routes to two runways

Figure K. Runway Distance Remaining Sign indicating 3,000 feet of runway remaining

Figure L. Taxiway Location Sign

Figure M. Runway Boundary Sign

Index